M-commerce

mCommerce

Boost your business with the power
of mobile commerce

Paul Skeldon

crimson

M-commerce

Published in Great Britain 2011 by
Crimson Publishing, a division of Crimson Business Ltd
Westminster House
Kew Road
Richmond
Surrey
TW9 2ND

Every effort has been made to ensure that the information in this book is correct to the best of the publisher's knowledge at the time of going to press. However, changes are constantly taking place in m-commerce, so readers are advised to undertake their own research before making strategic business decisions.

A catalogue record for this book is available from the British Library.

ISBN 978 1 85458 675 9

Typeset by IDSUK (DataConnection) Ltd
Printed and bound by in the UK by Ashford Colour Press, Gosport, Hants

For Thea and Elliot

Contents

About the author

Paul Skeldon is a freelance journalist, consultant, writer, podcaster and videocaster, who has been talking about all things mobile for more than 15 years. He is currently editor of the leading mobile retailing news source M-retailing.net at *Internet Retailing* magazine, managing editor of World Telemedia, the leading mobile content and billing media and events house, and is the co-founder and creator of Europe's first interactive webzine, Mobiledotcomms. Gadget-fan Paul has also written for major newspapers and magazines on mobile and its role in business and lifestyle, and he can regularly be found chairing mobile conferences around the world.

He lives with his wife, son, two cats, three iPhones, five laptops, a dongle and a garage full of mobile handsets dating back to 1992, in the Chilterns in Buckinghamshire, England.

Acknowledgements

Where do I start with thanking people? I would need to list everyone I have met in the mobile, telecoms, media, advertising and publishing industries who have inspired me, shown me all manner of great technology, predicted the future (sometimes getting it uncannily right and sometimes spectacularly wrong) and who have come up with ideas for things to do with mobile phones that no one else had thought of. You are an inspiration all.

I must first thank Ian Wallis and his team at Crimson for their patience, suggestions, guidance and, of course, advance – and for finally giving me an outlet for 15 years of information. My head is now clear.

I also need to thank a raft of analysts and companies whose data, insight and world views have shaped my opinion of mobile on an almost daily basis; and who have given me, over the years, a view through the murk and mist as to what is probably happening out there among businesses and consumers that are spending money through mobile.

Among them, in no particular order and with apologies for not naming specific people: comScore, Neilsen NetRatings, Forrester Research, Juniper Research, Compuware Gomez, Mobile Squared, ForeSee Results, eBay Infographic, Canalys, InMobi, JiWire, the e-tailing group, Experian, Performics, Chadwick Martin Bailey and iModerate Research Technologies, ROI Research, Retail Systems Research, Mobio Identity Systems, IBM, Adobe, Harris Interactive, and ABI Research.

I also need to thank the many staff and people connected to various industry bodies, who also provided data, information ... and the odd red herring: MEF, MMA, IAB, IMRG, AIME, PRA, Action4, PPP, Ofcom,

ITU, GSM Association, UK Trade & Investment, Tradefair, Mobey Forum, NFC Forum, and the Office for National Statistics.

There are, of course, the websites and other resources of Apple, Google, Microsoft, RIM, Nokia, Samsung, Ericsson, Sony, LG, Amazon, eBay and Facebook to thank as well – just for being there.

Clearly, thousands of people in the front lines of the mobile industry have also helped me get this far. I can't thank you all by name (nor can I individually thank all the PRs who have played their parts), but for this particular project I would like to thank: Adam Maxted (the most connected human being in mobile in the world); Emma Potter, Tim Dunn, Ben Cusack and everyone at MIG; Caitlin New at Ketner, and all the team at Digby; Merissa Arnold at LaunchSquad; Mark Adams and Rachel Wilkinson at Portaltech; Paul Maas at Usablenet; Sienne Viet at Marks & Spencer; Harriet Williams at Debenhams; Mark Challinor at INMA and the Telegraph Media Group; Damian Hanson from One iota Limited; Simon Harrow at Kiddicare; Mark Collin and Sophia Henri at Infogain; Cameron McLean at PayPal; Elliot Messenger at Hypertag; all the people at Placecast and O2 More; Steve Rothwell at Eagle Eye Solutions; Andrew Darling at OpenMarket; everyone involved with the FT Digital Media and Broadcasting conferences; Chris Cleave; Alex Miesl and Claire Armitt at Sponge; Esther Cochrane at GameOn Marketing; and many, many others. You all know who you are, so pat yourselves on the back and take yourselves out for a drink.

I must also personally thank Ian Jindal and Mark Pigou at Internet Retailing for channeling my mobile madness into the world of retail and commerce just before everyone got obsessed with it. Amazing what a chance meeting in a pub can do. I also have to thank Jarvis Todd and Annika Micheli at World Telemedia for being such cool colleagues, and for pretty much owning the m-commerce space and completing the circumference of the circle.

I would like to thank Reggie for his patience; and of course, I must thank my lovely, long-suffering, rubbish-phone-owning Luddite of a wife, Thea George. Sorry for all the lost weekends spent writing, the swearing and drinking all that cold coffee. I am so glad you hate social networking.

INTRODUCTION

On the move and on the money

When he was seven months old, my son picked up my iPhone, which he'd seen me use many times since he was born, and started jabbing at the screen. To him the device wasn't so much a phone, but more something you touched and prodded and, unbeknownst to him, enjoyed.

Anyone who grew up in the 1960s, 1970s, 1980s or even the early 1990s would have been beguiled by the prospect of a personal communications device as pioneered in *Star Trek* (due in part to the lack of a budget to create realistic space craft interaction), and then used in every sci-fi movie ever since. And lo, using radio waves, such a device came to pass – the mobile phone was born.

Early adopters were ridiculed, and many commentators suggested that such a thing would never take off. It would be too expensive, too cumbersome and would never achieve the critical mass of users needed to make it practical.

Well, as we know now, that wasn't the case. Mobile phones are everywhere, but as my young son – who is now 18 months old and can actually use, albeit rudimentarily, an iPhone – confirms, these devices are proving to be more than just phones. They have morphed in a very short period of time into computers in our pockets.

The modern handset is connected to the Internet, has processing power that outstrips by some margin that found in the Apollo spacecrafts that got humankind to the moon, has a full color screen, can handle multimedia, and is connected to everyone else with a phone. This has become a modern marvel and, to my mind, is one of the defining inventions of humankind.

But hyperbole aside, the mobile phone of today is a powerful beast – with a profile and ubiquity dominant enough to influence a small boy before he could walk or talk – and this makes it commercially interesting to us all.

But what is mobile commerce and how can it benefit you? Well, to most people m-commerce is simply an extension of online shopping – connecting these devices that people hold so dear and have with them all the time to the web and hence to online shops.

Online shopping took many years to get entrenched in the public mindset, but now it is a standard way of shopping. The mobile phone clearly offers an even more convenient way to do it than a computer, allowing people sitting in front of the TV to shop, without having to get up and turn on a PC or pick up a laptop.

This view of mobile commerce is indeed a vital part of the multibillion dollar m-commerce marketplace. But there is so much more to what mobile in commerce can deliver that, well, I wrote a book about it.

M-commerce, of which mobile retailing is a subset, is everything from selling content and goods, to delivering vouchers and coupons, to engaging with and entertaining potential shoppers. The phone becomes a tool to drive those shoppers into brick-and-mortar stores; a channel to turn TV, print, billboard and online advertising into sales; a payment device; a way of letting consumers share and recommend retailers; and even a tool that allows them to call you if they really need to.

M-commerce even covers a range of services and offerings that make the consumer experience in an actual shop more informative and productive; and it delivers a whole host of services that retailers can use on the shop floor to improve the efficiency and customer service of their staff, cut checkout lines and allow for more up-selling and cross-selling opportunities.

M-commerce is, frankly, commerce on steroids.

And as such, mobile is something that anyone who is in the business of selling, or buying, anything – be it digital goods, real world goods, services, content or ideas – should be looking into.

To many people m-commerce is a natural extension of e-commerce: the selling of stuff on the web moving to the mobile channel. In its basic form that is exactly what m-commerce is. As mobile phones have become more like wireless computers, so the difference between what constitutes m- and e-commerce has become a gray area.

In many cases, m-commerce is simply the mobile version of e-commerce, only using the phone rather than a desk-bound PC or a laptop. (Which is another interesting point. Is shopping on a laptop or a tablet m-commerce? Indeed, is shopping on a digital kiosk while out and about m-commerce too?)

But this belies some inherent differences between online web services and those accessed via mobile. These differences are often subtle, but are hugely important, such as taking into account how the phone's screen differs not only in size, but also in orientation and aspect ratio to a computer screen, the processing power of the phone, the ability – or not – of the phone to multitask, and the fact that the phone may be connected via a mobile network that will have variable – not to mention questionable – bandwidth.

But the subtleties of mobile go much deeper than these important technical considerations. Mobile commerce is also a psychological shift for the consumer. A person's mobile phone is sacrosanct to him or her and incredibly personal. It is also (ironically, considering it's a communication device) very private. This personal nature needs to be reflected in how a business uses the mobile channel to connect with a consumer.

Anyone looking to engage consumers in mobile commerce also needs to look at where and when the consumer is accessing a brand or a retailer's website with his phone. Making sure that the consumer's experience matches not only each device's peculiarities, but also the peccadilloes and even time and location of its user, is a huge challenge; and this is what separates m-commerce from e-commerce to an even greater degree than what separates brick-and-mortar stores from their online renderings.

That is what this book is here to do. It will take you on a wild roller-coaster ride of thrills and spills, providing a brief history of e-commerce, the rise of the mobile phone and, more pertinently, the mobile web, as well as looking specifically at how mobile is playing out in the retail space. I will also look at all the other aspects of mobile commerce – from digital goods sales; to the sale of media as a commodity using mobile; how mobile is streamlining other commercial offerings, such as in the health care, lifestyle and travel industries; as well as how football clubs, sports, live events and other brands are looking to leverage the unique selling power of the mobile phone.

This book will look at the opportunity to make the mobile a personal sales and buying tool, as well as a means of opening up one-to-one personal relationships between customers and brands – looking at how to do it and, in some cases, how not to do it.

With my young son set to be a consumer in his own right when I deem it time to start giving him pocket money, businesses like yours need to be ready for the fact that he and millions like him will not only be digital natives (that generation growing up now that has never not known the Internet), but they will be mobile digital natives. And they will want to do all manner of commerce using their mobiles. I would go so far as to say that computers as we know them will disappear, being viewed by my son's generation as clunky, bulky and bedeviled by poor interface (unless we get more touchscreen and voice control). Everything will be done on mobile devices, with touchscreens. These will be everywhere, an integral part of life.

We have some way to go before we get to this, but as we stand at the start of the long road that is mobile commerce, any business — your business — needs to know what mobile offers now, what mobile commerce is doing globally, and where this is likely to go in the next couple of years.

So, set your phone to silent and read on . . . .

CHAPTER 1

What's it all about?

To understand the importance and potential of m-commerce, it is essential to first understand how, over the past decade, consumers – and retailers – have come to embrace the concept of buying and selling goods over the Internet.

The web didn't really become a commercial tool, and certainly didn't feature much in the way of commerce, until about 2000. Although "invented" by Tim Berners-Lee in the 1980s, and pretty well cemented, albeit in a nascent form, in the public eye by the mid 1990s, it wasn't until the turn of the century that the security protocols and the general acceptance of the web as a commercial network really took hold.

In the 10 years since then, e-commerce has exploded, with the US e-commerce market alone worth some $173bn in 2010. And that doesn't include the fact that most of us these days do some or all of our banking online and routinely move trillions of dollars, pounds, euros, yen and even dinars between bank accounts using this public network.

E-commerce is simply the buying and selling of goods and services over the Internet electronically (hence the e). According to the Pew Research Center's Internet & American Life Project, 66% of the adults online in the US have purchased something over the web, whether it's books, shoes or a Caribbean cruise. If you extend e-commerce to the researching of products online – which is a big part of its appeal, and that of mobile commerce, as we will see – the number of adults who participate in e-commerce jumps to 93%. That's pretty much everyone.

Even with a slumping global economy, online retail sales continue to rise. In the US retailers plan to spend $220.9m on mobile in 2011, and the m-commerce sales volume there is set to reach $9bn in 2011. Predictions are that in three years, 24% of US retailers will have annual sales of 15% or greater coming from their mobile channels. Already 59% of consumers use their phones for mobile shopping activities at home, while 28% use their phones in retail stores to perform mobile shopping activities. That's around 74 million consumers in the United States shopping from mobile devices. This will spur around 78% of retailers to invest in m-commerce by the end of 2011.

In the UK, where mobile retail is booming perhaps more than anywhere else outside the US, shoppers spent a total of £4.9bn ($8.5bn) online during February 2011 alone – equivalent to £79 per person across the whole country, a 20% increase over the same period last year. Already in the first two months of 2011, UK consumers have spent £10bn ($18bn) shopping online, with the biggest sellers being booze, clothing, food and appliances. Everything else is doing well too: books, holidays, music and computers – not to mention a growing trend toward big ticket items such as furniture, cars and even yachts.

Where – and how – did it all start? As the price of personal computers (PCs) started to drop in the 1980s, thanks to the pioneering work of Sinclair, Acorn, Apple and others, entrepreneurs looked at how to monetize this new trend. Games clearly were the headline grabber, but companies such as CompuServe started to look at how to add tools to these computers, becoming one of the first to offer what they called networking services: e-mail, message boards and something called the electronic mall, where users could purchase items directly from 110 online merchants. While the electronic mall wasn't a huge success, it was one of the first examples of e-commerce and sort of set the scene.

In 1990, a researcher called Tim Berners-Lee at CERN (the European Organization for Nuclear Research) created a hypertext-based web of information that a user could navigate using a simple interface called a browser. He called it the WorldWideWeb, and in 1991 the National Science Foundation lifted a ban on commercial businesses operating over the Internet, paving the way for web-based e-commerce.

In 1993, Marc Andreesen at the National Center for Supercomputing Applications (NCSA) introduced the first widely distributed web browser called Mosaic. A year later, Netscape 1.0's release included an important security protocol called Secure Sockets Layer (SSL) that encrypted messages on both the sending and receiving side of an online transaction, thus ensuring that personal information such as names, addresses and credit card numbers could be encrypted as they passed over the Internet.

In 1994 and 1995, the first third-party services for processing online credit card sales appeared. First Virtual and CyberCash were two of the most popular. Also in 1995, a company called VeriSign began developing digital IDs, or certificates, that verified the identity of online businesses. Soon, VeriSign switched its focus to certifying that a website's e-commerce servers were properly encrypted and secure.

In July 1995, Jeff Bezos boxed up a book in his garage in Seattle and sent it to someone who had bought it over the Internet. Amazon had been born, and within its first 30 days of existence, the self-proclaimed "Earth's largest bookstore" sold books to online shoppers in all 50 US states and 45 countries worldwide.

Books were the natural place to start: they were cheap to ship and easy to order directly from publishers. Publishers had already created vast digital archives of their titles on CD-ROM, which could be uploaded to a website so that consumers could browse and buy online.

E-commerce hasn't really looked back from this point, and has become an entrenched part of most commercial businesses' modus operandi.

While all this was happening on the Internet, the strange bricklike devices that had once been the preserve of the Yuppie had started to morph from a glorified military field radio into something small and a little more useful – the mobile phone.

The mobile phone started out as an almost crazy novelty, taking the idea of the radio and turning it into a two-way conversation tool – in essence, a two-way radio. The first call from a "mobile telephone" was purportedly made in St. Louis in 1946. The device weighed 80 pounds and cost the equivalent of $330 a month to use.

It wasn't until the 1970s that the first practical – not to mention portable – mobile phone system was developed by Motorola. Martin Cooper, the Motorola executive in charge of the project, is widely credited with making the first mobile phone call on April 3, 1973, from the street outside his Manhattan office. He called his rival Dr. Joe Engel over at Bell Labs to crow over his team's success.

The first commercially viable automatic mobile telephone system, subsequently dubbed 1G, was eventually rolled out by Nippon Telegraph & Telephone Corporation (NTT) in Tokyo in 1979, and was eventually available to the whole Japanese population by 1984.

Meanwhile, 1981 saw the simultaneous launch of the Nordic Mobile Telephone (NMT) system in Denmark, Finland, Norway and Sweden. This was the first mobile phone network featuring international roaming. The first 1G network launched in the USA was rolled out by Chicago-based Ameritech in 1983, using the Motorola DynaTAC mobile phone. Several countries followed in the mid-1980s, including the UK, Mexico and Canada.

The first "modern" network technology on digital 2G (second generation) cellular technology was launched by Radiolinja in 1991 in Finland on the GSM (Global System for Mobile Communications) standard. This also marked the introduction of competition in mobile telecoms, as Radiolinja challenged incumbent Telecom Finland, which ran a 1G NMT network.

In 2001, the first commercial launch of a 3G network was again in Japan by NTT (now NTT DOCOMO) on the WCDMA (Wideband Code Divisior Multiple Access) standard. By this time, the mobile phone was becoming rooted in modern life, with more than a billion phones in circulation. In some Scandinavian countries, there was an average of more than one phone per person.

By 2010, there were more than five billion mobile phones in use worldwide, accounting for one each for nearly 70% of the global population. There is no avoiding the mobile phone, and once it reached massive mass-market penetration, it became clear that mobile phones offered a huge commercial opportunity – not just through making calls, but in the creation and delivery of a host of other services that could generate money.

Perhaps the most significant development in the rapid journey of the mobile phone to something that is now commerce-ready was the overwhelming mass public embrace – in Europe, Asia, Latin America, India, China and finally the US – of SMS (Short Message Service), also known as texting.

SMS

The simple 160-character alphanumeric messaging tool was originally built into the mobile ecosystem as a way for engineers testing the networks to communicate with one another. The first text message, or telenote as it was originally called, was sent on December 3, 1992, by Neil Papworth to colleagues at Vodafone in the UK. It said "Merry Christmas." The commercial launch of SMS took place in 1995. In the UK the key moment in SMS's commercial development came when O2, Orange, Vodafone and T-Mobile agreed to let messages travel from one network to another, enabling everyone with a mobile phone, whatever network they were on, to text anyone else.

Once the public got hold of this, the mobile phone was revealed to be more than its name implied. These devices that more and more people now had in their pockets were not just a way of calling one another, but a way of sending non-time-dependent messages. A new mode of communication was born and the potential for the mobile phone to be a data device was cemented.

This shift can't be emphasized enough. Getting people using their phones to message one another, as well as the creation of a whole new language of "lol"s, smiley faces and other icons, shorthand and abbreviations, was a "gr8" step forward, if not linguistically, then commercially. This alone made the phone suddenly more interesting to more than just phone companies.

This move to text use occurred at about the same time that consumers and business markets were coming to grips with e-mail; and text's popularity can be attributed, in some small part at least, to this sudden blossoming of new ways to communicate. For several thousand years those that could write had the option of sending a letter or talking face to face. The telephone changed all that, from a verbal point of view at least, some 150 years ago. The mid 1990s saw possibly the greatest leap forward in human remote communication since the invention of writing: e-mail. This transformed written communications to an instant electronic tool and revolutionized business and communications. Text, I like to think, became another new way of communicating and offered a way of e-mailing while on the move. It certainly filled that gap more than adequately, until mobile Internet and smartphones allowed for proper delivery of mobile e-mail.

It is also worth taking a short detour here into the world of instant messaging, text and e-mail. As said, all are revolutionary and, while

I hate to use the phrase, they actually did represent a paradigm shift in how people communicate, and initiated a whole new protocol of communications. Instant messaging does what it says on the box: allows almost instant "chat" in an informal and instant way between people. Text is typically also an informal though not so time-dependent way of communicating with people you know reasonably well, and it fills the gap between needing the immediacy of talking to them (face to face or by phone) and sending them a letter or an e-mail. It's that perfect tool for saying "I am running 10 minutes late," rather than having to waste more time calling up and doing the "Hello, how are you?" thing and then saying, "I am running 10 minutes late," and probably having to explain why.

This may explain why 6.1 trillion text messages were sent globally in 2010, compared to a trifling 4.1 trillion in 2008. When record keeping began back in 1998, a commercially viable 5.4 million texts were sent in the UK in just one month (April). The 1 billion messages a month mark was passed in December 2000. And still it grows.

The US has been somewhat slower to adopt the use of text messaging, preferring to converse by voice and e-mail, but slowly text usage in the US has grown. According to the International Association for the Wireless Telecommunications Industry (CTIA) in the US, text and data use on mobiles has now surpassed voice in the US, and the average US teen now sends some 1,500 texts a month.

E-mail, meanwhile, can still demand an immediate reply, but as texting, instant messaging and social networks start to cover the instant part of communication, e-mail is being relegated to an electronic letter, and so rather formal, instead of a way of chatting with people. That said, now that people are e-mailing from their mobile phones, e-mail may yet see a change in how it is used.

With consumers viewing their mobile phones as more than just an expensive alternative to phone booths, a whole industry started to grow up around the personalization of phones, starting with ringtones.

Back in the late 1990s, new Motorola handsets let you edit and create ringtones by typing in the actual notes – A, B, C, C#, etc – that made up a tune. (I should know. I spent hours programming my phone to play "Smells Like Teen Spirit" by Nirvana in a festival of beeps and swearing that nearly cost me my marriage.) This, of course, was not satisfactory, and soon clever people were doing the programming for you and letting you buy the ringtones to stick on your phone.

Mobile commerce had been born.

Ringtones

it is important to note that one of the other keys to making a mobile phone a commercial device is the fundamental fact that it is attached to a billing mechanism: the phone bill. This allowed – still allows – the phone to be used to pay for things, as the charges can be added onto the user's phone bill or, in the case of prepaid services, taken from the available credit.

This billing mechanism had long been running on the fixed telephone network under the auspices of Premium Rate Services (PRS), since the 1980s. These services, usually associated with sex chat lines, dating services and practical jokes, had in fact become very successful. Weather reports, sports scores, and dial-a-disc had all achieved high levels of commercial, if not quality, success. While most people associated these services with the seedy end of the 0898 numbers market as it then was, the most commercially successful PRS service on landlines in the 1990s was in fact a bird-watching service, where birders could report sightings of rare avian visitors to British shores.

So the idea that certain numbers would trigger a more costly call, from which revenue could be taken for services, had been well established in the fixed-line telephone world for many years, by the time mobile entrepreneurs started to look at how to sell strange bits of electronic ephemera to personalize the phone.

Accessories

The fact that text was, since 1998, a cross-network service embraced by all operators and, more significantly, one that the service providers could bill for, meant that much of the business know-how applied to the premium-rate telephone number services in the fixed-line world, could be applied to text. In fact, with SMS it could go beyond what fixed-line billing could achieve, allowing for different texts to be sent and the sender to be charged for a variety of goods or services.

Let me explain. When you send a text, it goes from your phone to a message center within your operator network, where it is stored and then forwarded on to the destination you have sent it to (usually another mobile phone, but not always). The delivery of this message from the message center to the device produces a delivery message that your message center logs and you get charged for. (Similarly, if the message doesn't get through, you don't get charged.) This charge appears on your bill. Thanks to the pioneering work of the fixed-line premium-rate services industry, this system can be used to charge you for various things.

For example, you can text a number – these days typically a shortcode of five easily remembered numbers – to vote for something. Or in Finland, you can buy a can of Coke from a vending machine and be charged for that can of Coke on your phone bill. This is Mobile Originated (MO) billing.

Conversely, you can, as is more common these days, send a text with a key word to a shortcode and get a text back with a passcode in it. The passcode lets you access whatever you are texting to do. (Often this is used to access websites or pay for content on websites.) The returning text or texts carry the charge. This is known as Mobile Terminated (MT) billing.

The upshot is that using SMS as a billing tool suddenly made it a lot easier not only to use the phone as a way of paying for things on the web – or from a vending machine – but also meant that buying things via your phone became quite simple. The operator knows who you are and, if you are a post-paid customer, has run credit checks on you. If you are post-paid phone user, the operator – who in effect owns your bill – knows if you can afford whatever you are trying to buy. It also has the billing delivery mechanism and the content delivery mechanism, and you, the consumer, have a device to consume the content on.

This seemingly complicated sentence is why m-commerce works and will be so prevalent in the coming years. It is simple, self-contained, secure and works. The stage is set.

Personalization

As the public warmed to buying stuff for their phones, so the manufacturers of the phones started to create handsets that were open to more customizing. Colored screens, better sound players, more memory and even processors and media storage cards all began to creep into the mix, and soon there was a burgeoning market for digital goods for use on phones. Phone users had the options to buy wallpapers – the backdrop on the phone's screen – sounds, moving images and games.

Content

Soon brands with suitable content – movie companies, TV producers, the music industry, the games industry and the gambling world, to name but a few – saw a small, but potentially useful, new outlet for not only selling versions of their products, but for taking advantage of mobile's unique marketing properties. Not only was there a thirst among consumers for more of this "content" on their phones, but it also afforded, say, a movie company a chance to market its latest release to this audience by getting it to pay for clips, images and sounds from said movie, to wow their friends on their mobile and to spread the word.

Apps

This foray into content-based marketing marked the birth of not only true mobile commerce, but also of viral marketing on a grand new digital scale. Further, it started the move to make mobile networks broadband, and saw network operators the world over look at how they could become the gatekeepers of this content. They largely failed to pull that off in the long run, but online at least, Apple, Amazon and Google have been hugely successful at cornering some markets with iTunes, iBooks, Kindle and the Android apps store.

So with better handsets, better mobile networks, and nascent markets in digital m-commerce, with a billing mechanism using PRS and Premium Rate SMS (PSMS) and a growing love and understanding of e-commerce via PC developing in parallel, 2010 saw a groundswell toward bringing the two worlds – mobile and online – together, driven by the potential to sell more goods, content and fripperies. It is the stuff of capitalist dreams: you need to sell better handsets with more expensive data plans to consumers who want to shop on impulse wherever they are. In doing so, you sell more stuff. Marxism it ain't.

This potted history of the mobile commerce market – oversimplified, admittedly, but enough to give you the heads-up on how it came about and why it works – shows just how the mobile phone has transformed from one thing (a way of making telephone calls) to a tool that presents a palette of communications colors (voice, SMS, instant messaging, e-mail and social networking chat), and now to a network-connected terminal that allows you to do all of the above, as well as buy and "consume" music, videos, films, books, newspapers, advertisements, coupons, tickets, ringtones, wallpapers, photos and, with the growth of apps stores, all sorts of other things far too numerous to mention here. (As I write, there are some 300,000 unique apps out there on the major mobile apps stores.)

Mobile commerce encompasses all of this, but is also now becoming more of an extension of how more traditional retailers sell things on the Internet, opening up the mobile commerce world to being not just a multibillion-dollar content-consumption business, but to being a multitrillion-dollar content-consumption, goods-selling and marketing and advertising business.

CHAPTER 2

Why does m-commerce matter?

Mobile commerce is important as it appears to be one of the key growth areas for a number of business sectors, including retail, media, games, music, art, social networks and many consumer-facing brands. But scratch the surface of what mobile can actually do in a commerce sense, and you realize that it is likely to impact virtually every facet of daily life: travel, transport, health care, well-being, shopping, entertainment, information, communication, banking and finance, and even real estate services, property renting, dating, religion, art, politics and, in some countries, revolution.

In Chapter 1 we touched on how e-commerce came about, how mobile morphed from a basic voice communications tool into something far more versatile and sophisticated, and how, in turn, the combination of e-commerce and this sophisticated, web-enabled, billable device is likely to shape how people buy things from now on.

However, the reach and ubiquity of the mobile phone means that it infiltrates every facet of modern life. Rather than looking at why mobile commerce is important, it is likely that by the time you have finished reading this book, you will be thinking how mobile technology can pretty much make everything in life easier. The commerce part comes in getting people to pay for this ease and convenience – and ideally, not at the expense of spending elsewhere in the economy. Mobile commerce can take its place in generating recovery, as opposed to simply cannibalizing already hard to come by revenue streams.

As we also saw in Chapter 1, one of the keys to mobile commerce is the increasing sophistication of mobile handsets. They used to be something of a laughing stock when they first appeared: bricklike in size, shape, weight and style. Early models were cumbersome, not very functional and required the transportation not just of the unwieldy handset, but also a large, and short-lived, battery pack.

Over the years the mobile phone shrank in size as it grew in functionality, as battery technology and processing power increased exponentially according to Moore's law. Ironically, in today's computerlike smartphone market, handsets are getting bigger again. They need to accommodate larger screens as they become media players and content creators themselves, though still they remain much smaller than their ancestors.

In fact, many people argue that it is these smartphones that hold the key to the success of mobile commerce – and they may indeed be right long-term – but much of m-commerce's growth over the past five or so years has come not from these devices, but from ordinary handsets and what have been dubbed feature phones. These Java-based handsets took the mobile telephone from something with a small screen that just showed the incoming or outgoing phone number of a call or the text you were sending, to something that offered a rudimentarily navigable screen. This allowed you to do a bit more with your phone, and featured the all-important sound-playing and graphics-display technology that let the phone play ringtones and music, and display photos and flashy wallpaper.

While the western world is embracing the smartphone with alacrity, the real growth in terms of people using mobile phones for commerce lies in the hugely populous regions of the developing world – India, China, Southeast Asia and Africa – where mobile phones have already given almost two billion people access to the telephone. Those people are now starting to look at how they can use their more basic handsets to do more commercial things.

The mobile phone in these regions allowed people who would never be able to afford a telephone – the cost of rolling out landlines being too much of a burden for most to shoulder – to get talking. The mobile phone is not another phone for these people, it is the only phone. Now, in these same regions, web-enabled, affordable feature phones (and possibly smartphones to come, following the agreement between Nokia and Microsoft) are letting these people in the poorer parts of the world leapfrog fixed-line Internet technology and reach the web via mobile.

This opens up m-commerce to a staggeringly large new audience, and it is therein that the real gold lies.

Mobile commerce in the developed world

First, we need to look at the developed world, its thirst for mobile phones, feature phones and smartphones, and how this is driving the market for m-commerce.

Before we get on to the very modern phenomenon of the smartphone and what it means for mobile commerce, we have to look at how ordinary mobile phones compare with feature phones.

It is hard to put a number on the penetration of ordinary phones in the developed world. Everyone's definition of what constitutes an ordinary phone differs as the line between them and feature phones blurs. Also, with an average turnaround of 18 months in the life of a phone, by rights there should be hardly any ordinary phones left. Their role in m-commerce these days is also minor, since they typically do not have access to the web and are not able to run apps.

But they can't be discounted completely, as they can be used to pay for things using SMS as discussed in Chapter 1, and can consume ringtones and wallpapers, often sold through operator portals. They can also receive text-based marketing, which may lead to the owner of the phone entering a store and buying something. I think we can consider that part of the mobile retailing experience, so they are not to be totally dismissed.

Anyone reading this book in order to get an idea of how mobile phones may have an impact on their business in the developed world and what they should do to service the needs of their mobile customers, should always have some lo-fi version of their mobile offering available for these ordinary phones. There is an ever decreasing number of them in circulation, but they are still there.

More pressing is looking at how many feature phones are in circulation. According to comScore research, 60% of the US consumer market is using what is dubbed a feature phone. That number is falling rapidly as the penetration of smartphones is rising. A similar, though slightly smaller percentage of Europeans are also using feature phones as their primary mobile device. The number of ordinary phones in the US and Europe combined is 200 million handsets: a not insignificant number. While the sales of smartphones are rapidly increasing and are likely to pass those of feature phones early in 2011, there are enough feature phones in circulation to warrant any m-commerce based business to cater to the needs of these devices.

As with all things mobile, the difficulty is in developing any sort of content or service that will work on the vast and varied number of handsets, each with their own operating-system quirks, screen sizes, network connection speeds, processor capacities, processing power, memories, menus and networks. In fact, mobile phone technology has to be the most fragmented technology yet devised by man, with very little in the way of hard and fast standards (apart from network operating technologies such as GSM, EDGE, UMTS, WCDMA, 3G, 4G and LTE . . . hang on, even this is getting totally fragmented).

It is estimated that anyone wanting to roll out any sort of third-party mobile service that will work on the majority of (note, not all, but most) handsets in a given geographic area has to be prepared to create around 6,500 versions of their offering to cater to the different manufacturers' phones, operating systems, various screens and so on. In fact, even different models made by the same phone manufacturer don't necessarily have the same OS, screen or processors. It is a vastly complicated market.

One apps developer I visited, and who wishes to remain anonymous, has a cabinet with literally thousands of handsets in it. On visiting his offices, I assumed it was just a display of the history of mobile phones. When I complimented him on his collection, he told me that no, they weren't a display, but rather *some* of the phones they had to use to test that their apps worked on as many phones as possible.

The arrival of the smartphone, for now at least, alleviates this difficulty to some degree, since there are really only four or five major operating systems in the smartphone world and they are all fairly standardized, but more of that anon.

The feature-phone market has boomed over the past few years, driven by the vast majority of people who were not able to afford early smartphones, but who were eligible for an upgrade nonetheless. They have played an important role in getting consumers used to the fact that they can do a lot more with the cell phone than just make calls and send text, and, as such, have started to act as a loss leader for the raft of smartphones starting to deluge the market. Get the customer used to using handsets for more than just calls, and then move in for the up-sell.

Feature phones introduced the market to 3G networks, some mobile web-surfing, the idea of apps, better cameras and video, and the use of the mobile phone as a music player. They also generated a lot of revenue for people selling ringtones and wallpapers for mobile phones, as typically the feature phone screens are larger, full color and more functional than those of previous mobile devices.

While the feature phone has seen success over the past five years, their demise is speeding up, as smartphones not only grip the public imagination, but thanks to competition in the market, become cheap enough for mass-market penetration. This falling price of technology (again, part of Moore's Law) has had a dramatic effect on the mobile handset marketplace, not only by displacing the feature phone as the top dog in the mobile space, but also by ushering in something that no one really saw coming: the beginning of the decline of the PC.

In the fourth quarter of 2010, the sale of mobile smartphones — essentially a phone on steroids that combines a voice telephone with the capabilities to access e-mail and calendars via the web, as well as download software applications, or apps — outstripped those of desktop PCs globally. That means that in the latter part of 2010, more people bought a smartphone than a computer. That is considered by many in the computing, mobile phone, retail and commerce industries as a crucial tipping point in how people use the web.

The fact that it has taken only about three years for the smartphone — characterized by Apple's iPhone, which was launched in April 2007, but also exemplified by the BlackBerry, which preceded it by a few years — to sell more than the desktop PC shows that, while the parallels between mobile and e-commerce are strong, the timeline for mobile is considerably shorter.

It also shows that how people want to use computers has changed immeasurably during the 21st century. They have embraced portability, and manufacturers have combined the ever-increasing cheapness of computer processing power with the need to do things on the move, creating a sophisticated device that puts more computing power into a person's trousers than was used to fly the Apollo moon missions.

The smartphone phenomenon sits at the heart of the interest surrounding mobile commerce in the developed world's markets, and sales and penetration of such devices compared with those of desktop PCs is considered by many as a bellwether of how m-commerce is shaping up against e-commerce.

Of course e-commerce still outstrips m-commerce by a factor of between 10 and 100, depending on whose statistics you read. M-commerce is a large potential market, but still a nascent one compared to the hundreds of millions of dollars spent online via computers. That said, we cannot forget that while I was writing this book, smartphones outsold new desktop PCs.

In fact, in the US smartphones are about 40% of the market for phones and growing rapidly. There are 234 million mobile phone users of one kind or another in the US, believes comScore, so consumers there own around 94 million smartphones. IDC Research estimates that European smartphone sales grew by 99.4% in Q4 2010 compared to the same period in 2009, with some 25.6 million smartphones being shipped in that period. That brings the total Western European mobile smartphone market to just shy of 60 million units.

For a market seeded by Apple's frankly revolutionary iPhone in 2007, the fact that the number one operating system in the market is Google's Android OS is remarkable and shows how dynamic the mobile phone market is. Android was developed by Google to be an open operating system that developers could freely develop for. Like Apple's iOS operating system, it comprises a set of development tools called SDKs (software development kits) that third parties use to turn their ideas into small software apps that sit on the phone. As we shall see in Chapter 3, there is a lot more to this than meets the eye.

Keep taking the tablets

One spin-off from the smartphone revolution is the creation of what seems to be a wholly new type of mobile device: the tablet computer. Exemplified by the Apple iPad (now in its second iteration), but also leading to a raft of devices by, among others, Samsung (the Galaxy), BlackBerry (the PlayBook), and even Hewlett Packard (the TouchPad), the tablet computing world combines the computing powers of the laptop with the keyboard-less touchscreen technology and portability of the smartphone, producing a device that is at once genius and absurd.

For a while anyone who wanted to do computing, not least connect to the web and engage in commerce on the move, had to buy a laptop. For many years these powerful yet portable computers did us all proud. There was a push to create a smaller version of the laptop — the netbook — which did away with a lot of the heavy and bulky internal workings of the laptop, such as hard drives and the like, relying instead on all that sort of thing happening remotely in "the cloud" (remotely hosted within the Internet). But netbooks never really caught on. They seemed like smaller, less effective laptops.

Then along came the tablet computer, and through the power of style over substance, the tablet became a whole new kind of portable computing device: part smartphone, and part web-enabled media consumer and creator. The fact that the iPad and its chums are essentially netbooks in a different, more stylish skin, has passed us all by and now we all use them. (Me included. In fact, just to prove how I really needed an iPad, I am writing this section about tablet computers on my iPad, so there).

But sentiment aside, the tablet computer, and the same goes for the less sexy netbook, is an important part of the m-commerce tale. According to Neilsen NetRatings, which analyzes who does what online with what device, as of the end of 2010, penetration of tablets in the US market (by far the most advanced tablet market) was 4%: a small but significant number, and only 2% lower than e-book readers and 4% behind netbooks. Significantly, among the kind of people who consider themselves to be early adopters of technology — you know the type, skinny jeans, black-framed glasses, beards — tablet penetration is 48%. Those in the know have embraced them with alacrity.

Tablets are an important part of m-commerce as they open up the possibility of different ways to consume things while on the move. Where the mobile phone and smartphone are ideal both as payment tools and devices to consume small things on, tablets are much more suited to game playing and media consumption, watching video footage and reading books. They are also more likely to be used as videophones.

All these add a whole new outlet for selling everything from videos, books, newspapers, games and videophone calls – not to mention apps that do all sorts of other things – which means more m-commerce revenues. The fact that tablets also blur still further the line between computers and mobile phones means, statistically at least, that the amount of money deemed to be spent on m-commerce as opposed to e-commerce will become more of an opaque distinction over the next few years.

In a retail context, tablet computers offer a chance to extend the mobile retailing experience to include video demos of clothes or goods, to see video reviews, demos, instructions and much more. As such, as we shall see in Chapter 4, tablets will play an increasing role in mobile commerce in the coming months and years.

The developing world

While tablet computing is very much a trait of the (over?) developed mobile market in the western world, mobile is increasingly the central pillar of both the communications and Internet revolution in the developing world. India, China, Southeast Asia, Russia, Latin America and Africa all have huge populations, and they are becoming more mobile-phone oriented.

The cost of rolling out old school fixed-line telephone networks to remote habitations, often in or beyond inhospitable landscapes, has become prohibitive, even for state-controlled telecom companies.

Mobile, relying as it does on connected towers that service vast areas using radio, means that rolling out country-wide networks, while still expensive, is much more affordable than it ever was. Further, the vast number of mobile handsets created in the west means that the unit price per handset of basic design is low enough for even the poor to afford. Together, these two factors mean that mobile is becoming a booming consumer business in developing countries – and where there is a booming consumer market, there is booming mobile-commerce opportunity.

A similar argument applies to the rollout of the Internet. Many developing countries have bypassed the fixed-line Internet, going from nothing to mobile web in a single bound. The mobile networks have been built relatively recently, often by western telecoms who have future-proofed them, and so we are seeing a surge, especially in India and China where there is a burgeoning middle class, in mobile web use and all the commercial opportunities that brings.

According to Mobile Squared, there are more than 500 million mobile users in India alone, and it is expected to see some 260 million mobile Internet users by 2011. This massive market is, however, dwarfed by China, which is already seeing some 800 million mobile web users – 58% of all Asian mobile web users.

In Africa mobile phones account for 90% of all telephones in use across the whole continent. Thanks to very good prepaid mobile phone deals, about 500 million Africans (half the estimated population of the continent) have mobile phones. While not as developed as markets in India and China, and lacking a sizable middle-class market segment, Africa offers a different, though no less enticing, mobile-commerce environment.

In Kenya, mobile phone users have already embraced mobile payments, using Vodafone subsidiary Safaricom's M-PESA mobile money transfer offering. (*M* is for mobile, while *pesa* is Swahili for money.) While not m-commerce in the conventional sense, M-PESA is interesting as it reveals how what was an undeveloped market five years ago has been transformed by using mobile. In many ways, with the mobile buy-in of the people, it can be an m-commerce pioneer.

M-PESA is a low-cost money-transfer service that lets anyone with a mobile phone — they don't even have to have a bank account — put money into their mobile phone account, transfer it and cash it in at the other end. The service, launched in Kenya in 2007, has gone from strength to strength, and now sees several million users, who typically had never used a bank, using their phones to move money about and pay for things.

Typically across these developing markets, m-commerce is limited to distinctly lo-fi GSM handsets; but as I said earlier, the alliance between Nokia and Microsoft could well provoke a surge in the use of smartphones, and hence the mobile web, for m-commerce across these markets too.

Nokia has pretty much cornered the market in Africa and India. In fact, many people in both regions call their mobile phones their Nokia, in a bit of brand eponymy bettered only by Band-Aid, Xerox and Hoover in the 20th century. (The Germans, incidentally, call mobile phones a "Handy".) A partnership with Microsoft to put the latter's operating system on Nokia smartphones could well see the economies of scale coming to bear, as highly functional smartphones hit wireless networks across Africa and other developing geographies. This would put Nokia back on the top of the smartphone tree in number terms, if nothing else, and open up the vast markets of Africa and other areas to the joys of mobile commerce.

So what is it all worth?

M-commerce is a hard beast to tie down and measure. Defining exactly what it is and then measuring the money that goes through it, the profit extracted from it and the general value of the market, regionally and globally, is a tough one. The picture is muddied still further as smartphones and tablets blur the line between whether a transaction was mobile or just online.

That said, there are clear areas that are revenue generators and are purely mobile commerce, and these have been measured through the tried and true technique of guesstimation: the technical term for licking one's finger and holding it in the air. Guesstimators have arrived at some startling figures.

In Japan, by far the most advanced and long-lived mobile commerce market, ABI Research values the m-commerce market at some $10bn. In the US, relatively immature as a mobile commerce market, ABI suggests the figure is closer to $2bn, despite tripling in size between 2008 and 2009. Worldwide, ABI predicts that m-commerce in all senses – from buying tangible goods to buying content and services that will be used on the mobile device – will be worth about $120bn by 2015.

Where is it going?

What is interesting about m-commerce is that, while it looks like it will be a $120bn global market by 2015, it has yet to reach its true potential. To date we have seen only the beginnings of mobile commerce and what it can achieve. So far we have largely concentrated on how the mobile phone can be used to buy and consume content, and touched on the fact that it can also be used to buy tangible goods, like a phone-based version of e-commerce.

But there is so much more that mobile can do, and much of the value it brings to commerce overall is impossible to measure directly. Mobile commerce, to my mind, extends from these beginnings of simple purchases, turning the phone handset into a wallet, a media player, an infinite shopping mall, a ticket machine, a social buying and selling platform, a tool to interact with other media, a games console, a bank, a credit/debit card, a television, a computer and my ID.

It is a platform to consume paid-for and free software apps, a device to access the web and to delve into location-based services and augmented reality. It will also be a conduit for advertising and marketing, tokens, offers, loyalty programs, plane tickets, satellite navigation ... and a phone. All these things will generate money, directly or indirectly, and so trying to predict what it will all be worth is impossible. Mobile will sit at the heart of so many everyday commercial activities that it is almost of limitless value.

So where is it going? Well, this whole book is devoted to answering that question, but before we get stuck in those details, here are some key areas where mobile will be making a huge impact over the coming years.

M-commerce will continue to be driven by the sale of content and services consumed on the device itself. It will also see the rapid and exponential growth in retail, both as a mobile e-commerce tool, and as a tool that can be used to enhance the retail experience online and in a store.

These two will be the pillars that hold up m-commerce. But around them will grow a huge eco-system of payments, banking, marketing, location-based offerings, augmented reality and much more. Will it surpass e-commerce? For sure, but only in the way that e-commerce and m-commerce will blend into one: it will all just be commerce, and will be more about how to best serve each channel a consumer uses to access your business, delivering the right experience and joining it all together. As a man of a certain age I like to think that m-commerce means I will never have to go to a shop again, but that might be fanciful thinking. It will, I am convinced, mean that when I am taken shopping, I will be able to augment the experience with my mobile device or devices and have a much more pleasurable time of it.

CHAPTER 3

Apps, mobile web and all that

- Where do apps and m-web fit into mobile strategies?

- What impact will HTML5 have on m-web?

- How will mobile networks cope with increased data?

Since this book hopefully has a long shelf life, it seems wise to stick to the assumption that, as time marches on, we will move ever closer to 100% penetration of smartphones, at least in the developed world. So it is worth considering what makes them tick technically and why they are important.

Technically, smartphones and tablets are pretty much mini-computers, featuring the some sort of processing power, an operating system that runs on the processor, memory (both RAM and storage memory) and software that makes various things like the clock, camera, e-mail and so on work. All phones typically have this. It is only now with smartphones that there is some degree of homogeneity of how they work, as well as a greater degree of sophistication regarding what software can be run on them and the myriad applications that you can get your phone or tablet to do.

In essence, the modern mobile smartphone device (and when I use that term I am, from now on, including tablet computers) allows its user to do two things, aside from making phone calls and sending texts: connect to the Internet and run software that makes the device useful. These two things are at the heart of what modern mobile communications technology brings us, and are why mobile suddenly has a commercial side to it. These multifunctional devices that we carry around can do so much so securely, they are effectively storefronts and web browsers in our pockets.

And this opens up two things that have until recently been seen as in competition with each other, but which are rapidly becoming highly complementary: apps and mobile web (m-web). These are the two main ways that a smartphone (and even feature phones) can make themselves useful. Both rely on the device connecting to the web (apps when you have to download them and m-web to actually work) and both are means of getting things to work on your phone, and to offer things to buy and ways to pay for them.

Until recently there was often an air of either/or about apps and m-web. Many people thought that apps were more versatile, since you only needed to connect your device to the web to download them, and you could then use them whether you were connected to the Internet or not. M-web, on the other hand, let you do much the same tasks, but without having anything sitting on the handset. M-web, the old thinking had it, allowed businesses to update their offerings whenever they wanted without users ever doing anything; it could work on multiple devices without having to develop the same app over and over again for a variety of handsets and operating systems; and it was more akin to cloud computing and the netbook idea discussed in Chapter 2.

Conversely, the champions of the app believed that while all that might be true, apps had several distinct advantages. They could be personalized; they could offer a richer, faster and more pleasant user experience; and, perhaps most important of all, they kept the data usage on the phone down and thus were much cheaper to run.

All very valid. However, what has happened since is that operator data plans for consumers are increasingly cheap and often uncapped, so the data cost issue is cut. Most smartphone devices have Wi-Fi access, so you are not always using mobile data anyway and, heck, it's even better if you combine the functionality of apps with the connectedness of m-web. So today we tend to see anyone who wants to deliver an app developing web-enabled apps for key operating systems – typically for Apple and Android devices, some Nokia and various mobile Windows offerings – and also creating a mobile website that any other device can connect to. The best of all worlds.

But before we get on to how all this works together, how to make it happen and where the commerciality lies, we need to take a look at apps, m-web and, ahem, operator portals, in more detail.

App, app and away

Back in the 1990s everyone was talking about finding "the killer app." Today, everyone is urging consumers to download their app. But what are they? In short, *app* is an abbreviation for application – and in that sense, the killer app of the 1990s that we searched for (and never found!) and the downloadable apps are, semantically, one and the same thing. Since we now live in the 21st century, however, we shall concentrate on what apps mean today.

An app is essentially a piece of software that can run on the Internet, on your computer, or on your phone or other electronic device. There are currently thought to be about 300,000 individual third-party apps sitting on a variety of apps stores. Somewhere between 150,000 and 200,000 of those are created for Apple's iPhone/iPod/iPad range of devices – many of which are slowly being replicated for Android, Nokia, Windows, BlackBerry and other OSs – while the remaining 100,000 or more don't work on Apple devices.

At the time of writing, a total of more than 15 billion apps have been downloaded worldwide onto handsets, covering everything from games and shopping apps, to photographic processing services, to productivity and workflow tools, to things that pretend to turn your phone into an x-ray machine and others that deliver a joke every morning. Many of these apps are free to download and use, and it is estimated that about a quarter of the rest carry a charge – from a few cents for some simple applications, right up to hundreds of dollars for sophisticated satellite navigation offerings.

Apple is far and away the biggest apps deliverer, having notched up its 15 billionth app download from its store as of September 2011.

However, since the vast majority of those apps are free, and those that are paid for generate very small revenues – on average about $700 per app per year, with half of all paid-for apps costing no more than 99 cents, and the mean price paid for an Apple app being just $2.70 – it is widely believed that Apple (and you can extrapolate downward for all other app sellers) has made only a few hundred million dollars selling apps.

That said, it is still a nascent business and, as we shall see in this chapter, as the technology surrounding apps and the mobile web evolves, the possibility of making money through apps incrementally is on the rise, as they increasingly sit at the heart of mobile commerce. And with Apple taking 30% of the list price of each app – and poised to take 30% of all in-app billing and apps-subscriptions revenues too – it has the potential to net the company an ever-growing amount of money.

How they work

Apps are simply software typically developed by third parties – so not by Apple, or Google or whoever owns the phone's OS, network or apps store – using an approved set of development tools (or Software Developer Kits or SDKs), so that they are compatible with the device's operating system. The app can then tap into all the other functions of the phone's hardware, such as its web connection, location, orientation, accelerometers, calendars, e-mail, browser and all other apps on the device, if need be.

The genius behind apps, and why so many of them have been downloaded, is that they have become an easy way of accessing mobile services. Anyone familiar with an iPhone, Android phone or any other modern smartphone knows that apps sit on the home screen as a collection of brightly colored, clearly labeled buttons that, when touched, connect the user to something useful that is either run locally on the device or increasingly out there on the web.

When mobile phones started to morph into feature phones and got access through 3G networks to mobile data services – the Internet, to you and me – one of the biggest drawbacks was actually getting the device to connect to anything useful. Typing in a URL (a web address) by using the phone's alphanumeric dial pad tested the patience and dexterity of even the most ardent SMS user. And even if you did manage to do that and had a good enough connection to actually get to a website, those sites weren't optimized for mobile phone screens, processors or the tools used to navigate around a website. In short, you had a website on your phone screen that didn't fit, couldn't be moved around and didn't have a cursor to click on anything. It was a tawdry and dispiriting experience for us early adopters, I can tell you.

The app, however, changed all that dramatically. Suddenly the phone could do all sorts of new and exciting things, and those things were optimized for the screen of the phone. Even if they weren't running from the Internet cloud but locally on the device, we suddenly had a lovely new experience, and the power of the smartphone was unleashed.

Now, many people get angry about the lionizing of Apple Inc. and the iPhone, but let's give credit where it's due. This device and the apps-based approach – in fact, the whole ecosystem of device, store, apps, screen and software – created by Apple for the iPhone was revolutionary, and it is the only reason why today we have smartphones, the promise of a highly lucrative m-commerce market and probably the reason you are reading this book (and certainly the reason I am writing it).

Until the launch of the iPhone, which leveraged Apple's skills in understanding how consumers use things and how they will buy beautifully designed devices, the feature-phone experience was awful. Left to the geeks at leading handset manufacturers such as Nokia, Motorola, Sony Ericsson and so on, things would have become more complex and we probably wouldn't be talking about m-commerce in the terms that we are today. These guys, all very clever indeed, were steeped in mobile. The only problem was, they never really thought about how the devices were used, could be used and how people wanted to use them.

Along comes Apple and decides, primarily, that people want an MP3 player, a camera and access to the web and e-mail on a device; and lo, a device is designed that offers a large screen, a (relatively) high-powered processor and Wi-Fi connectivity – as well as a phone and texting capability. Suddenly, everyone gets it.

From this the apps market is born as Apple realizes that many software developers can make light work of creating a whole range of other things that can be done using this device – and that Apple can control the entire process of getting those things to people's handsets – and an entirely new ecosystem is born.

Google sees the potential and launches Android, and a set of phones – created again by more consumer-goods-oriented companies such as Samsung and LG – flood the market, and we have a whole new way of using mobile phones. All because people like pressing buttons.

Of course, phone makers such as Nokia are not going to give up on making handsets, and soon they too are offering a raft of these new-look smartphones, their own OS, their own apps ecosystem and store, and in three short years the mobile phone market has taken one almighty leap forward.

Currently there are really six main operating systems for smartphones that you need to consider when developing your apps:

Apple's iOS

Originally known as iPhone OS and developed, as the name implies, for Apple's iPhone, iOS – now on version 4.3 – is a common operating system for iPhones, iPods, iPads and Apple TV. The latter is the company's web TV stream service, which we don't need to worry about too much here. Apple does not license iOS to run on anything other than Apple devices, and it is tied directly to Apple's iTunes store, which runs the Apps Store. ITunes is essentially a music browser that sits on the user's PC or Mac desktop computer or laptop, and manages music, media and apps, offering a payment gateway and back-up service. Essentially, it lets Apple manage everything any iOS user does. In the mobile world, it is known as a walled garden.

Android OS

Google's answer to the iOS, Android was developed by a consortium of interested parties from the computer world called the Open Handset Alliance (OHA). Based on a similar OS for computers called Linux, it is an open software platform, whereby developers are free to tweak the operating system itself to improve it, so long as they share those tweaks and improvements. It too has an apps store and billing tools, but Android apps are also available through other third-party stores such as GetJar and, soon, Amazon's apps store, cementing the OS's credentials as not being a walled garden. And the approach seems to work, since as of Q4 2010, Android is the most widely used mobile OS on the market, accounting for 31.2% of the US handset market and a staggering 44% of the Western European handset market. It knocks Nokia's Symbian (see below) off the top spot after 10 years as the most widely used mobile OS.

Nokia's Symbian OS

Originally developed by Symbian Ltd. for the Psion range of personal digital assistant (PDA) devices in the 1990s, it was created by merging and integrating software assets contributed by Nokia, NTT DOCOMO,

Sony Ericsson and Symbian Ltd. Nokia then used the OS as the basis for its S60 series of feature phones and beyond, refining the OS over the years. Until recently – December 2010, to be precise – Symbian OS on Nokia handsets was the most widely used mobile operating system, accounting for 43.8% of all worldwide smartphone handset sales in Q2 2010. There are in fact 235 million Symbian OS handsets out there currently, so while it no longer grabs the headlines, it is worth developing for.

Windows Mobile OS

A mobile operating system developed by Microsoft, this is designed to be similar to desktop versions of Windows, feature-wise and aesthetically. Additionally, third-party software development is available for Windows Mobile, and apps can be purchased via the Windows Marketplace for Mobile. Originally appearing as the Pocket PC 2000 OS, most Windows Mobile devices come with a stylus pen, which is used to enter commands by tapping it on the screen. As Android and iOS have gained ground, Windows Mobile's share of the smartphone market has fallen yearly, leaving it now as the fifth most popular smartphone OS with a 5% share of the worldwide smartphone market (after Symbian, BlackBerry OS, Android and iPhone). In the US it does, however, have a 24% share of the enterprise users' market.

Windows Phone 7 OS

This is a mobile operating system developed by Microsoft. The successor to its Windows Mobile OS, it is aimed more at the consumer market instead of the enterprise market, where Windows Mobile is relatively successful. With Windows Phone 7, Microsoft offers a new user interface with its design language named Metro, integrates the operating system with third party and other Microsoft services, and plans to strictly control which hardware it runs on. Windows Phone 7 was developed quickly, resulting in the fact that Windows Mobile applications do not run on it. That leaves many apps developers with the onerous – and costly – task of rewriting their Windows Mobile apps for Windows Phone 7. However, the pill may be sweetened by a deal done in February 2011 between Nokia and Microsoft, which will see Windows Phone 7 becoming the OS of choice on all Nokia phones from now on. That means that WP7 is likely to become the most widely used mobile OS globally, and will make apps development much simpler, with just iOS, Android, Windows 7 and BlackBerry to develop for.

BlackBerry

This is a proprietary mobile OS, developed by Research In Motion (RIM) for its BlackBerry line of smartphone handheld devices. The OS allows multitasking, and has been adopted by RIM for use in its handhelds, particularly the trackwheel, trackball, trackpad and touchscreen. The BlackBerry platform is perhaps best known for its native support for corporate e-mail, through MIDP 1.0 and, more recently, a subset of MIDP 2.0, which allows complete wireless activation and synchronization with Microsoft Exchange, Lotus Domino or Novell GroupWise e-mail, calendar, tasks, notes and contacts, when used in conjunction with BlackBerry Enterprise Server. Third-party developers can write software using the available BlackBerry API (application programming interface) classes, although applications that make use of certain functionality must be digitally signed. In September 2010, RIM announced a new unrelated QNX-based platform, BlackBerry Tablet OS, to run on its upcoming BlackBerry PlayBook tablet computer. QNX is going to completely replace BlackBerry OS as of BlackBerry 7, says the company.

Apps stores

An intrinsic part of all mobile OS these days – driven by Apple and Google, with the others playing catch up, adding them to their roster of services – are apps stores: the storefront where the apps market really comes to life.

Apps stores are the repositories of all the 300,000+ apps out there, and the main means of getting them from the developer to the consumer's handset. All the above OS players now run their own apps stores, but there are also a growing number of independent apps stores that sell apps for all of these operating systems, bar Apple's walled garden, and share the revenue between developers and handset makers. They are, in effect, apps aggregators.

The most well known of the apps stores is Apple's App Store, which at time of writing had some 300,000 unique apps for iPhone, iPod and iPad on its virtual shelves. The store is part of Apple's highly successful online content-management iTunes Store, which in turn is part of the iTunes browser that sits on many thousands of Mac and PC computers all over the world.

Opened on July 10, 2008, the Apple App Store is essentially an app itself that lets Apple iOS devices download apps onto that Apple device. It allows users to browse and download applications from the iTunes Store that were developed with the iOS SDK or Mac SDK and published through Apple. Depending on the application, they are available either for free or at a cost, and the App Store – via iTunes, which requires that a user sign up with a credit or debit card – handles the billing for that app. Of the store's revenues, 30% go instantly to Apple, and 70% go to the developer of the app.

Following the popularity of the Apple App Store, competitors developed their own app stores and, despite "App Store" being an Apple trademarked name, most people call them that, regardless of device. They include:

Android Market
Launched on October 22, 2008, the Android equivalent of the Apple App Store comes preinstalled on most Android handsets, so that users can immediately fill up their handset with all manner of useful

and exciting apps. Android has the highest proportion of free apps of all the apps stores (57%) and passed the 200,000 apps milestone in December 2010. Like Apple, the Android store offers a 70:30 split on the revenue of all apps sold through the store; and it has become the first mobile apps store to let users pay for their purchases on their mobile phone bill. T-Mobile in the US – the launch customer of Android back in 2008 – is the first telecom to offer this. Like Apple, Android Market does vet applications and has banned several, typically in the adult market, though it is not viewed as being as zealous about this as Apple.

Windows Marketplace for Mobile

Microsoft's apps store for its soon to be phased out Windows Mobile platform allows users to browse and download applications that have been developed by third parties. The applications are available for use directly on Windows Mobile 6.5 devices, and on personal computers. Again, the store offers a 70:30 split on the apps revenue with developers, although it also levies a onetime charge of $99 on developers to list an unlimited number of paid applications, or up to five free applications yearly in the marketplace. After five free applications have been listed for the year, each additional free application can be listed for $19.99. Windows Marketplace for Mobile is also unique in that it offers mobile network operators the ability to create a branded section of the store, in order to market carrier-specific applications and services for their customers.

Windows Phone Marketplace

Created to service Microsoft's new Windows Phone 7 mobile OS, it offered some 10,000 apps as of March 2011. The store supports credit card purchases, operator billing and ad-supported content. It also features a "try before you buy" scheme, where the user has an option to download a trial or demo of a commercial app before paying for it. Other features are similar to Windows Phone Marketplace's predecessor, Windows Marketplace for Mobile (see above), and will have 61 categories split into 16 main categories and 25 subcategories. Apps can only be placed in one category. Windows Phone Marketplace will feature downloads for podcasts and music provided by the Zune Marketplace. Windows Phone Marketplace will also feature downloads for 3D games that will have integrated Xbox LIVE connectivity and features.

Nokia Ovi Store

Ovi is Finnish for door, and was introduced by Nokia back in 2007 to cover all of its then mobile Internet services, in a world where apps stores and smartphones didn't yet exist. Ovi initially focused on games, maps, media, messaging and music, but has since branched out to cover a much richer range of apps, many from third parties and even operators. The current Ovi Store was launched in May 2009 to tap into the burgeoning world of smartphone apps, and it lets users download a vast array of apps, videos, music, media, games and more, totaling some 35,000 items by the start of 2011. Now that Nokia has partnered with Microsoft to put Windows Phone 7 on next generation Nokia devices, it is likely that the Nokia store will become part of the wider Windows Phone Marketplace and eventually disappear, though at the time of writing no plans were forthcoming.

GetJar

GetJar is the largest independent mobile phone application store in the world, founded in Lithuania in 2004. Offering more than 75,000 mobile applications across major handset platforms, including Java ME, BlackBerry, Symbian, Windows Mobile and Android, it reaches more than 15 million consumers. It has notched up some 1.05 billion individual downloads at a rate of 3 million downloads per day, making it the second most used apps store behind Apple. GetJar allows software developers to upload their applications for free through a developer portal, and has some 300,000 software developers currently using the service.

BlackBerry App World

BlackBerry maker RIM's apps store offers some 10,000 apps and sees around 2 million downloads per day, many skewed toward business use rather than consumers. It charges developers $200 to load up to 10 apps onto the store.

Palm App Catalog

Palm's apps store offers third-party apps for Palm devices that use WebOS.

Samsung Apps

Launched in the UK, France and Italy, as well as in Asia, Samsung Apps provides mobile applications developed specifically for Samsung mobile phones. Apps cover set categories of: games, health/life, e-book, music, video, news, navigation, productivity, reference, social networking, utilities, theme and brand.

Nintendo DSi Shop

Not strictly speaking a mobile phone, this portable handheld game console is rapidly becoming a web-enabled device that uses Wi-Fi to connect it to the Internet either in home or when out and about, and so is worth a mention. It has a games store that it can connect to, and therefore counts as an apps store of sorts.

Sony PlayStation Store

As with the Nintendo DSi and its store, the Sony PlayStation's portable PSP also has web connectivity and a store for buying games.

Others that are planning to enter the apps store race include Amazon, which is set to extend its online/mobile e-books store and music download service to the delivery of apps. Amazon currently boasts one of the most widely used mobile commerce apps, and the move to add apps to what it sells could be a game changer. At the time of writing however, Amazon had yet to set a confirmed launch date.

Challenges app-plenty

This mushrooming of devices, operating systems and apps stores has its drawbacks. Apple devices (iPhones and iPads in particular) have a niche market, dictated by the price of the goods and the brand values that aim it at a certain kind of person – or demographic, as marketeers politely refer to it – so to get your app out there to the largest possible audience, it has to be developed for other smartphone OSs too. While the basic premise of the app is pretty much the same across all devices, each will have its own quirks and differences. Suddenly we are back to a world where, while not quite having to prepare things for more than 6,000 devices, you have to build apps for at least three or four, if not all six, major – and distinctly different – operating systems.

This can be a time-consuming and costly process. Not all devices that you want your app to run on will offer the same functionality. So, for example, you may end up being able to offer a full bells-and-whistles experience with your app on iPhone and Android, but not have quite the full functionality on a Nokia or Windows phone. They also all, once again, tend to have different screen sizes and dimensions, different user interfaces – Windows Mobile using a stylus and BlackBerry using a trackball, for instance – and so the process of app development is not one that ever can deliver a uniform experience across devices.

Perhaps the biggest challenge with apps, however, is in getting people to find them. With more than 200,000 different apps out there, unless a consumer or business user is actively looking for a particular app, knows what it is called and can be bothered to search it out on the apps store, you have practically zero chance of your app being discovered if you don't do anything to push it.

Most apps stores will do a "featured" section, which, depending on the apps store, is either free and run by people on the store, or is paid for as a marketing expense. That is one way to be discovered. But with such a huge turnaround in apps entering stores each week, it would be foolish to rely on this as the only way to get found.

Another extension to this is to get as many people as possible to rate (ideally highly) your app and to recommend it. This too will sit on the apps stores as a community endorsement. However, this is something of a catch-22, as you need people to find it, and once they've downloaded it, to rate and review it.

Which brings us to the irony at the heart of the apps market: despite this being a high tech marketplace for cutting-edge software for mobile phones, which can do some frankly amazing things, you often need to rely on good old-fashioned marketing and traditional media channels to get people to find your app, especially if you are a commercial organization looking for mass downloads of your app.

This, of course, adds to the expense in developing an app, as you have to invest in marketing to get anyone to know that it is there. But with 10 billion apps now downloaded, the process does seem to work.

Once people have apps on their handsets, you hit the next problem, which is really the crux of the apps verses m-web strategy debate, and which reveals the way people view apps is subtly changing – how do you update apps or connect them to the web?

Prosaically, most apps end up having to be updated – with more features, to fix bugs, to refine compatibility with changes to the phone's OS. To do this on current devices, you need to connect your apps-store app to the Internet, it needs to ask the store's servers what needs updating, then you have to manually download those updates and install them. What if you want to update your app all the time to make it more timely and interactive, not to mention useful on the fly?

Until recently you couldn't. Increasingly, though, developers are seeing that apps are not static things that sit on the phone. They are gateways to doing specific things on the mobile web, and in many ways are becoming a way of delivering users to specific parts of the web easily and simply (back to just pushing a button again!).

For example, I have a New York City Subway app in my iPhone that provides me with a range of useful things, such as a line map, a route finder and even a guide to where to stand on the platform so that when I disembark I am opposite an exit. I also have them for the London Underground, the Barcelona Metro, the Hong Kong MTR and the Moscow Metro. All this runs natively on the phone, so I can use it underground while riding the subway.

So far so good. But what about when I want to get live information as to the running of those trains, to find out which lines have delays and which don't, so I can plan my route even more effectively? Well, I can't. First, I am underground, so no connection; but even if there were, a static, locally-run app on the phone is useless. To get this updated, it needs to be connected to the web and pull information down from the web without me noticing.

Increasingly, this is where apps are going. They are a way of delivering m-web with a better user experience with some functionality run locally as software on the handset, and so speeding up what is done on the mobile web. As we shall see in the next section, the mobile web offers much to the mobile commerce experience too. For the sake of making this book more structured, I have chosen to break up apps and m-web into two sections. In reality, though, anyone working with mobile commerce is going to find that the two are inextricably linked, and each makes the other work better. Sure, there are instances where you want one rather than the other, but realistically we are living in a mobile world where m-web and apps are one and the same thing.

There is also the issue of the fickle nature of people. A study by Localytics found that while smartphone and tablet owners are willing to give applications a try, 26% of the time they never use the same application again. The study also found that another 26% of people become loyal repeat customers, using a new application more than 10 times. But that still leaves 50% who are neither loyal nor onetime users, which might be even worse: they are ambivalent to your app. And the pattern is pretty consistent across all OSs too, Localytics found.

Spinning the m-web

While much attention has been placed on the mobile apps market, as we have seen, apps are becoming ever more web-enabled. And sitting behind this web-enablement is the mobile web. The mobile web is very interesting, not least because it doesn't exist. Well, there is no such thing as a mobile Internet, it's just the Internet, but it is called mobile web (or m-web) when it is accessed and used by browsers or apps running on a mobile device or mobile OS.

It's a bit like quantum physics (the Heisenberg Uncertainty Principle, to be precise): the mobile web only exists when the device connecting to it is connected to it.

Let me explain. The Internet is just there to be accessed. When you do it the "normal" way with a PC, the servers that your PC connects to know that you are a PC (in fact, they increasingly know what kind of PC you are, screen size and so on), and you receive the right experience of the websites you are looking at for that combination of browser, PC, screen and so on. In the mobile world it is much the same: pointing a mobile device at the Internet delivers a version of that website tailored to a mobile device. That version typically contains less data, is formatted for smaller screens and adheres to some slightly different standards.

The mobile web is significant because, as of 2008, more people accessed the web via a mobile-based browser than via a fixed PC browser, and this trend is accelerating. This means that today, more people access the web through mobile than PCs.

The drawbacks of m-web

While there is much to be said for the mobile web, it does have some inherent disadvantages for anyone wishing to access the web on the move. Many of these can be overcome, and indeed are well on their way, but it's worth pointing out where the limitations of accessing the web via mobile lie before we look at how they are being overcome.

Small screen size is probably the number one drawback to using the web via a mobile device. Small screens make it difficult or impossible to see text and graphics that are dependent on the standard size of a desktop computer screen, and if the website is not mobile-optimized (as we shall get to), then it can severely reduce functionality. Modern phones such as the iPhone, with its pinch to zoom in touchscreen technology, go some way to overcoming this, but for many people, having a normal PC website load up on their phones with unreadable text usually results in instant abandonment. And if you are running some sort of commerce site, that is a lost shopper you may never get back.

Connected to this is the inability to have more than one window open at any one time – a function of both the screen size and lack of processing power in these devices, compared with your average PC or Mac desktop, or laptop computer. A desktop computer's ability to open more than one window at a time allows for multitasking and for easy reverting to a previous page. Historically on mobile web, only one page can be displayed at a time, and pages can only be viewed in the sequence they were originally accessed. The most recent smartphones in the iOS and Android market do allow multitasking, but there is an element of awkwardness in flipping between windows, especially when online.

Navigation is also hindered in the way mobile phones work. While touchscreens have come a long way in creating control over the phone screen environment – so much so that next generation Mac laptops will likely to have some form of touchscreen technology in them as well – the lack of a mouse or cursor in most smartphones makes scrolling, and especially scrolling within a webpage, tricky.

BlackBerrys still have a trackball to move a cursor about, but these are being phased out, as are Windows Mobile phones with a stylus. It looks like the finger is the mouse of the future, but OS and software design on smartphones, while very good today, needs to up its game to give an even better navigation experience on mobile.

The webpages themselves are also problematic, although as mobile web access increasingly becomes the way most people access the Internet, one must assume this will be addressed at the web's core. Most feature phones can't access JavaScript and cookies, the minicomputer programs that let a website pop bits of software and script onto its page to enhance the experience. However, most of today's smartphones can, so there is a distinct disparity between what a user experiences from one handset to the next. It also means that basic web analytic tools – the cornerstone of making websites a commercial proposition by measuring who does what on each site – can't always be applied to mobile web access. There are increasingly ways around this, but they are costly, and they also don't always allow for access to the web via domestic Wi-Fi on a mobile.

Many sites are also poorly designed for mobile, not taking into account the low processing power and absence of large cache memories; that is, memory that remembers large elements of websites you've been to before on your PC, so that it can load those while waiting for other bits to come up.

A study carried out by Compuware Gomez, which analyzes the performance of websites and mobile websites, finds that many retailers' mobile websites are too jam-packed with information and images, and as a consequence take far too long to download to be competitive. The worst offenders currently are Netflix – an online streaming service for TV shows and movies – and DIY store Home Depot, which had average download times of 24.377 and 11.977 seconds respectively. Among the best were QVC at 2.194 seconds, and Amazon at 4.787 (both poor compared to UK grocery chain Tesco, whose mobile site fully loads on an iPhone in just 1.6 seconds).

Overall, the benchmarking of mobile sites across the US finds that the average is about five to six seconds, which is acceptable, but as consumers get evermore impatient for instant access, even that could be a problem.

According to Compuware Gomez, the key factors that affect these speeds are page structure and page weight. Generally, the bigger the page weight – or how much data it contains in bytes – the longer it will take to download. One problem can be that a site has too many pictures of too high a resolution – too high quality, especially for a simple phone screen – and that these pictures, along with other elements of text and graphics, are being drawn from a range of different servers to build the page. This page-structuring issue goes hand in hand with page weight and leads to a terrible experience. On some sites, there are more than 20 page elements from numerous domains that make up the page. The page appears to be optimized more for desktop browsing than mobile browsing, and so is very slow on a mobile phone.

In contrast, the home pages of the UK's Tesco mobile site are relatively light – around the 100k–140k byte range, with fewer than 20 objects to download. This site appears to be the fastest in the known world. Its average download speed of 1.6 seconds is on a par with the website performance achieved via a standard PC browser.

But perhaps the biggest hurdles of all are the mobile networks. While there are clearly issues with the way in which websites are rendered onto handsets, they are addressable (as we shall shortly see) at a relatively low cost. In fact, they will be addressed as a matter of course, since the volume of traffic coming into the web from mobile is only going to grow. The networks, however, are not really up to the job – not when everyone now wants to access the web and get a good, fast broadband-like experience of it, via mobile networks.

Increasing use of mobile to access the web, so called mobile data, means that networks are typically running at their maximum capacity these days for much of the time. These third generation, or 3G, networks were designed to offer fast (or fast-ish) mobile data downloads, but it is clear that when they were designed and built in the early 1990s, no one anticipated quite how many people would be undertaking massively data-hungry tasks. Nor did they foresee the vast array of always-connected devices on which people would be undertaking these data-hungry tasks.

Along with dwindling oil reserves, dwindling bandwidth is becoming a headache for many businesses. As early as 2009, UK network operator 3 was warning that there would be issues with capacity on 3G networks in the UK by 2010 – and that was before the advent of the iPad and mass uptake of smartphones. Network capacity is being reached, and this is invariably slowing down what people can do with mobile.

In the US, many of the major national and regional mobile network operators are already looking to counter this problem by building 4G networks – also known as LTE (Long Term Evolution) networks – with T-Mobile and AT&T working on rolling them out in certain areas as early as the end of 2011. Regional US carrier U.S. Cellular is doing it already in Iowa, Wisconsin, Maine, North Carolina, Texas and Oklahoma.

Other operators in Europe are looking at how to augment their increasingly congested mobile networks with Wi-Fi services, in an attempt to take some of the data-hungry traffic off the cellular networks. LTE/4G is also being built (albeit slowly) across Europe, but arguments about standards persist and hold it back.

Will this have a huge detrimental effect on how mobile commerce works? Well, yes and no. No, m-commerce won't stop developing, since it is becoming entrenched in the consumer psyche; but yes, overfull bandwidth will start to put people off – especially those that come late to the party.

But many of the issues with mobile web are being tackled and, as we have already seen in the section on apps, mobile web is a necessary part of the mobile commerce experience. Without the connectivity it ceases to be a live transactional tool, and m-commerce disappears in a puff of logic. So there is a vested interest in making it work, as we shall see.

And now the good news

Modern smartphones, not to mention tablets, have largely overcome the screen-size issues by installing screens that are as large as the device itself. This has also prompted devices to cease their Lilliputian shrinking act and start to get bigger again – one of those weird examples of backward evolution, like the end of supersonic air travel, heralded by the removal of the Concorde from service.

The very fact that smartphone screen sizes are becoming uniform means that it is expedient for those wishing to mobile-optimize their websites to do so around these new dimensions.

We are starting to see a new approach to the web, tailored more to how mobile devices work. The use of the finger to work a touchscreen – making mobile commerce literally digital – is prompting many e-commerce sites to be re-designed for mobile (or rather, to have a whole new website that is served up to mobile users).These sites take into account how the web will be used on different kinds of phones and the overall experience of websites on mobile.

One of the earliest protagonists of this was renowned UK retailer, Marks & Spencer (M&S). Not generally considered an innovative retailer, the company, famous for selling sturdy, practical underwear, saw hundreds of thousands of customers buying, or trying to buy, merchandise on its website via mobile. So in May 2010, the company rolled out a mobile-optimized website. By September 2010 the m-web site, designed and built by Mobile Interactive Group and US mobile web specialist Usablenet – two of the biggest names in mobilizing commerce websites – had attracted 1.2 million visitors, more than 10 million page views and 13,000 orders from the site – including one single order of £3,280 for a pair of sofas.

M&S was an early leader in mobile-optimization of its website. It took the view that, to work in as many handsets as possible, it had to go down the mobile web route rather than develop an app. Still, it decided that that site needed to look and behave, on high-end smartphones like the iPhone, as an app.

The technique that M&S, and now countless other retailers and other commercial sites, have employed to make this happen, is a technique called web scraping. In its simplest form web scraping (or web harvesting, as it is also known) is simply the taking of information from websites. In the mobile-optimization sense, it has come to mean taking web data from a server and repurposing it for mobile use. This can be as simple as just reusing the data, but with certain constraints on it, so that only the bits that work on mobile get delivered; or delivering the data from a website and repackaging them into an entirely different design that works on mobile phones.

M&S opted for the latter and created a mobile website that, to the iPhone and Android user, looked like an app and behaved like an app. For those hitting it from lower spec feature phones, the website still enabled the consumers to see what they needed to see and, most importantly, to buy things in the same way and with the same account as they did online at Marksandspencer.com.

Case study

Juicy Couture woos US shoppers with m-web and apps

Back in 2009, like so many retailers, women's clothing retailer Juicy Couture saw a growing proportion of its e-commerce traffic coming from mobile. In this case, it was just 4%, but the company deemed it significant enough to build a mobile-adapted version of its website to try to better serve those customers.

As demand has grown, the company has decided to implement a proper mobile web and apps strategy to better deal with the variety of devices and requests hitting its e-commerce servers from shoppers. Working with technology provider Usablenet, it has built a mobile-optimized commerce site that has the look and feel of its e-commerce page, but with elements – such as better product detail that displays better on mobile – built in. It has also studied how users use the mobile site and has started to work, again with Usablenet, on developing a parallel apps strategy too.

Since the relaunch, the retailer's m-commerce site has generated 15% of digital traffic and 6% of online sales.

This was, in mid-2010, revolutionary, and in the few short months since then, there has been a surge in retailers adopting this sort of technology for their websites (as we shall see in Chapter 4).

But in some instances, these scraped websites that are mobile-optimized have become victims of their own success. Over Christmas 2010, when mobile and online shopping hit its peak in the UK and US (due in the main to poor weather, but also, so popular wisdom has it, because men finally got to do their Christmas shopping without leaving the house: the best Christmas present of all) many retail and commerce websites crashed. Not only were they being inundated with browsers coming in through the traditional Internet, the same servers were being scraped repeatedly by an unprecedented number of mobile browsers. The result was that, just at the busiest and most lucrative time of the year, their servers crashed and no one could sell anything.

The impact can't have been that great, as more was sold online and on mobile in Christmas 2010 than ever before. In fact, on Super Sunday, the Sunday before Christmas 2010, more was sold on mobile in the US than all previous Christmases put together.

But as user tastes regarding mobile shopping get more sophisticated, so web scraping — which has been a nice entry level way of relatively cheaply and effectively mobile-optimizing a website — is starting to look jaded. The quality of pictures, for instance, is exposed as poor on the new super high resolution iPhone screen. The pages often look low-rent on the even bigger screens of the iPad; and, in testament to how consumer demand outstrips supply, many people now consider the way websites function to be clunky and old-fashioned when compared to the slick user experience they are getting with apps.

The answer then could be something called HTML5. HTML (Hyper Text Markup Language) is basically the computer code websites are written in. Devised in 1990 and then updated in late 1998 to XHTML, these two languages are what have made the web and all its spin-offs tick. But like many of us who were there in the 1990s, it's tired and increasingly has to be jury-rigged to get websites — especially those that are accessed on various devices — to work properly. HTML5 is the latest iteration of this language, and aims to make websites easier to build for multi-device use and much easier to program in video, audio and other flashy new content, and to get that read by the software and processors on all sorts of devices.

I won't go into any more detail about HTML5 (one could write a book about it) as this isn't really the place or time. What is pertinent, however, is the effect HTML5 is set to have on mobile websites. In a nutshell, HTML5 makes the creation of highly functional and interactive websites much easier. It also means that so much more can be done with a mobile website, adding proper geo-location, better graphics and moving images, and generally letting website designers create mobile websites that to all intents and purposes look and act like apps.

Case study

M-commerce gets a new look with HTML5

UK high street fashion retailer New Look became the world's first retailer to use HTML5 to create a highly functional mobile website that brings much of the user-friendliness of apps to the mobile web. But it has been followed by a number of key US retail launches as HTML5 gathers pace as the design tool of choice for mobile commerce sites. New Look worked with Mobile Interactive Group to develop the site, and the retailer now offers mobile shoppers an array of easy-to-use functions not normally seen on a mobile website.

Meanwhile, US m-website technology provider Usablenet rolled out an HTML5 version of its development platform, and delivered new HTML5-based mobile websites for Shop NBC, Expedia and ASOS.

Key features of HMTL5 sites include fast "one click" checkout for registered users; quicker journey from homepage to products, with engaging zoom functionality; easy-to-browse products in one, two or three column formats; seamless viewing with accordion navigation to reduce page refreshes; and a single consumer shopping basket between the website and mobile site.

New Look's site also boasts multiple calls to action and a prominent search bar on the homepage to enable users to get to relevant products quickly and easily. Within the product pages, users can refine category searches without leaving the page and define how they want to display their product-results page. Users will be notified if that particular product is running low in stock or is out of stock.

Usablenet's US clients get all that as well as a range of other rich media delivery - such as image galleries - that look good but don't cause huge network demand. Both Usablenet's and MIG's HTML5 sites also allow different experiences tailored to the handsets that access the site. High-end smartphones such as iPhones get the full HTML5 experience, but lesser feature phones that can only handle HTML4 get that version of the same site - less functionality, but still geared to work on the phone more smoothly.

This combination of innovation, new technology and the simple evolution of websites so that they offer an unparalleled mobile experience solves the problems facing the commercialization of the mobile web. The other issue of networks isn't so easily – or cheaply – solved.

The current setup in much of the developed world is what is known as third generation, or 3G, networks. You have probably seen the moniker 3G appear on the signal bar on your phone from time to time. These networks were billed as being mobile broadband, and were set to meet all the needs of mobile voice and data long into the future.

In reality, within three years of them being licensed, and even before many of them were fully rolled out, it was apparent these networks were soon going to be swamped. The arrival of the iPhone in 2007 and the revolution in mobile connectivity that this ushered in has since seen these networks across the developed world start to creak under the strain. And now, as mobile looks set to become the centerpiece of modern life, being responsible for everything from simple messaging and phone calls, to paying for and delivering tickets, groceries and even furniture, the shoring up these creaking networks – or better still, replacing them with higher speed and much higher capacity alternatives – is becoming imperative, not just commercially, but for the good of society.

In the US, 3G licenses change hands for enormous amounts of money, with two changing hands back in 2004 for $41bn and $38bn apiece. Globally, 3G has been a license (if you'll pardon the pun) for governments to print money as operators raced to roll out high-speed mobile-data networks. Now that these networks are clogged and operators need to invest in 3G, there is, understandably, some reluctance to invest similar amounts of silly money in more licenses. Instead, radio spectrum formerly used for other things is being allocated to high-speed 3G, 4G and LTE networks globally.

Of course, the natural progression that this is spotlighting is the rather unimaginatively named 4G. Fourth generation networks have been defined by the International Telecommunication Union (ITU) as a "service set with a peak download speed at 100Mbit/s for high mobility communication (such as from trains and cars) and 1Gbit/s for low mobility communication (such as pedestrians and stationary users)." These super fast networks will all be based on the kind of digital packet data service that makes the Internet work (called Internet Protocol, or IP networks), and will supposedly offer a way out of the black hole of data network overload. But, in a time of recession, falling profits and lower call costs, network operators are struggling if not to find the money to build these networks, but the will to do so.

While that debate rages on, so-called 3.9G solutions are already making some impact. These are faster, fatter networks than 3G but, since they don't meet the 100Mbit/s from a train, 1Gbit/s from stationary stipulation, they can't be called 4G. These solutions include WiMAX, a sort of Wi-Fi on steroids, and 3G Long Term Evolution or LTE – networks that manage to squeeze more out of existing networks.

More simple still is the plan by UK operator O2 to expand a second network, this time of free public Wi-Fi around the whole of the UK. Well, it will be free to O2 customers, and cheap and easy to use for everyone else. The idea is that, for a relatively low cost of "several tens of millions", it can take a lot of pressure off the existing 3G network, making it faster and more reliable. It will also, in theory, lure more people to sign up to O2 and so drive more paid-for traffic across its networks; and third, people using it who are not O2 users – which is more than half of the UK's mobile device toting populace – will pay to use it, so it will recoup costs.

Public Wi-Fi has a patchy history, but has managed to deliver connectivity to people, albeit slowly. Perhaps ramping this up could be the interim solution needed to make mobile web access on the go more attractive.

Either way, something has to be done. While much of 2010 was taken up with the debate, especially among retailers looking to dip a toe in the mobile waters, as to whether apps or m-web were best, as we start 2011, that debate has evaporated. Everyone now sees that not only do apps and m-web fulfill different roles, they also kind of need each other to work. And it all comes back to how people find you.

The theory has it that loyal customers and those who have had great online and mobile service from a brand, will remember that and will seek out that brand's app in their apps store of choice, download it onto their phone and use it regularly. Those who are looking more generically for, say, a pair of socks to buy when on their mobile, will do what everyone does and Google "socks." This will spew out results that are m-websites. So to be found by the browsing consumers, you need a website that is mobile-optimized. Provide a good experience, and you may well convert that customer into someone who will then download your app and use that.

For this reason, you need both an app and a mobile website. But the link between apps and mobile web goes further still. As we saw earlier in the chapter when we were looking at apps, the modern app needs to be web-enabled, not just to update itself and to offer better content, but also, in the context of m-commerce, to provide a payment channel. For this reason, if for no other, apps will increasingly become web-enabled; and they will morph into a special button that takes you to VIP areas of the web, where you get special offers and better deals. And you can't then have a strong apps market without the mobile web and vice versa: the two now coexist and offer a bright view of what m-commerce has to offer in terms of content sales, extending online commerce, what can be done in the retail sector and how mobile has such a significant part to play in all other commercial businesses — as the rest of the book reveals.

ACTION POINTS

- **If budget's an issue, build apps for one operating system.** It's a quicker, easier way into mobile and gets the app into that OS store fast.
- **Consider the customer.** Be warned: your board of directors may all have iPhones, but not all customers do. Research your customer base.
- **Build for other operating systems if you can.** Apple's iOS and Android are priorities, and then Windows Phone 7. If you have the money, do as many as possible.

- **Use developers with knowledge of multiple operating systems.** This cuts development time and cost, takes responsibility of getting approval at multiple apps stores off your hands, and gives you the widest possible coverage.
- **Build a marketing plan.** Without marketing, both mobile and through traditional channels, how will people know your app is there? Apps don't pick up much in the way of passing trade.
- **Mobile-optimize your website.** This lets people who enter your company name in Google on their mobile find you. It also lets you carry over membership and other details from any online presence you have.
- **User experience is critical.** M-websites have to be carefully designed so they can render on multiple handset screens and processors, offer a good experience and must NOT just be a repurposed version of your online presence.
- **Pare your website back for mobile.** Consider how users will use the mobile version of your site on their phone and remove all the stuff from your "normal" website that isn't needed
- **Keep data levels down.** Make sure your mobile web properties are made up of small images and files. The name of the game is to deliver as small an amount of data over the air as possible.
- **Ideally you need both m-web and apps.** Once consumers are downloading your app, start to build a better relationship by sending offers and treating them personally, thus making the app the destination of choice.
- **Build up to the money.** The m-website drives browsers. A good m-web-based commerce experience will drive those people to download your app, and then you can get

them spending by using the app to treat them as individuals.

- **Play to the device's strengths.** Whether app or m-web (or both), play to the strengths of the phone - portable, localized, has a camera and so on - to create something compelling, extending what you would normally do online.

CHAPTER 4

Mobile in retail: shopping from the comfort of your own phone

- 🔊 Why is the sophistication of mobile devices so crucial?

- 🔊 How can mobile augment rather than mirror traditional retail services?

- 🔊 Where do location-based services, barcode scanners, augmented reality and social media fit in?

To many people, mobile commerce means shopping. As such, the retail sector has attracted much of the attention lavished on m-commerce over the past few months. While this misses the point that mobile is a commerce tool that can help anyone sell anything (as we shall see in Chapter 5), retailers are certainly the largest economic sector that mobile has so far made inroads into. Given the success of e-commerce with ordinary retail, conventional wisdom has it that m-commerce is assured similar success.

As we have seen already in earlier chapters, m-commerce neatly divides itself into the use of the phone to sell virtual goods – music, games, content – and tangible goods – washing machines, books and so on. The retail sector largely falls into this latter grouping, with inherent challenges and rewards that differ from the sale of other stuff over mobile.

Retail, globally, is the cornerstone of all economies, so large that it is almost impossible to put a value on it. E-commerce (online shopping) is thought to account for about $400bn to $500bn globally, if you average out the often wildly differing statistics available. Mobile retailing is, currently, a fraction of this e-commerce revenue. Still, at just 1% it already counts as a multimillion dollar business and has huge growth ahead of it.

In 2010, mobile retail was thought to be worth about $4.1bn globally, and is expected to hit at least $12bn by 2014, according to some figures. However, growth has been so rapid over the first half of 2011 that it is likely that these figures will be revised upward as mobile continues to gain traction with consumers; as more retailers come on board with mobile offerings; and as retailers, brands and marketeers all discover new and innovative ways to use mobile as a shopping channel, an in-store augmentation device and a payment tool.

In the US, mobile in the retail sector is seeing some spectacular growth already, as the nation moves from something of a mobile hinterland (back in the early 2000s, the US lagged behind the rest of the world in mobile use for anything other than voice calls; the arrival of the iPhone in 2007 changed all that) to leading the charge in the western world in mobile commerce.

Figures for the US suggest that some 74 million Americans are already active mobile shoppers, and that between them they will spend around $9bn through the mobile channel in 2011. Nearly 80% of retailers are planning to invest to some degree in mobile this year, and are looking to spend around $221m on servicing this growing demand for mobile shopping. Within three years it is expected that a quarter of all retailers in the US will see at least 15% of their sales come through mobile.

Now, the role of mobile in retail is multifarious, being everything from a mobile extension of the storefront, a portable version of an e-commerce website, a store-finder tool, a place to do reviews, a way of finding more information about products from scanning bar codes, a way of paying for goods, a place for a retailer to market its wares, and even a way for shops to improve the in-store experience and cut wait times at the checkout. Mobile is also increasingly a part of the omnipresent loyalty schemes, and provides a great medium for the propagation of money-off vouchers and coupons, as well as letting your customers virally spread news about your offerings among one another.

According to research company ForeSee Results' annual retailer survey, this is how most shoppers used their phone for retail purposes:

- 47% to compare price information
- 34% to compare different products
- 20% to look up product specifications
- 15% to view product reviews.

And retailers are now starting to get it. In 2010, mobile started to figure more and more on retailers' wish lists for developing what they call their multichannel strategies: the rollout of selling things through brick-and-mortar stores, with catalogs, online and through mobile. In many ways, mobile isn't really a channel in this multichannel strategy anymore, but is increasingly being seen as the glue that binds together all the other ways of reaching and interacting with customers.

From this position, I, as an advocate of a totally mobile-centric world, believe that mobile will become the key way in which retailers sell things – even in brick-and-mortar stores – with mobile replacing the catalog and becoming just another way of using the Internet (although I accept that this means a world where everyone has Internet access and a mobile device ...). Eventually m-commerce and e-commerce will be one and the same thing. But for now, we live very much in a world where mobile retail is seen as a separate entity, and while some retailers are starting to make use of parts of it, we have yet to see retailers anywhere making use of all the facets of what mobile can bring to what they do.

So, while we live in this fragmented mobile commerce market, it is worth taking a look in detail at each of the constituent parts that make it up; but, as I say, keeping one eye on the future, where all of these things together will be what consumers expect to get from all retailers on their mobile handset.

M-web and apps

As the previous chapter showed, mobile web and apps hold the key to exploiting the potential of mobile in a commercial sense, as they form the way into a mobile world of experience and adventure on the humble handset. Once you have accessed either, innumerable possibilities open up, which we will come to in due course in this chapter.

But first of all, it is important to look at the business case for m-web and apps, and to look at which – if indeed you need to make a choice – any business in the retail sector looking to go mobile should invest in and why.

It is interesting to note at the outset that this is all very new to the retail sector. In fact, a joint survey of UK retailers – among the most advanced in the world technologically, in a market that is extremely mobile – that was conducted in mid-2010 by the Association for Interactive Media and Entertainment (AIME), the Internet Advertising Bureau (IAB) and the Interactive Media in Retail Group (IMRG), found that just four out of the top 20 most frequently visited retailer websites were optimized for mobile, while only eight of the top 20 had any kind of smartphone app. This despite the fact that each month in the UK, a staggering 4.2 million consumers visit retailers' websites using the mobile Internet.

Interestingly, 59% of the senior-level representatives from the UK retail brands that took part in the study expected their mobile revenues to increase over 2011, with 94% seeing mobile as a real opportunity for their business and 41% planning to have a transactional mobile site or application in place within the next year.

The research, albeit UK-centric, highlights the need for retailers in any market to move faster to keep up with the consumers already seeking out retail websites via their mobile phones. But with so few of even the top most frequently visited retailer websites being optimized for mobile, many retailers could be missing out on additional revenues from the ready and willing mobile consumer traffic.

While most retailers believe their mobile revenues will increase over the next few years, currently around 63% either make less than 1% of their total revenues via mobile, or don't measure their mobile revenues at all, citing a lack of knowledge and expertise about the mobile platform.

The majority of retailers do, however, welcome the opportunity for further training in mobile commerce and advertising, recognizing the increasing part the medium will play in the customer journey. Three-quarters say they would like to receive training in this area. Currently one in 10 retail marketers cites himself as a "mobile expert," while 43% believe they have a basic knowledge of the medium.

But progress is being made. Consumers are already using mobile apps and m-websites more than catalogs to browse and buy retail items, as well as rating mobile higher than its paper counterpart. Such was the finding, again in the UK market, in a study by e- and m-commerce implementation consultancy Portaltech and research company eDigitalResearch.

According to the wide-ranging research into the habits and views of both smartphone and non-smartphone users across the UK, 25% of those surveyed use mobile to research, browse and buy goods on a weekly basis, compared with just 16% who said they did the same with catalogs. The study also found that on average, across 20 key brands surveyed, 2.55% of shoppers have purchased using an app or an m-website in the past 12 months, compared with 2.27% using catalogs.

All this points to the beginnings of a thriving market for mobile retailing, one driven not by the retailers, but by customer demand. All this research also highlights how mobile is more than just a transactional tool for buying things, but plays a much more central role in the whole experience of shopping, be it remotely from the sofa on a cold winter's night, or when traipsing around the shops on main street, or traversing the aisles of a supermarket.

Who buys what where?

The French buy clothes and accessories; Germans like to buy World Cup football tickets; Americans buy cars and trucks; and lonely gamers worldwide buy more games on Valentine's Day than any other day. These are the findings of eBay's m-commerce Infographics data for who bought what on mobile in 2010. Ebay has seen more than 30 million downloads of its app this year, and mapped who bought what and where using mobile from January 1–December 21, 2010. And the findings are at once much as you'd expect and extraordinary.

So what are the key m-shopping moments worldwide? Well, according to eBay's Infographics, the trends make interesting reading for anyone looking to go global online or on mobile.

- **High-end holiday spending:** During the holiday shopping season (November 25–December 25), US eBay mobile sales grew 134%, generating nearly $100m in sales. Worldwide, mobile sales grew 166%, generating $230m in gross merchandise value. Designer handbags, diamond jewelry and Rolex watches topped last year's most expensive holiday purchases.
- **Sports shopping spree:** Major sporting events drove fans to shop on eBay mobile to commemorate some of the most highly coveted competitions. Based on mobile sales, the sports memorabilia category peaked in Canada during February's XXI Olympic Winter Games, held in Vancouver. The category also peaked in Germany in June and July during the 2010 FIFA World Cup South Africa, where Germany placed third; and in France during July's Tour de France.
- **Gaming lovers:** Valentine's Day has become a boon for the video game industry, as World of Warcraft and Final

Fantasy hosted special online gaming events. Video game sales through eBay's mobile apps spiked 68% for the week ending on February 14.

- **Must-have gadgets:** In the US, tech lovers flocked to eBay as the iPad made its debut on April 4, 2010, driving the consumer electronics category to its highest point of the year the day after the iPad first arrived in retail stores. On June 24, the day the iPhone 4 launched in the US, the cell phones and accessories category hit its annual peak as a flurry of new and pre-owned iPhones were listed on eBay.
- **Fashion fanatics:** As eBay released its fashion app for iPhone this summer, clothing and accessories was a consistently popular category on mobile. In Canada and France, clothing and accessories was a top category overall based on mobile sales. It was a top three category in Australia, Germany, the UK and the US.

Demonstrating the breadth of merchandise people are purchasing on their mobile phones, the top three categories by sales for the year in each of eBay's top six mobile commerce markets are:

- **Canada:** clothing and accessories, jewelry, cars and trucks.
- **France:** clothing and accessories, jewelry, computers.
- **Germany:** auto parts, cars and trucks, clothing and accessories.
- **Australia:** cars and trucks, home improvement, clothing and accessories.
- **UK:** cars and trucks, clothing and accessories, auto parts.
- **US:** cars and trucks, clothing and accessories, auto parts.

Store finders, price comparison and bar code scanners

Back in 2009 when apps started to gain mass appeal – and sufficient people had smartphones on hand – one of the first things that retailers built into their apps was store finders. Making early use of the fact that the phone and network know where they are (roughly at least), these neat apps allowed consumers on the move to start using their phones to find the nearest branch of a coffee shop, a supermarket and so on. This is pretty much where mobile and retail first came together, and store finders now provide a standard service on virtually all mobile web and apps offerings from retailers that have entered the mobile fray.

This simple function, something that had already gained traction on e-commerce sites, is ideally suited to the mobile. It's one thing to look up your nearest branch of Megacorp Ltd when you are online, but quite another proposition to be able to do that while actually out and about and looking for things to buy.

Many retailers rapidly cottoned on to the fact that these simple store locators could actually increase foot traffic through their stores, and so started to see that mobile, rather than being a costly addition to what they did with an unproven return on investment, could actually aid sales. It is the simplest form of location-based marketing (something dealt with in more depth in Chapter 6).

The other tool from the online e-commerce world that has gained enormous traction on mobile is price comparison. Price-comparison websites are huge earners for both their operators and the businesses that pay to be listed on them. They have also forced down the cost of various things from insurance to utilities to socks. It doesn't take a genius to see that the combination of price comparison and store finders makes for a very powerful tool. And so we are starting to see services such as Google Shopper and Amazon introducing price-comparison apps, so that consumers can search out what they are looking for and either find where it is and at what price, or, with Amazon, usually find it in a store and buy it cheaper via the app.

So powerful has this combination of location and price comparison become that people are basing whole businesses around it. Start-up company Udozi is aiming to harness the power of the mobile web to help retailers drive consumers back into their stores and get them shopping "the old-fashioned way". The company has launched an online and mobile service that offers a stock comparison experience, allowing consumers to search out goods that they need based on where they are in stock in relation to their location, reserve them and then go and collect them in the store. Originally developed as an online service, with the rise of the smartphone and apps Udozi has been aimed at mobile users who can use the app to do stock and location searches for goods and services. The service works by getting retailers to pay a £750 a year membership fee, which gives Udozi access to each company's stock databases and websites. The software within Udozi then uses this information, in conjunction with the consumer's location data and preferences, which are supplied when the consumer signs up for the service, to search for stores holding certain items in stock, listing them in increasing distance from the consumer.

Consumers can search by product or brand name, product code, or even just generic search terms such as "orange T-shirt" or "fridge," and the service will display a list of stores that stock the particular item, based on how near they are to the user and marking whether the item is in stock or not. It will even show how many items are held in stock and how often the stock update is amended, if the retailer allows.

Once the consumer has found what he or she is looking for, he can then e-mail, call or even Skype the shop and reserve the item to collect later on.

Initially the company is focusing on clothing, electrical goods and books, but aims to increase this as retailers buy into the idea. The company is also so confident of success that it is waiving the retailer fee for 18 months, to allow retailers to really see that it works. Retailers can pull out without incurring any cost.

The whole purpose of the service is to help drive consumers back into shops. Foot traffic is crucial to retailers, because unlike online or mobile shopping, when a customer walks into a store to buy a particular item, once they are there they are more likely to browse and leave with more than they came in for. This is one of the advantages Udozi helps deliver.

The next step in the evolution of mobile's role in retail is the integration of bar code scanners into the device. These let consumers scan bar codes, calling up details of those goods on their phones. Originally designed to let retailers disclose more information about their products to mobile users while in a store, bar code scanning technology for mobiles, as developed by companies like RedLaser and StripeyLines, soon found an ideal partner in price-comparison offerings for mobile. Now a mobile user can search for a store, find what he is looking for, scan its bar code and see if he can get it cheaper anywhere else – in the real world or online.

This process has become a staple of many services. Amazon's mobile app features a bar code scanner so that you can see if you can find anything you want to buy cheaper on the web. Retailers such as kiddicare.com, which specializes in selling infant products – car seats, strollers, cribs and so on – has long been a leader in using technology, pioneering online sales and embracing mobile with alacrity.

It launched an all-out assault on mobile retailing in 2010 with the rollout of both an iPhone app and a mobile-optimized website, both of which offer secure transactional capabilities. The app, however, features a bar code scanner to deliver the must-have mobile experience du jour, which also acts as an adjunct to the in-store experience. The idea is that you can use the scanner in the store to see more information about the products on offer, including instructional and testimonial videos, but increasingly consumers are using it to price compare in other stores – something kiddicare.com is very happy to facilitate.

Case study

Kiddicare

With some 7% of its web traffic – or 70,000 unique users per month – coming to its online portal through mobile, UK online nursery equipment retailer kiddicare.com launched both an m-website and an app in late 2010 to make mobile shopping as easy as possible for its increasingly mobile-oriented customers.

The app has been developed to support kiddicare.com's drive for a multichannel strategy, and integrates secure payment, bar code scanning, video, price comparison and search, alongside core e-commerce features. It is designed to be easy to use both as a mobile storefront when shopping from home, as well as allowing shoppers who are out and about to use the bar code scanner to price-check goods in a store with Kiddicare's online offerings, and make an informed decision about what they buy and where. (Though Kiddicare obviously wants the shopper to buy from them.) The app also allows access to video demonstrations of products, and delivery details and tracking.

The Kiddicare app is unique in its front-to-back-end integration of data and services - joining up user search to live data, secure wallet transactional payment and delivery specifications. The system links IBM WebSphere, Endeca Search, CyberSource Payment Service and Liveclicker Video Commerce, among others, to produce a seamless, intelligent application that truly adds value for the customer.

Meanwhile, the fully transactional kiddicare.com mobile site enables shoppers to browse and purchase items on the go in a more conventional e-commerce manner. Customers can access their personal kiddicare.com account that they have, in theory, been using online already, providing them the option to store credit card details safely yet conveniently, and to review their previous orders. This one-basket-per-user approach means shoppers can browse and select items while on the go, but save their order and then check out at home, if they prefer.

In fact, the use of mobile for comparative shopping is growing rapidly. According to ForeSee Results, while in physical stores, more than two-thirds of mobile shoppers (67%) used their phones to visit the store's website, but one-quarter (26%) used their phones to access a competitor's website. This proportion is up substantially from 2009, when only 17% of mobile shoppers accessed a competitor's site from within a store.

Show me the money

So retailers are bringing together location, bar code scanning and price comparison in one mobile service. But what if you could actually pay for things as well? Well, while early adopters of mobile service — especially apps — opted not to offer any sort of payment channel, due to complexity, others are now doing so. In consumer's minds at least, apps and mobile websites that don't offer the chance to actually buy things, no matter what other sophisticated offerings are on show, are not really worth bothering with.

I touched on sorting out mobile payments in Chapter 1 and will look at them in much more detail in Chapter 9, but in essence, collecting money through mobile is easy in theory, but fraught with challenges in practice.

Mobile websites offer the simplest way around this: if your website takes payments, then you can easily replicate that on the mobile. With apps it has been trickier to get what is now known as in-app billing to work, due to constraints regarding who owns the app and who owns the billing platform, but slowly this is easing up.

The real problem, however, is much more prosaic: the user interface. In other words, the screen size and the keypad on a mobile device, even high achievers like the iPhone or the Samsung Galaxy S, are not really designed to make the inputting of long strings of credit card numbers easy.

Apple's iOS has some useful tools built in that let you navigate from field to field on a web payment page by hitting next, but not all website payment pages are formatted for this, and you still have the problem of having to enter the 16-digit card number with tiny keys on a tiny screen (and by the nature of mobile, there is a good chance you will be trying to do this while riding a train or sitting in a coffee shop). It's not easy, and you don't know you've done it wrong until the payment won't go through and you have to start the whole annoying process again.

There are many payment tools available for mobile, but what seems to be gaining ground with users is the use of accounts with which you can preregister your card details online — using a normal keyboard and screen. You then use the account to pay with just one click on your mobile phone.

Apple's and Google's apps stores allow this process to happen seamlessly. The stores need the payment card details once, and then use this information to handle any subsequent transactions through the apps. Amazon, meanwhile, has cornered the market in what is dubbed one-click payment, letting Amazon users set up their accounts so that they can pay by clicking on a card registered online to that account. The service has proved so successful that Amazon is looking at white labeling it and letting other retailers add it to their sites as a quick and easy payment tool.

The other payment service that is seeing a boom thanks to mobile is PayPal. PayPal, as revealed in more detail in Chapter 9, allows for secure payments between accounts without either party seeing the other's bank details. It is a payment intermediary. PayPal has already been hugely successful in the online world, overcoming the security issues many shoppers felt were a barrier to shopping online. In fact, they are so easy to set up, something like 96% of people in the UK and US have PayPal accounts. Fewer than this use these accounts regularly, but it still shows massive penetration. And PayPal is eyeing mobile as the next big thing for payments.

Proving the point, UK eatery chain Pizza Express recently launched an app that enables customers to pay their bills at the end of the night via their smartphone, without having to attract the attention of a waiter. The free iPhone app links to the customers' PayPal accounts, allowing them to pay in "less than a minute." To support this, Pizza Express offers free Wi-Fi and cloud access across 370 restaurants. Users of the app can also view menus, find restaurant locations, book tables, and access vouchers and receipts.

Location, location, location

The ability to locate a mobile phone and then use that location to send it relevant information about nearby stores is just the start of it.

Location-based services have long been considered one of the killer apps (remember those?) for the mobile phone, but until iPhone arrived with its built-in maps and Nokia picked up the mantle of being a mobile navigation specialist, location hadn't really delivered on its early promise.

But now, as we have seen, using the fact that, like an ancient mariner, the network can triangulate the location of a phone, location is becoming one of the key services used by mobile to create new value around old propositions. Retailers are using it to great effect to let users find the nearest store. Many services such as AroundMe and the newly launched Near Me have picked up this idea and created a sort of location aggregation service, which lets the user find the nearest shop, bar, restaurant, hospital, taxi firm and much more, all from one app and in one location.

These services add a whole new paradigm to how the retail sector can use mobile location, paying a third party to carry additional information or even act as Google does with advertisements, giving preference to those that pay the most to appear. The services also allow for users to not only find what is around them, but to see reviews, photos, videos, and to contact those institutions and effectively do business with them.

But location is not just your position on a map, nor should the onus on finding a business with mobile be in the hands of the consumer. Using some of the other technology built into mobile phones — Bluetooth, SMS and, increasingly, Near Field Communications (NFC) — retailers can actively target mobile users as they pass by their shops.

As we shall see in more detail in Chapter 6, mobile is an ideal marketing tool, and these geo-targeted services — a fancy name for pushing things to mobile phones as users enter certain areas or walk past certain shops — have a specific relevance to retailers.

Case study

Facebook Deals serves up new location twist

In a twist to the location-based retail idea, social network Facebook, which is now used by more people on mobile than on desktop PCs, is proving a new channel for retailers looking to utilize both mobile and social media as a storefront.

In the US, American Eagle Outfitters is using the check-in component of Facebook - Facebook Places - to give money-off vouchers and special offers through Facebook's foray into e-commerce, Facebook Deals. The idea is that American Eagle customers share their location with their friends on Facebook by checking in on Facebook Places, revealing that they are in an American Eagle store. Special offers, typically 20% off any purchase, are sent to their Facebook accounts on their phone when they check in.

In the UK, fashion brand Republic is trying a similar offer, which triggers special deals when consumers check into Facebook Deals via Facebook Places when in or near the store.

The move by both Republic and American Eagle - and a growing number of others worldwide, too numerous to mention here - to use Facebook Deals as a mobile storefront is a canny one, especially for businesses that are targeting the 18-25 year old market and already have a critical mass of customers as friends on Facebook.

Turning Facebook friends into money has long been a goal of retailers and Facebook alike, and this seems to be the way to do it. It encourages shoppers who are already in a store to shop - that is, to actually buy rather than browse - and it can also inspire their friends to come to the store and also be converted to buyers via the special offers.

Bluetooth and proximity marketing

The simplest form of what is becoming known as proximity marketing uses the short-range wireless communications technology called Bluetooth. Many of you will be more familiar with this as the technology that allows you to use a wireless mouse with your PC, but it is built into all modern mobile phones, and is a great – if slow – way of sharing things between phones and other Bluetooth-enabled devices that are no more than a few meters apart.

How it fits into retail is simple: you use it to ping (if I can use the technical term) short marketing messages, advertisements or even money-off vouchers to passing phones as their owners walk past your store.

Still very much in its infancy, Bluetooth-based proximity marketing has the potential to reach the bulk of phones out there and to deliver a very simple message to the passing trade: come into my shop, show me this message and get 10% off.

In the US, proximity marketing is gaining traction in shopping malls, pulling consumers with mobile into stores with tokens and offers. The beauty of proximity marketing in a mall is that you have access to a mass of people who are in the mood to buy. Sending rich media and targeted advertising, or coupons and money-off offers, through Bluetooth – or even Wi-Fi – to handsets when people are in a shopping place (mentally and physically) leads to great sales.

It is also a form of advertising that is highly measurable. With each redemption logged, the advertiser can see exactly who is buying what, where and when – information that can prove invaluable. This is one of the key things with mobile in the retail space (in fact, in almost all mobile commerce applications): it is trackable and traceable and ultimately extremely measurable, giving unprecedented insight into how customers buy, where and when they buy, and who they are.

Case study

Mall marketing

The key to proximity marketing is to situate it in areas where lots of people tend to congregate, and this is precisely what a mall owner and a media company - EYE and Ace Marketing & Promotions, respectively - are doing in malls in New York, New Jersey, Colorado, Arizona and California. The two companies have partnered to launch a Mobile Proximity Marketing mall network in EYE malls. Ace's Mobile Proximity Marketing technology allows advertisers in EYE malls to reach shoppers on their mobile devices through Wi-Fi and Bluetooth, with rich media content in a very targeted manner.

The technology is embedded in digital Eyelite units strategically placed in high traffic areas of the mall - such as the entrances, food courts and escalator areas. Collectively, the 10 malls in this initial rollout represent some 10 million consumer visits per month, which gives EYE and Ace a tremendous opportunity to deliver relevant advertising content to a huge audience that is in a shopping frame of mind.

One of the earliest and most successful rollouts of Bluetooth proximity marketing in Europe was a trial carried out by Burger King at London's Luton Airport. The trial, conducted for a month in 2010, saw 2,265 people download the offer pinged to their phone from a billboard in the check-in hall – representing around 10% of the people who received the Bluetooth nudge.

Working with advertising company JC Decaux and with Hypertag, proximity marketing specialists, Burger King decided to try to use Bluetooth marketing for a 15% off promotional deal to attract more customers to a tucked away outlet, located between the check-in desks and the departures terminal. Running between December 17, 2009 and January 16, 2010, the Bluetooth-enabled coupon reached some 20,000 passing people, with 2,265 actually downloading the offer.

As to how many people then redeemed the offer at that Burger King branch is not being revealed, but Elliot Messenger, Hypertag's rather appropriately named proximity marketing manager, says that Burger King was more than pleased with the trial. "What is interesting," says Messenger, "is that one person tried to redeem the offer at a Burger King in Manchester, showing that this form of marketing lives on in consumers' minds much longer than paper vouchers. He couldn't redeem it there, but it was interesting to note."

On redemption, Messenger says that, because the Bluetooth trial was part of a wider newspaper and TV advertising campaign, the redemption mechanics were simple. "Burger King can centrally add a button to the checkout screen," he explains, "that the salesperson just presses when presented with a voucher in whatever form. This makes implementation very easy."

However, Hypertag recognizes that the redemption issue is the key thing that will hold back widespread adoption of m-vouching. "We are at least three years away from any widespread adoption of this, as the redemption technology isn't cheap enough to appear in all shops", Messenger says. "Personally, I think we will see big stores like Tesco and Asda doing this in the next two years, but until the technology is cheap, it won't be ubiquitous."

Other Bluetooth marketing campaigns have started to appear — often as trials — for major brands across the US and UK, with some in Europe. They have covered everything from cars to radio shows to cakes to . . . mobile phones.

Case study

Bangalore phone shop leverages proximity

Bangalore-based mobile phone store Sangeetha Mobiles was one of the first retailers in India to start using proximity marketing, opting to make use of what it calls its BluFi network, a combination of Bluetooth and Wi-Fi. In fact, the retailer used Bluetooth and Wi-Fi, along with memory cards, to sell upgrades of phones to consumers, using a clever campaign based on setting up networks in stores, shopping malls, cafes and teen hangouts to target its core market of teenagers and young adults. Its intention was to get them into stores to upgrade their handsets.

Customers were segmented by phone sophistication and messaged accordingly. The messaging was not only appropriate to the phone type, but also to the location where the user was receiving it. If he was in a mall, he would get an offer directing him to the store. If he was in a café, he was messaged about how much better life would be with a better phone, and where to find the nearest store. The beauty of the scheme was that each recipient felt like he was getting a message unique and personal to him, and that he was the only one getting the good deal.

The promotions reached more than 50,000 users through 20 or so locations around Bangalore, and the company saw the foot traffic of users with Bluetooth turned on in different retail locations increase from 20% to 150% during the campaign, claims the retailer. More than 4,000 users visited the store after receiving the message. A staggering result.

This active messaging of consumers as they walk past your shop or get down in your nightclub, or hang out in a café or wander the mall, has produced surprising uplift, showing that people are generally quite open to receiving marketing material this way. Uplift for Burger King at Luton Airport was around 10%. Sangeetha Mobiles' was closer to 45%. Compare that with traditional forms of marketing such as direct mail and magazine inserts, which typically yield 1% uplift or less, and you can see that mobile marketing is a useful tool for driving retail trade.

The only caveat is that you have to be careful whom you target. Burger King's trial at Luton, Sangeetha's in Bangalore or the plethora of other trials happening across the world, were tempered by the fact that the recipients had to have their Bluetooth turned on. Any mass use of this form of marketing – or any form of proximity marketing, as we shall see – would have everyone doing it. A simple walk through a downtown area or across the departure lounge at the airport would result in a blizzard of pinged marketing messages hitting everyone's phones.

For this sort of technology to take off, it has to be opted into. It also has to have some degree of targeting to it, so that not only has the recipient opted to receive messages, but the marketer is sending appropriate messages to that person. Vegetarians are not going to look too kindly on being offered 10% off a burger as they sit around the airport in their hemp shoes, now are they? And this makes the whole process of using mobile proximity marketing more difficult than at first it appears. But there are ways around it.

Geo-fences and opt-in location marketing

While Bluetooth is, in many ways, a trial run at how mobile proximity marketing can work for retailers, proper geo-location-based services are tied into users preregistering their likes, dislikes and habits, along with opting in to a marketing service. Geo-location services also use much more sophisticated network-based technology to locate and deliver the marketing messages, and can offer a range of content to suit the handset as well. This makes for a more design-led and, frankly, funky campaign that recipients are more likely to want to share with friends, thereby doing some of the marketing work for you.

A prime example of how this works has been pioneered, as so much mobile technology and services to date have, in the UK by operator O2. It has gone live with a location-based SMS service that pings to opted-in consumers vouchers and other information regarding specific stores and products, whenever the consumer enters a "geo-fence" around that store. The launch customers are Starbucks and L'Oreal, and O2 already had a million people opted-in and following a soft online launch in late summer 2010.

Called O2 More, the service has been developed in conjunction with Placecast, which runs similar location-triggered couponing and vouchering services for leading retailers, and MNOs (Mobile Network Operators) in the US – including American Eagle, the restaurant chain Sonic and the sports apparel store REI. The service is interesting as it can be adapted to a specific store and specific offer, and uses text to reach as many consumers as possible. It offers location-time-relevance triggering and adds a whole new dimension to mobile advertising.

In the US, retailers are using geo-targeting to create awareness of local stores and goods through simple messaging, as well as sending offers to phones that cross into virtual geo-fenced areas around stores. Placecast, which built the service and has white labeled it for O2 More, is also rolling it out across the US with brands such as The North Face and American Eagle Outfitters. It has also signed a deal with AT&T to create a similar setup to what O2 is doing in the UK, launching it in New York, Chicago, San Francisco and LA. Users opt in on AT&T's website, its Facebook page or through advertisements in magazines, papers and on billboards (by sending a text to a shortcode).

They then receive targeted ads when within a mile of relevant places that advertisers have paid to geo-fence.

Advertisers so far include HP, Kmart, JetBlue, SC Johnson, Kibbles 'n Bits, Nature's Recipe and the National Milk Mustache "got milk?" Campaign. Consumers receive MMS or SMS alerts, depending on the sophistication of their handset.

In the UK, where much of the work on geo-targeting has been pioneered, Starbucks has built 800 geo-fences around stores all over the country, and is using the O2 More service to launch Starbucks Via, its brand of instant coffee. Opted-in users — who when they sign up to O2 More online can select what sorts of offers they are interested in receiving — will then be sent a money-off voucher as they pass through the geo-fence around one of the Starbucks stores. If they have a smartphone, they get a nice colorful MMS. If they have a feature phone, they just get a text.

L'Oreal, meanwhile, is doing it around the launch of a new shampoo, and has had its geo-fences built around branches of Superdrug. When consumers enter here, they get a similar experience to Starbucks'.

In each case the voucher is redeemed simply by showing it to the shop assistant. In the future, when the infrastructure is in place for wide-scale mobile coupons and vouchering, the vouchers will have a more sophisticated redemption channel, says Placecast.

Since its launch one year ago of O2 More, O2 Media has provided personalized media opportunities for brands, including Adidas, Cadbury, Blockbuster and Interflora, by leveraging O2's unique customer data. Success stories include a NatWest campaign that targeted its app at iPhone owners, which received a 26% response rate. Targeting families with teenage children gave Thorpe Park a near one-in-three download rate for its app. O2 Media has since expanded into new areas, like Top-up Surprises and Priority, to offer different brands unique and innovative solutions that stand out from the traditional clutter.

Vouchers and coupons

A common theme that you may have noticed emerging in this chapter is that one of the main forms of engagement between retailers and consumers is the practice of sending mobile vouchers and coupons to handsets to drive users to buy things. Typically, customers go to the store or buy online, using a PC or a mobile device.

In the US, it is estimated that around 3–4% of retailers that claim to be multichannel – that is, using web, mobile, catalogs and stores – are using mobile coupons to entice users into their shops and onto their e-commerce sites. In fact, some $1.2bn of digital coupons were issued in the US in 2010, and redemption rates on mobile are extremely high. Groceries are the most popular – unsurprising, since that is the traditional ground for money-off coupons – but other retail sectors are also doing well with mobile coupons, often delivering unheard of redemption rates. One Dunkin' Donuts SMS voucher campaign generated 21% redemption.

Statistics from the UK market, where mobile couponing is very advanced relative to most other markets, finds the logic behind doing it is sound enough: research from the cashback site fatcheese.co.uk has revealed that almost a third (31%) of Britons rarely or never pay full price when shopping, as they take advantage of a plethora of vouchers, discounts and cashback services. Fatcheese has labeled this new breed of consumer the lemon squeezers – shoppers that will do anything to secure the lowest price and best deal.

Similar levels are found in the so-called frugal cities of the US: Oklahoma City, Las Vegas, New Orleans and Philadelphia.

Research has found that in the UK and US, the average shopper now spends one to two hours a week searching for the best prices and hunting down vouchers for two-for-one deals and money-off shopping discounts.

And one in 20 (6%) Britons are hardcore bargain hunters, spending more than five hours each week surfing the net and shopping around for the lowest prices and best deals. These lemon squeezers feel disappointed and frustrated (69%) if they are forced to pay full price for an item − and for some it has a serious psychological impact, leaving them feeling physically ill.

The research also includes some fascinating quotes indicating just how far consumers will now go to save a little money − and how quickly a business can lose custom if it doesn't offer a discount. Some of the peachier consumer comments include:

- "I left a well-known burger restaurant because the couple next to us had a half price voucher and I couldn't cope with sitting next to them and paying full price."
- "I drove an extra 20 miles to get petrol at 5p per litre less . . . before realizing the distance driven cost more than the saving."
- "I got up at 4:30 am, two hours earlier than I needed, to save £20 on my flight."
- "Bought enough antiperspirant for two years because it was seriously reduced."
- "I stayed up all night for three days in a row to enter an online competition that had a winner every hour, as I thought less people would play at night. I won £200 for three sleepless nights."

In the mobile world, further research − albeit by a company that specializes in messaging technology, mBlox − has found that as many as 71% of consumers in the UK want mobile coupons sent to their phones while they are out shopping, and 59% want retailers and brands to contact them using SMS.

In the US, where text is still very much a teen sensation, this figure is likely to be a lot lower, and many consumers and brands are bypassing SMS as a contact tool in this instance.

That said, consumers the world over love a coupon – especially on mobile. More than three-quarters of all consumers use coupons when shopping, with 29% of UK and 15% of US consumers having already used a mobile coupon. Furthermore, 71% of UK and 42% of US mobile users say they would be interested in receiving mobile coupons while they are shopping in a store to alert them to a special offer or promotion, indicating a pent-up demand for these services.

And this is backed up by the industry. "Our clients, who range from small businesses to large restaurant and retail chains, media outlets and professional sports teams, are seeing mobile coupon redemption rates of up to 25%," says Chad Manning, vice-president of sales and marketing for mobile couponing company eNowIt. "This success drives a lot of repeat business, but it is surprising that more companies are not yet embracing this medium. Delivered in seconds and redeemed in minutes, no other advertising channel can reach consumers in such a contextualized way."

Kids are also a great driver for this, with a study by Placecast finding that mobile phone owners with children under 6 years old were the most receptive to mobile couponing and money-off offers, with 35% being at least somewhat interested in receiving opt-in text alerts about new products, sales or promotions from their favorite merchants, restaurants, or stores. Of households with children ages 6 to 17-32% showed interest, while only 25% of those without children in the household showed interest in such alerts.

When asked a series of seven questions about promotional activity, adults with children under 6 years old outpace comparative demographics every time. The most marked difference is found in the "Signed up to receive coupons online, ie from Groupon, DealOn" category, in which adults with young children showed double the interest of those with no children: 36% compared to 18%.

Though many in the mobile industry are tuned into the idea that early-adopter males drive the use of consumer electronics, the Placecast survey shows that families with younger children place more importance on their cell phones than those without children. Women, especially between the ages of 35 and 54, are rapidly embracing the device and using it to simplify their lives. Of women aged 35 to 54, 28% showed interest in mobile marketing messages, compared to 22% of men of the same age.

Placecast CEO Alistair Goodman says, "This report points to great potential for marketing to people with kids via mobile devices. Mobile Moms and Dads may not have the time to open an app and search for information, but they see the value and ease of receiving text alerts. In today's economy, more people are seeking money-saving opportunities that savvy mobile marketers can provide."

Kathryn Koegel of Primary Impact is a full-time working researcher and mother. She says, "My mobile usage is largely driven by convenience. I want on-the-go information for where to find products. Right now, I'm trying to enjoy my summer, but I have the daunting task of back-to-school shopping for both clothes and supplies. I'd like marketers to be able to tell me through my mobile media device what they've got in stock and at what price. Kids get really specific lists of what they need to bring and I want to go to one place and get it all — then get back to the beach."

But mobile coupons and vouchers work well for all markets, with fashion retailers using them, coffee shops and supermarkets. Even online-only businesses see that mobile messaging can drive traffic to their sites if they tap into that basest of human needs, the need to save money.

The issue with mobile vouchers has always been how to redeem them. Will the retailer need to invest heavily in new technology to allow the point of sale (PoS) – that's the cash register to you and me – accept the voucher and log it with the retailer's back end systems? On more sophisticated smartphones and feature phones, bar codes are being tested, so that the mobile-voucher technology ties into the paper-based voucher technology that retailers have been using. Issues with smudged screens (they are, after all, held up to people's greasy heads on the odd occasion that they're actually used as a phone) have sometimes made this inoperable. The simplest form of redemption seems to be imbuing the virtual voucher with a unique numeric code that the sales assistant can tap into the PoS. Not ideal, especially as the line lengthens behind you, but workable for now.

So workable in fact that mobile vouchers and coupons are becoming, along with transactional apps and m-web sites, the staple of how the retail industry is using mobile to service its customers and generate new revenues, driving traffic into stores and online.

Case study

Karen Millen launches SMS-based voucher service

High-end UK fashion chain Karen Millen has launched a range of SMS-based gift vouchers. When someone buys a friend or loved one a Karen Millen gift voucher as a present, instead of getting a paper token in a card for money off at the high-end fashion retailer, the lucky recipient gets a text featuring the value of the voucher, the sender's name and a unique PIN code. When the user goes to the store to redeem the voucher, she simply shows it to the store assistant, who enters the code into the store's existing Electronic Point of Sale (EPOS) system, and the discount is lodged.

Currently, Karen Millen gift vouchers come in incremental values between £10 ($14) and £300 ($490) and are available to buy online via a special part of the retailer's website. The buyer enters the amount, the recipient's mobile phone number and a short message, pays using a payment micro-site, and the voucher is delivered via SMS.

The program has been running for a little over a year, and early evidence indicates that these mobile vouchers already outsell paper and plastic card vouchers in terms of online sales of such gifts, by about three to one.

Augmented reality

While we are out and about and talking about location, it is worth mentioning a relatively new mobile technology that is long on potential but, to date, short on actually generating money: augmented reality (AR).

Now, when I was a student, augmenting reality usually involved a few bottles of my roommate's home brew, but here in the 21st century, AR is something that looks pretty much like the future, available in the here and now.

AR is essentially the overlaying of digital information onto the real world, either using a camera-enabled smartphone or online with a webcam and some clever software. It has become the latest buzz technology to grip the digital world, as everyone from game designers to retailers to health care companies to estate agents gear up to use it commercially somehow.

Ever since Apple introduced its iOS 3.1 upgrade in September 2009 – an enhancement that made it easier for developers to integrate services with the camera, location data and electronic compass functions of the iPhone – AR has shifted from its hard-core beginnings at aerospace firm Boeing, where it was used to overlay schematics of complex wiring diagrams onto actual wiring via a headset, to being a tool that offers to bring together the real world and the Internet. Such a confluence of the actual and virtual worlds would, you'd have thought, offer a GPS-accurate route to riches untold. But while AR's benefits to users are clear, how they can be commercialized is still a long way from settled.

But first, what is AR? The term was coined by Tom Caudell, a senior principle scientist at Boeing, in 1996 to describe the company's wiring helmet. It is now defined as computer-generated content – which typically includes graphics, audio and other sensory enhancements – that is superimposed over live images to enhance the real environment around us.

In mobile, where AR's future seems to be heading, it uses everyday technology such as cameras, GPS and electronic compasses that are built into the phone, in combination with Wi-Fi and broadband networks, to bring together location, orientation and context – all adding up to a richer experience of the world around the user.

But what you then do with it is where it gets interesting. Some early non-commercial examples of AR have seen apps – the small downloadable programs you stick on your smartphone – that will, if you turn them on and hold the phone's camera up to the street you are on, show you the nearest subway station. You can even point the Stargazer app at the night sky and it will overlay – even through the clouds – the constellations, stars and planets and facts about them. Others offer the chance to see reviews, menus and comments added onto the view of a restaurant or bar.

Case study

Using AR to locate the nearest Quiznos restaurant

Fast food restaurant chain Quiznos in the US has become one of the first businesses to make use of augmented reality (AR) to not only help people find the nearest of their 3,000 restaurants across the US, but also to layer animations over key landmarks.

Designed by Hoopla and Winvolve, the idea is to use an AR app on iPhones to create amusing animations of key landmarks – such as the Bull on Wall Street, the Hollywood sign, that sort of thing – that involve Quizno products. Not only does this offer something amusing for the consumer, but it also delivers a lovely bit of product and brand placement for the restaurant chain.

This overlaying of information onto the real world has huge potential in mobile marketing (see Chapter 6), but is also starting to excite retailers. Not only can it allow vendors to let people see what they have in stock as they pass the store, it also allows them to see where stores are, and to track down what they are looking for using a combination of mobile technology and their eyes. Something like a Yellow Pages of the real world.

Which is exactly why business directory owner yell.com – owner of the UK's *Yellow Pages* – has added augmented reality to its iPhone app, allowing users to "see" local shops, offices, restaurants and other useful services through the iPhone's camera viewer – even if they're around the corner or in the next street.

In essence what the service offers is a new way for businesses to advertise with yell.com. They pay to have their details added to the augmented reality overlay, so that when a user holds up his iPhone with the app running, the software places around it details of the business that the camera can "see."

As you move the iPhone around, yellow boxes are displayed over the live feed of the world directly in front of you. If you touch one of those boxes, information is displayed about that specific business, such as address, phone number, opening hours and website.

AR has also attracted the attention of über-mobile-retailer eBay, which is using AR to let shoppers try on sunglasses without actually doing so, and is planning on adding AR to its local auction services. Consumers can hold up their mobile in any given street and, with the AR-enabled eBay app working, see who is selling, or buying, what on eBay.

It is hard to see right now how AR can be truly commercialized, but it does at least play a role in getting people to buy things. One to watch.

Social media

While a lot of attention has been focused on using vouchers and coupons, as well as apps and m-web, to get consumers shopping on mobile, the converse is often more true. Let's not forget that consumers are often driving retailers to invest in mobile since they want to use it. Part of this customer-powered revolution can be attributed to social media and, more precisely, the rise of mobile social media.

Social media are things like Facebook, Twitter, foursquare and to a lesser extent, LinkedIn, Bebo, Flickr, Myspace, Digg and so on. They are online sites that let people share information about themselves, usually of the prosaic "I am watching TV" variety, but not always. Increasingly the postings of the 500 million or so people on social networks globally now feature more information as to what they are doing, where they are doing it and, most importantly in this m-commerce environment, what brands they like using while they are doing it.

Shopping in retail stores has become a prime example of how mobile social networking is becoming a force to be reckoned with. An IDC Retail Insights survey in the US at the end of 2010 found that mobile shopping "warriors" (hyper-connected individuals) and mobile shopping "warrior wannabes" (moderately connected individuals) accounted for 28%, or $127bn, of the $447bn that the National Retail Federation (NRF) predicted US consumers would spend over Thanksgiving 2010. The survey was designed to explore how consumers' growing comfort with mobile commerce (m-commerce) and social media commerce (sm-commerce) will play out. According to results, m-commerce and sm-commerce are giving consumers greater advantage as they engage retailers on their own terms, even when inside the store, within arm's reach of merchandise.

But it goes much further than that. MSM-commerce is not driven by retailers — despite their best efforts — but again by consumers. The power of mobile social media in retail is when friends advocate retailers to each other, not when retailers reach out to shoppers per se. In general, social media doesn't have widespread influence on shopping decisions, but friends influence one another's shopping behavior on social networks, and sites that have earned consumer trust will influence this behavior as well.

MSM also is clearly a young person's game. People aged 25 to 44 constituted nearly two-thirds of the mobile shopping warrior group in IDC's findings, while they constituted slightly less than half of consumers surveyed. In addition, adults aged 45 to 54 years were the most inclined to use their mobile information advantage; for example, asking for a better price to match one they found on their mobile device while in the store.

For retailers, the impact of mobile shopping warriors will be significant across the board, and, as ever, retailers' m-commerce competence greatly influences consumer perceptions about the brand.

The study also found that an easy-to-use mobile website significantly influenced consumers, across all age groups, on where to shop during the holiday season. Results also suggest that while the influence of social media outlets on buying decisions is growing, retailers continue to serve as the most important source of information for consumers before they make their final purchase decisions. As such, retailers who have met the critical need for consumer-generated website content and easy-to-use product information will have the advantage.

In-store

One area of mobile in retail that is often overlooked is the power it has to embellish the in-store experience and influence purchasing right when the consumer is poised to put his hand in his pocket. IDC Retail Insights finds that more than one third of smartphone-carrying consumers — who represent 24% of all US consumers — are ready to use their mobile devices in ways that transform how they shop everywhere and, in particular, how they shop in retail stores.

These new in-store behaviors facilitated by mobile include searching for price and product information, checking merchandise availability, and comparing prices at nearby stores, browsing product reviews, and purchasing goods. There is also the concept of using mobile in the store to help create a sort of hybrid experience of web and real world. It may all sound a tad like *Star Trek*, but the reasoning is sound. Why just let the handset be a conduit to vouchers and some stock information — and indeed a channel to let consumers see that the same item is cheaper down the street — when it can be used to add a whole range of information to their shopping experience?

One of the key things often cited is the ability to add environmental or source data to goods, so that the more eco-aware shoppers can see where things came from and how much damage to the world they have actually done in traveling from China to Chicago. A bit grim from a marketing perspective, but this shows that there is more that can be added to the in-store experience. More exciting to most retailers is the ability, through bar code scanning (see earlier) to let consumers order goods in their size, or to see video footage of items in use, customer reviews of the items, and all the things you can do when shopping online.

Customer reviews and how-it-works videos are among the key unique selling points of online shopping, and are responsible for huge amounts of both up- and cross-selling. Witness how Amazon works if you don't believe me. These can now be added easily to the in-store experience through the mobile channel. You can even let consumers upload their reviews and photos while in the store.

This isn't the ravings of an addled mind; it is, again, something that is being driven by consumers. A study in the UK by British Telecom (BT) in 2011 found that 68% of shoppers are excited about prospects for technology to revolutionize their shopping experience and want to see this happen. They are almost banging on your shop window, demanding that you let them use their mobile phones in an innovative way.

This is all part of creating an all-around mobile experience in retail that brings together the remote shopper, the window-shopper, the customer in the shop and the well-connected social networker. This is why mobile is seen as the glue in the multichannel retail environment. It brings together all aspects of how consumers shop and can play to the strengths of each. It is a marketing tool, a sales tool, a reviewing tool and a payment tool, and consumers are making widespread use of it already. They just need retailers to catch up.

Case study

Apps-and-sleeves let micromerchants take card payments

The combination of smartphones, apps and a bit of lateral thinking have turned simple iPhones into point of sale devices that can help reduce lines or empower mobile tradesmen, such as plumbers and electricians, as well as market stall holders, into people who can take credit card payments.

PAYware from VeriFone, is pushing its app-and-sleeve card reading solution at micromerchants in the US, with plans for a second generation solution that will work in chip and PIN markets in Europe later this year. The solution features a sleeve that fits over the iPhone, connecting to the base port, and works in conjunction with a free app that is available at the apps store.

The sleeve allows for card purchases, as it has a magnetic card swipe slot. The customer/merchant opens the app, swipes the card through the slot, and gets a beep that signifies the data have been scanned, encrypted and sent. The screen then clears for a signature, which the customer provides. With the push of one more button, the transaction is complete. Another click and you can e-mail a receipt to the customer.

The service is aimed at micromerchants such as stall holders and independent traders, and offers them the chance to upgrade from clunky credit card carbon machines or no credit or debit card facilities, to full live card approval.

PAYware is cagey about costs, but Tony Saunders, VeriFone's marketing director, does say that "This solution is being targeted to support the micromerchant who doesn't typically have a customer present card payment acceptance solution, and is a customer who doesn't necessarily have a high volume of card transaction opportunity. For these merchants, the solution has to have a compelling price point to ensure, as a merchant, they can realize a return on their investment."

Meanwhile, accounting software supplier Intuit and iPhone sleeve and charger maker mophie have become the latest pairing to develop a device that turns the iPhone into a credit card reader for the US market. Together, the companies have developed a device that incorporates Intuit's GoPayment credit-card-processing app with mophie's credit card reader, so that the phone can become a credit card reader.

ACTION POINTS

- **Assess where mobile fits business aims.** Anyone in any form of retail business can benefit from mobile – unlike e-commerce, which can exclude those that are sole traders, stall holders and the like.
- **Apps versus mobile web – select well.** In an ideal world, any retailer would have both. But that is expensive, and they service different forms of customer action.
- **Use apps for loyal customers.** It's ideal for those that want a richer experience with cool content and interesting features, such as augmented reality.
- **Use mobile web for customers who shop for goods, not your brand.** These are browser-based shoppers. M-web is good for attracting passing trade and is relatively straightforward to build if you have an e-commerce property.
- **Make it easy to use.** You can get bogged down using all the attributes mobile offers, and this can make things complicated and hard for users to fathom. Build your

mobile strategy around clear aims – and add things later if it takes off.

- **Make it transactional from day one.** The mistake many early adopters made was to create mobile offerings that didn't let you buy. Consumers want to buy when they see things. They are not going to find things on mobile and then wait to buy online.

- **Increase sales by using mobile to enhance an online or in-store offering.** It can get shoppers to interact with ads and buy things, to look for things while out shopping and to seek more information when in the store.

CHAPTER 5

Mobile business:
interacting, playing,
buying, selling, consuming
and enjoying from the
comfort of your own phone

- How is mobile shaping up in the spheres of entertainment, music, travel and books?

- What kind of products and services will enable brands to reach the mobile generation?

- How can mobile enhance experiences and interactions with brands?

Mobile commerce is a broad church, and while many people think of it mainly in terms of buying goods from traditional retailers, in reality mobile is a platform for the sale and consumption of many, many things. As a result, industries outside of the pure retail space are all also seeing mobile as a huge commercial opportunity.

While many of the principles and technologies involved are much the same as encountered in the retail space, each business sector has its own proclivities and peccadilloes that are worth looking at on their own.

Broadly, it is media companies, TV companies, brands, games companies, gambling operators and other content producers that gain all the headlines, and offer mobile as a way of marketing, engaging and delivering content to consumers. But, as we shall see, it isn't limited to these areas. Travel, ticketing, live events and most businesses out there have something to gain from embracing mobile commerce to some extent. Of course, this is far too broad a subject to look at every single business type and how m-commerce may impact it, but by focusing on some of the key areas, with some interesting case studies, I hope that anyone reading this who runs any sort of business can adapt and amend the ideas here to create their own mobile-commerce side to their business (and I look forward to hearing all about it for the second edition of this book!).

Media

Media companies were early adopters of mobile commerce, being among the first large organizations to add the sale of ringtones and wallpapers (see Chapter 1) to their small ads at the back of most tabloid newspapers and many magazines. But the role mobile has to play in the media is split into two distinct areas: using mobile to interact with services and generate revenue through messaging; and the use of mobile as a way of delivering content, ideally in a format that consumers will pay for.

This same split applies nearly universally across all media types, from print to TV to the web.

Print media and interaction

For many years newspapers and magazines have had their own chat line services, dating services and horoscope services on their webpages, usually run on their behalf by a collection of third parties, who shared the not inconsiderable revenues they generate. This has, in fact, been the backbone of most premium-rate telephone services, as discussed in Chapter 1.

The fact that these sorts of services – chat, dating, psychic and horoscope – translate well into mobile has been a boon for publishers for many years. They are becoming a staple of digital TV channels too, using the same premium-rate services and mobile offerings to allow interaction and generate revenues, as we shall come to shortly.

But concentrating on our friends in print media for now, these types of services that require engagement between people are a godsend on mobile. For starters, they usually run on non-geographic numbers (they used to be in the infamous 0898 number range, but now have a variety of dialing prefixes) and so, when called from a mobile handset, cost lots of money. However, their real power with mobile especially in this smartphone age, is that they can be much more content rich and interactive.

Take, for example, dating services, a staple of newspapers from the highbrow to the tabloids, in women's and men's magazines, and often in Sunday supplements and specialist magazines. These used to involve calling a premium-rate number to leave a message in a mailbox. With mobile, these services can deliver images, videos and all sorts of much richer content through dating apps, often branded to the publication or other brands, or mobile-optimized websites. These enhanced, mobilized services take full advantage of the phone's inherent technology, camera, video, media services, text, and so on, to enhance their offerings to consumers. And they probably lead to much better dates and chat, I am sure.

What this yields the media company is a better service for the consumer that, in theory at least, delivers more users to the service and so more incremental revenues. In fact, dating is a good bet. The UK's Office of National Statistics (ONS) has added money spent on dating sites (fixed and mobile) to the "shopping basket" of 100 essential items purchased by the average citizen that it uses to estimate the ongoing cost of living. Dating services are now a well-accepted part of people's lives.

In the US, online and mobile dating is predicted to generate some $932m, with much of this being spent on advertising chat and dating services in newspapers – and in their online properties – and on classified services such as Craigslist (which is expected to earn some $120m in 2010 from these sorts of ads in the US alone).

In Asia the dating marketing is harder to quantify, since many of the sites aren't aimed at the domestic dating scene, but at those overseas looking for Asian brides and partners. The cost of these services is borne largely by the users rather than the advertisers, and is also international.

The challenge with using dating and chat services as a revenue stream – whether mobile or online – in newspapers and other media channels is that they face stiff global competition from operators such as eHarmony, Zoosk and PerfectMatch on the web and on mobile.

While psychic and horoscope services are not used to calculate the cost of living – well, not officially (whether the ONS uses them to predict future cost of living has never been revealed) – they do, especially in these uncertain economic times, play a growing role in consumers' lives. The fact that many of them are morphing into life-coaching offerings also adds a renewed drive to their uptake. And mobile, again, plays a central role in enhancing the delivery of these services.

In the old days you had to call a premium-rate number and either hear a recording of your star sign for the day, week or month ahead, or, for substantially more per minute, talk to a real live psychic. The system was beset by fraud problems and regulatory issues, and had been on the wane. But mobile saved the day. What mobile brought to the party was not only ways of enhancing the offering along similar lines to those found in dating services; it allowed for the creation of something much more powerful: a way of keeping the consumers coming back.

And dating is hot. Consider the value of the online dating market in the US in 2010:

- 17% of all marriages were between couples that first met online.
- From 2009 to 2010, nationwide use of online dating increased by 15%, while overall Internet use increased by just 9%.
- Over 40 million Americans used an online dating solution last year.
- Match.com alone has 15 million members.
- On average, the online dating customer spent $239 per year on Internet dating services.
- Online dating was a $4bn industry worldwide in 2010, with $1.049bn coming from the USA.
- The average age of an online dating user is 48.

Mobile adds a whole new element of interaction and richness of content around dating, a richness that can easily be monetized. While there are many dating sites and services out there, media companies are adept already at tying into these services, repackaging them and selling them on.

And it's not just something you find in women's magazines, either. One of the most successful print media examples of a dating service with both online and mobile components can be found in the *Guardian*, a left-leaning UK broadsheet favored by media types, academics and teachers. It's all about bringing like minds together.

Case study

Isomob sees dating boom on mobile

Having successfully launched its Flirtfinder.mobi mobile dating product during the height of a recession, Isomob has witnessed an unprecedented increase in flirty conversations over the months.

The company has seen a two-fold increase in use of its mobile flirting service, and sees spikes in use when the weather is good. This is in line with Juniper Research's prediction that mobile dating is set to be worth in excess of $1bn worldwide by 2013. As Isomob's commercial director Alisdair Anderson explains: "While we have worked hard to get the database to critical mass, the weather certainly made the job much easier. Being out and about with a mobile phone gives members the ideal opportunity to interact with one another."

Contrary to the current vogue for free or nearly free mobile social networking platforms, Isomob's Flirtfinder.mobi monetizes consumers by charging them to send messages to one another using the MNOs' billing solution, PayForIt. Its success is due to its ease of use coupled with convenient micro payments, allowing it to neatly fill the gap between casual flirting and serious dating.

Back in 2008 Isomob announced a partnership with leading social networking company 4D Interactive. This forms part of Isomob's strategy to work with leading service providers who have not developed mobile dating platforms in-house, so that companies - such as media companies - can start to easily integrate, and derive revenue from, mobile dating services.

Mobile, as we have seen, with its multifarious messaging tools and connectivity, allows psychic, horoscope, life coaching or any other advice or information service to reach anyone who wants it using simple SMS, which can be billed on transmissions and which can run every day if need be. In essence, it keeps customers loyal, if they like what you are giving them.

Now, of course there are many moral, not to mention regulatory, issues about this, and I wouldn't want anyone reading this to think that you can send people whatever you want. You can't. However, there is a huge opportunity around print media to use mobile services, even just with text, to engage consumers.

The real benefits of mobile here are the same as they are in all other sectors: ubiquity and the fact that they can reach into an individual's most personal space. Services on mobile can be targeted very precisely to individuals; and, with canny use of the data you can glean from how they interact with you, you can create services, especially in the psychic/horoscope/life-coaching space that are pretty much individual to that user (or at least appear so to the user, which is the same thing).

Many of them work simply using text. You text a key word ("psychic") followed by your question to a shortcode and get back a psychically led answer. Same applies to many horoscope and life-coaching applications. It is all about instant help and reassurance – so long as it stays within the rules.

Print content

While the back pages of newspapers and magazines still do a roaring trade in mobile services around chat, dating, psychic and so on, the editorial and commercial bodies at publishing companies have long been facing a quite different conundrum: how to monetize their content.

The Internet has become a hotbed of news content and media sharing. It is a great place to find up-to-the minute information, read pretty much any news story from any news service or publication anywhere in the world, and to share that content. For free.

Great news for consumers (we all like a bit of free media) but terrible news for the media companies. The print media was spooked by what happened online with music. Music content online was shared for free, and soon everyone expected to get it for free. Instead the record companies decided to take their customers to court and sue them for sharing it. Not great customer relations. In the end Apple and others managed to make it a paid-for service, but at vastly reduced revenues to the record companies.

The print media does not want this to happen, and is wrestling with how to make online content something that can be charged for. To digress from mobile for a moment – although you will see that it is relevant – media companies such as Rupert Murdoch's News International have decided to erect paywalls. Users now pay a $1 one-time charge or $2 for a week's access to News International's US titles, including the *Wall Street Journal*. Similar things are being done with the company's UK titles, including charging a £1 one-time charge or £2 for a week's access to *The Times'* online content.

It hasn't gone well so far. Other print media companies worldwide are toying with other ways of doing it – such as giving some of the content away for free and then charging for more in-depth reporting (the "freemium" model), while others are just letting people get it for free (the BBC model), much to the chagrin of Mr. Murdoch.

One success online that is worth noting is the UK's *Daily Mail* newspaper, which is the second most accessed website online in the world after Google, with an international audience of around 18 million unique visitors, and many million page impressions each day. It doesn't charge. Draw your own conclusions.

Why this is pertinent to mobile is that mobile offers a ready-made way to sell media content at a profit. Traditionally, consumers see the web as free, apart from retail services from shops (where many of them think that the web should be cheaper, but that's another story for another book). The same consumers, brought up on the mantra that mobile is expensive because you pay for the convenience of having it in your pocket, believe that they have to pay for mobile.

The days of mobile call charges being astronomically higher than their landline equivalents no longer really applies, but you do pay more for calling to and from a mobile phone, and everyone accepts that fact. The same applies when trying to sell people the idea of using the phone as a web-accessing tool: it's very handy, it's on a mobile network, ergo, it must be costing me an arm and a leg.

This is partly true, but a move to wholesale all-you-can-eat data packages with smartphones has largely seen this die out. But anyone on one of these packages is paying £40 ($65) at least per month, and you can bet your bottom dollar that that is far more than they were paying before the advent of mobile Internet access.

Anyway, this quirk of how consumers perceive mobile as being expensive to use plays right into the hands of media companies – and most content and entertainment companies, come to that. They believe that they can charge for anything they offer over mobile. This is reinforced by the fact that, with the phone being connected to a network operator and often an apps store, there is, unlike on the web, a payments gatekeeper of sorts that can make the charge.

This has become a boom area for media companies – especially when they decide to turn their content into an app and look more closely at tablet computers. Here, media companies see a chance to make up for all the revenue they have lost by giving away their information online. Apps designed for tablets allow the media company to create an excellent, device-centric means of repurposing their print output *and* charging for it. Newspapermen the world over are excited.

Newspapers such as the *Daily Telegraph* in the UK and *USA Today* in the US are pioneering this model, creating an excellent interactive app with news, videos, 3D graphics and more that users subscribe to. And users are buying into it. The *Daily Telegraph* has some 70,000 users of its new iPad app.

News International has gone a step further with the creation of *The Daily*, the first newspaper designed specifically for the iPad, which aims to make quality journalism on the mobile handset pay. Their model is one that was pioneered online by the UK's *Financial Times* (FT), whereby readers get access to certain amounts of content for free, and then have to pay to get deeper or additional content.

The Daily does this slightly differently by letting users have the first two issues of this app-only newspaper for free, and then sets up a subscription for subsequent weekly downloads of $0.99. It has, at the time of writing, only been going for a few weeks, but has not proved the hit that everyone thought it would.

In fact, all online charged-for news (bar the FT) is not hitting the mark. The problem is that there is still far too much free news out there, so when newspapers start charging online or on mobile, many readers simply go elsewhere. Not until everybody charges for quality journalism will this catch on – which it will, but it takes time.

That said, mobilizing media content is fraught with all the usual problems associated with taking things mobile: screen size variations, huge number of handsets, different capabilities of handsets, network connection and how to bill for it. For this reason, most media companies have concentrated on simply delivering media content either as text alerts, which users sign up for, or have gone for the land grab on smartphones and tablets.

Tablets and smartphones offer the chance to develop rich offerings that largely replicate in many ways how a typical newspaper or magazine works. Their mobility means that, unlike online news services, these smartphone and tablet news offerings are portable, just like good old-fashioned newspapers and magazines (although, while they pass the you-can-read-them-on-the-toilet test that your PC probably doesn't, as the UK *Daily Mirror's* head of online said at the launch of a rival newspaper's iPad app: "No one ever got mugged for their copy of the *Daily Mirror*"). The advantage that mobile brings is that, since it is connected to the Internet, the content in the electronic publication can be much more interactive.

This can manifest itself in a consumer being able to tap on a particular story and see a video about it, or sharing it on social networks or e-mailing it to people. Either way, it offers a huge added dimension to how newspapers work – and this is something that people will pay for.

Right now, mobile news is very much in the realm of getting early adopters to pay for this sort of interactive media. However, as more and more consumers get used to interacting with shops, TV shows, newspapers and brands through their PCs, phones and tablets, soon this sort of experience will be the norm.

Where that leaves the paper-based newspaper remains to be seen, but there are already moves afoot to make them interactive too. *Le Monde* in France is testing the use of Quick Response (QR) 2D bar codes printed next to articles and ads, which when "read" by the QR code reader on the *Le Monde* mobile app, open up some video content for the news stories. When used on the advertisements, readers can request a brochure.

It is quite a low-tech solution, but one that works and one that, for virtually no money, suddenly makes the ads in a newspaper come to life. It also means that the value of the advertising to the advertiser can be tracked, and the details of who is accessing those ads can be logged. Suddenly newspaper advertising is not only an interactive medium, but also one that can show advertisers its real worth (see Chapter 6).

On the editorial front, this sort of mobile-enablement of newspapers has brought *Le Monde*'s sports pages to life, letting readers not only read about football matches, but also see video of the highlights and goals (if that's not tautological: I guess for one set of fans, the goals are definitely not a highlight).

It is in its infancy, but this sort of mobilization of static media is not only likely to reshape how media work commercially, but also can be applied to any business. Why just have a brochure for your company when you can make it interactive and bring the full weight of your website to bear on something you can hand to people?

Case study

Financial Times opts for app to drive ads as much as subs

The *Financial Times* has always been different. In the old inky days, it stood out for being a newspaper printed on pink paper.

When the Internet came along, it was the first – and remained pretty much the only – newspaper to charge a subscription to view its content. So, while its compadres in Fleet Street search for ways to monetize content internationally, it has a whole different set of problems.

While the *FT* charged for access, it never got the levels of readership that the other free web channels got. Now it's looking at new technology to help drive more people to subscribe to its services. As a result it has become one of the first publishing entities to develop a business strategy around iPhone apps.

Users get the app for free from iTunes, which gives them access to 10 free *FT* stories. After viewing two, they are asked to register for free. After looking at the remaining eight, they must then sign up for a subscription to FT.com at the newspaper's website to continue to use the service.

The iPhone app complements the company's mobile website, m.ft.com, and is part of its overall goal of making sure users get the best possible *FT* experience on any device.

Aside from using the app as an arresting way to reach a certain demographic, the move also gives FT.com a new channel to offer to advertisers; and while *FT* won't be drawn on this, it is perhaps the advertising side of apps that is really making this tick.

Interactive advertising is carefully blended into the application interface, and advertisers have the opportunity to take advantage of the ability to deliver tailored content to the individual, with advertisements that can be geo-tagged by country.

The *FT* example is interesting because it works, but as many of its competitors point out, the *FT* has two things in its favor. First, it is a niche title, covering a specialized field; and second, most of its readers are either well-off or pay for it corporately, so cost isn't really an issue. The model the *FT* has adopted, therefore, is often run down as being one that suits niche titles in markets where people spend money. However, the counter argument, which is gaining momentum, is that quality journalism and reportage from experts is of value in a world overrun with blogs and personal opinion. And that is something people may just pay for. Time will tell, as other mainstream newspapers look at how to monetize their content through mobile.

We have so far focused on how newspapers can use mobile to produce incremental new revenues, but magazines face much the same issues. Magazines do tend to have more loyal readerships and can follow, to some degree, the FT's model of being niche content. If you like cars, you buy a car magazine; if you like celebrity gossip, you buy *OK!* or something similar. These niche magazines are also looking at how to create money through mobile, and are doing much the same as their inky newspaper colleagues – through interactive premium third-party services, adding interaction to the ads and creating smartphone versions that people will subscribe to and which offer a range of innovative services.

Chief among these is the offering of video footage that backs up articles and reviews; something that again uses mobile as the access technology to a world of added value.

As in the newspaper world, this is turning magazines from print publications into multimedia outlets, with mobile – as it is in retail – the glue holding the different media channels together. This certainly looks on the face of it like something that users will pay for, even if it uses footage that is freely available online if you search it out, since the media brand is now acting as an aggregator of content. Longer term, this content is going to have to be unique and only available to paying users of the magazine brand if it's to gain any traction.

And the handset, again, will be the launch pad for this. It is in the hand while the publication is being read, and it is easy to fire up and use to augment the content the reader is reading. Similarly, if a reader is using a mobile device to read the publication, then there will be a subscription attached to doing that and incremental revenues will flow.

It is also possible to use the handset as the billing tool to access the content online, using a simple SMS pass code that carries a monetizable message to or from the consumer.

Many publishers are also looking at mobile – not just tablets, but smartphones too, especially in the youth market where tablets are less affordable – as the main means of web-content consumption, and are designing for mobile.

As I say, mobile is the glue as well as the device on which web content around media is consumed.

One thing that is worth mentioning at this juncture is that much of this will center on getting people to subscribe to services so that they are paying regularly. To date much of this has been done online, even for the mobile component, as it is easier to add credit and debit card details that way. Recently, however, both Apple and Android opened up their apps stores' billing mechanisms to allow for subscription services. This means that any media app that requires a subscription can be paid for in app or via the apps store. One caveat, however, is that both Apple and Android are taking their 30% off that, so if you are looking at this, be prepared to share nicely.

As Arthur Sulzberger Jr, chairman and publisher of the *New York Times*, told a conference in London in early 2011, this is no big deal. "For years we had to pay our newsstand franchisees to sell our newspapers. This 30% is just the cost of the digital newsstand." Quite.

Books

While mobile is revolutionizing the way print media works, it is also shaking up the book market. E-readers and e-books were pioneered by Amazon's Kindle and Sony's E-Reader back in the mid-2000s, and have slowly gained traction in the market and are becoming a force to be reckoned with.

Sales of e-books – which are essentially mobile books – grew dramatically in the first quarter of 2010, jumping from just 1.5% of total US book sales in 2009 to 5% of the market in the first quarter of 2010, according to analysts R. R. Bowker. The International Digital Publishing Forum (IDPF) reported US wholesale e-book sales for January 2010 were $31.9m, up 261% from the same month a year earlier.

Amazon, which has cornered the market in sales of both paper-based books and e-books, claims that e-books are now outselling hardcover books on its site, with the company selling 180 e-books for every 100 hardcovers. Jeff Bezos, founder of Amazon, told *USA Today* that he predicts Kindle e-book sales will outsell all books (including paperback) within a year.

Amazon believes that it owns 70% to 80% of the e-book market. Apple and Barnes & Noble each claim to own 20%, so the numbers don't quite add up, but it is a fledgling marketplace and one that is still in flux. The iPad has certainly upped the ante in the mobile book space.

Author James Patterson leads the pack in terms of sales, having shifted 1.14 million e-books to date. Of those, 867,881 were Kindle books.

Charlaine Harris, Stieg Larsson, Stephenie Meyer, James Patterson, and Nora Roberts have each sold more than 500,000 Kindle books.

And authors are generally welcoming of what e-books bring to the book market. Unlikely as it may seem, the traditionally stuffy book publishing world is now one of the most engaged industries in new digital technology, and one of the most likely media outlets to make money from new mobile devices and social media. Further, it comes from an unlikely source: an author. Chris Cleave is a *New York Times* number one best-selling author, and he is very much an advocate of what digital media brings to the world of book publishing.

Cleave is all for digital book reading, as well as embracing all the social media that goes around it. Let's hear it in his own words:

> **"For me the new digital world of publishing is here and it has changed what I do in two ways. Firstly people now want to see the process behind writing the book and what I do, so I produce video and photos of me doing the research and giving them updates. Then post publication they effectively come on the book tour with me. Secondly, it has opened up the world of book clubs through the social media angle - now people can discuss the book all over the world and engage with me about it. It has been very rewarding."**

Book clubs are an exciting nexus of digital book publishing, e-book readers, mobility and social networking. The book is now a multiplatform piece of content. And adding in the ability for readers to interact with the content, with one another and with the author offers some interesting new ways to engage people in books, as well as some monetizable opportunities.

> **"At the end of the day everything is just content," says Cleave. "And a paper book is just one way of distributing that content. I personally don't mind people sharing my books for free electronically - the more people that read it the better - but I understand that we need to make money**

> **from this, so I see a world where you can freely share the basic content, but if you pay you get all the rich add-ons."**

The book business has certainly learned from the music industry and its finger-burning experience with online and mobile. The music business was hit hard by file sharing. What the industry should have done is allowed for free sharing of the basic content – the track – but charged for the add-ons. That is a much more customer-friendly strategy than taking your customers to court and threatening them with huge fines or jail. This is essentially what the book business is now doing.

TV content

As print media companies embrace all things digital and glue them together with mobile, they run the risk of encroaching on the turf of TV companies and broadcasters. We are rapidly heading for a world where different media channels cease to exist. It will all just be content, and different bits of it will be delivered in different channels for different kinds of consumption – and for a variety of different prices.

So as newspapers add video footage to their news and entertainment, what are TV companies doing to mobilize their services? Well, the same split applies as it does to the print media. There are content models that work on mobile; and there are a raft of new interaction services that can enrich the experience of watching TV and deliver new revenue streams to not just the broadcasters, but program makers and advertisers that advertise around these shows.

Kicking off with the way TV companies are looking to mobilize their content, we find that much the same challenges apply as do in the print media world. Online there is a plethora of free stuff – often there illegally, but does anyone really want to sue their customers?

– that the people who made the content want to be paid for. Mobile again offers a channel to treat that as premium content that consumers will pay for, if it fits with what they want to do with it.

With tablets there is a strong argument that people will watch whole TV shows on them, as the devices are more suited to that – big screen and so on. There is a burgeoning market around devices like the iPad for episodes of TV shows that can be bought or rented and downloaded to view, much as people buy or rent DVDs. I know I have watched many of my favorite comedy shows over and over again on my iPad, or on the TV via my iPad.

This, of course, is a revenue generator for the program creators and broadcasters, much as selling DVDs and DVD box sets has always been.

The tablet also lends itself to the viewing of "catch-up TV" services, such as offered by BBC iPlayer, ABC online, Fox on Demand, Nova and Cartoon Network. These offer already-broadcast TV content in a streamed capacity, to be viewed if you missed it. Despite the proliferation of DVD players, hard-drive TV recorders and video, these services have proved extremely popular, and tablet viewing of them is expected to grow as the penetration of tablets grows. This time-shifted TV viewing has a commercial angle. On commercial stations there are ads, so there is a revenue stream for the broadcaster – not to mention a second hit at the audience for the advertisers.

Now both of these methods for watching TV are great on a tablet, and even workable as legitimate revenue generators on smartphones that are hooked up to a TV screen. (Again, I speak with some knowledge as I used to connect my iPhone to the TV and use the phone to stream BBC iPlayer from my wireless router. Before that I had an old laptop connected to the TV doing much the same thing.) However, this sort of TV consumption is not really workable when on the move.

For starters, smartphone memory is not going to hold too many entire TV shows, and, while it is possible, watching them on the smallest screen can be a challenge. On feature phones the problems are compounded by lack of phone memory and other processing issues. If you want to watch streamed TV from a catch-up service while on the move, you will soon find that, with flaky networks, mass use of mobile data on the train home from work and the general problems of signals dropping, it becomes so arduous as to be not worth the bother.

Also, the mobile user is typically looking to snack on things. Mobile is there to fill those little five minute gaps while waiting for someone to meet you at the pub, or while waiting for a bus, or in boring meetings. Or, if you are like some people I know, even visits to the bathroom. Anyway, the point is this: TV content for mobile has to be very carefully thought through. It has to be short, sharp and to the point, not too bandwidth heavy, and has to give the user what he wants, while satisfying the commercial demands to make some money.

I wish I could now point to a prime example of someone getting this right, but to date TV companies and the rest of the mobile industry have struggled with this. Mobile TV just seems to be a bridge too far. What people seem to like are clips that they can share that are either funny, amazing, gross or all three. Short sharp bits of things that they can pass around.

To date, this has largely become the preserve of the movie trailer, the TV show trailer or, perhaps most intriguingly, advertising. Trailers serve an indirect revenue generation purpose, getting eyeballs to the main event and the advertising that sits around that, be it at the cinema or on the TV. Advertisers, however, have seen the power of creating mobile snippets of video that are funny/amazing/gross enough to be virally circulated by consumers, acting as what is charmingly called viral marketing. This has become a staple use of mobile video as a revenue generator, but again falls firmly into the mobile marketing camp and thus the preserve of Chapter 6.

What seems to be working for TV companies and broadcasters on mobile is the creation of extra content and "behind the scenes" content that again augments mainstream TV programming. The raft of talent shows on TV – *America's Got Talent, American Idol, The X Factor*, and their myriad all-singin', all-dancin', all-ice-skatin' brethren across the world – are increasingly coming to use mobile (mostly through apps) to keep people hooked into the program brand while the show is not on the air.

During the season of *X-Factor* in the UK, ITV, the company behind the show, put up an iPhone app that saw 64,000 downloads after one plug on the Saturday night live TV show. By the end of the run, the app – which, bearing in mind, only worked on iPhone and iPod touch – had been downloaded more than 500,000 times, and had seen 3.9 million individual uses, with each one averaging 6.7 minutes.

This shows the power of an app connected to a TV show. What this app offered users was the chance to see behind the scenes clips, interviews and things that were not available on the show nor on the show's website. What is interesting is that it attracted a great deal of user attention on the night of the show – as you'd expect, people seeing the show being reminded that they had the app – but more surprisingly, people kept coming back to the app during the week, between airings. More surprising still, reveals Mobile Interactive Group, which built the app, is that even after the show was finished, the last song sung and the winner consigned to obscurity or singing on cruise ships, people still come back for more.

In effect, what the show creators have managed to do is to extend the TV show brand beyond when it is aired on TV. Not only into the dead time between episodes, but to the dead time between series. Quite a feat, and a demonstration of the power of mobile.

Commercially, since this was more of a trial than anything, ITV got the app sponsored by Domino's Pizza and built into the app the ability to order a pizza for delivery – a perfect link between the app, the show and the need to sit on the sofa and eat pizza.

For forthcoming shows, the reach of the app is to be extended in order to build upon this and to add the all important element of interaction, as we shall see in the next section . . .

TV interaction

Many people liken the mobile phone to a remote control for your life, but in TV terms, the phone – mobile or otherwise – if not exactly a remote control, is a device that easily lets you get involved.

Phone-ins to radio shows and phone-ins to TV shows are nothing new: witness the *Golden Shot* in the 1970s for instance, or the profusion of radio phone-ins that use the views of the ill-informed to pass as editorial content. But using the telephone to shape the outcome of a show has become hugely popular and, for TV companies, a lucrative new revenue stream.

Like so much in m-commerce, it comes back to premium-rate services (PRS), with fledgling TV shows that required a vote using PRS to let users vote for their favorite gifted amateur in talent shows. This worked well as a voice call on fixed line or mobile, until someone had the brainwave of getting people to text in. It was simple, involving just a five-digit shortcode and the word vote, followed by the name of who or what you were voting for. The message would be charged at a premium, and the return message thanking you for voting would carry another charge. This money, plus the network charge for the message, would be divvied between the program maker, the broadcaster, the service provider who made the SMS voting work and the network operator. This is big in Germany and the UK, but things are different in the US.

US TV shows have turned to the more traditional channel of sponsorship to find interaction services, getting AT&T and PepsiCo to sponsor the phone and SMS voting channels on *American Idol*, thus making them free to callers. It has also helped the TV company that makes the show maneuver around the complex regulations surrounding the use of voting and paid-for telephone services, yet has still generated revenue for the company. Since the sponsorship and advertising features on the TV screen and in the message heard over the phone, it still sort of counts as a mobile commerce revenue stream, but isn't as exciting as what has happened with these shows in the UK, which has largely pioneered TV interaction.

And it was, for a while, rich pickings. Until someone realized that SMS is not a direct messaging service, but is what is called store-and-forward. The message goes to a message server on the network, is then passed on to the recipient's network message server, and then on to the recipient. The problem is it doesn't go straight through, so when many people are all voting, near the very end of the voting process, not all messages arrive before the cutoff time. They may have been sent before the deadline, but thanks to store-and-forward, they arrive after it.

This meant that each time the vote was on, several thousand people were being charged for casting a vote that wasn't counted. In reality, it wasn't such a big scandal, but it was whipped up by the press (most of whom also use PRS for their chat, dating and other services, as discussed earlier in this chapter) who condemned PRS SMS as a frauds charter, and dubbed one poor service provider company MD (whom I know to be a lovely chap) a Premium Rat, and printed his photo in the newspaper.

Anyway, the upshot is that, while TV interaction should be a prime area for m-commerce, SMS voting is not allowed while an adequate solution to store-and-forward issues is arrived at. (That is now largely thought to be a robust refund mechanism, but I digress.)

But all is not lost. In the interim, as we have seen with *The X Factor* and the like, the app has surfaced as a tool that a large number of viewers of event television are keen to use, and so furious work is being done to make this interactive.

In ITV's *X Factor* app trial last year, as well as giving extra unique mobile footage and the ability to order a pizza, the service also featured a big red button that you could hit and make an amusing noise with, to indicate to your friends and family gathered about the TV with you that you thought an act was rubbish. It wasn't connected to anything more than the iPhone/iPod's sound card and speakers, but it demonstrated that people could play along.

The next iteration of the app, for the 2011 series of *The X Factor* in the UK (which is under wraps as I write, but may well have aired as you read) is set to not only work on Android, Windows Phone 7, BlackBerry and Nokia, but will also allow users to become a judge on the show. This is interaction writ large. The idea is that the app will be web-enabled, so people watching the show can use the app to vote on the acts. Their results will be displayed on the screen as a fifth judge, letting viewers shape the show (well, sort of) as it proceeds.

This is, as said, not yet out in the open as I write, but will at some point become reality, and it brings mobile into the realms of being a truly awesome TV adjunct.

Back in the real world, it is worth noting that mobile already plays a huge role in TV interaction, even in the UK where you aren't allowed to do it using SMS. For starters, most of these big TV shows let you vote using PRS calls, which many people, despite the cost (in fact, despite the fact that you can't actually see how much it costs until you get your bill), call with their mobiles. Primitive, but still mobile interaction and therefore m-commerce.

There are also a raft of digital-only TV channels of a more adult nature that let viewers text in messages to the "performers," requesting subtle nuances to their on-screen positioning and the location of their undergarments. It's all a bit sordid, but it does illustrate that in the right context, people do want to use their mobiles to interact with the TV and are willing to pay to do it.

As TV content becomes ever more than just another form of content, I believe it is important for TV companies to look at how else they can use mobile technology to augment what they do on the TV screen, for that is where the next generation of revenues and eyeballs are going to come from.

Music

The music business was one of the first industries to embrace mobile, seeing it as not only a handy device to consume music on, but also that it could be delivered over the air to users. If you wanted to listen to Beethoven's Ninth Symphony on the way home from work and you didn't have it, you could just buy it and download it to your device. Of course, back in 2000 when the music and mobile industries were talking about this, it was pretty much impossible to do. The networks, devices and billing tools – not to mention the music industry itself – just weren't up to it.

Before we got to this nirvana (or indeed before we got Nirvana) on our mobile phones, the market for ringtones had already taken off (see Chapters 1 and 2), opening the eyes and ears of mobile users to having mobile music. Since then the market has grown and expanded; and thanks to better phones, buy-in from the music industry, and iTunes and Spotify (to name the two main players; other mobile music stores and streaming services are available), mobile music downloads and streaming are now an accepted part of life and a lucrative part of the mobile commerce mix.

And boy does it make money. Worldwide recording industry revenues from mobile are put, by Juniper Research, at around $6.2bn in 2010, broken down roughly as $4.9127bn on ringtones, $72m on streaming audio, $65.1m on music downloads and $489m on ringback tones.

Mobile music is one of the key, and largely overlooked, money makers in m-commerce; and like mobile in other industries, it is increasingly being seen not just as a means of selling only music content, but as part of the whole music experience. It provides video (often exclusive video content), the ability to get tickets to shows and to purchase merchandise, and the sharing and viral marketing of content using social media from the device. The fact that most smartphones are now handy pocket-sized multi-gigabit music stores with excellent audio processors just adds to their appeal.

Ageing dance legend Faithless (which has recently split up) may be a bit passé with the kids, but the band was certainly at the forefront of marketing its new album and tour, turning to music recognition service Shazam to turn a TV ad into a downloadable track and ticket booking service.

TV ads for Faithless will feature the Shazam logo, and fans with the Shazam music recognition app on their mobile will be able to tag the Faithless track, "Feelin Good," that is playing during the ad. Shazam — which is a really neat audio recognition algorithm that identifies what it is listening to and tells you what it is — will then match the music from its database of nine million tracks and deliver the Faithless track and album cover, offering Shazamers links to buy the music instantaneously, as well as tickets to the gig, directly from their mobile.

The project was a groundbreaker and deemed a success by Faithless's management, but was sadly not enough to keep the group together. Still, it sows the seeds of how this could work.

DJs, the new rock and rollers, are all over mobile, as they see it as the ideal marketing channel to get people listening to their stuff, and, more crucially, buying tickets to see them perform and to buy merchandise.

Marketing and merchandise manager for UK act DJ Shadow blogged recently that "mobile is the future" for artists, and that a bare-bones mobile app is enough to bring traffic to artists' websites and social networks, where other merchandise can be purchased. Furthermore, in a recent tour, DJ Shadow used his iPhone app during his gigs to encourage the audience to interact with the music.

Other DJs such as Armin van Buuren and Markus Schulz have signed up with social location service Flowd from Finnish company Digia, which positions itself as a foursquare for music. The iPhone and Android app allows users to check in and let their friends on social networks know where they are. Crucially, DJs can also use it to let their fans know where they are, and they can also be messaged by their fans with the option to reply.

Then there are iPad apps such as mix.dj HD, whose makers claim that it streams more than 25,000 DJ mixes from around the world. These let DJs stream what they are doing to a global audience, who can then track them down more specifically and start spending money. These are the guys who are shaping how mobile music works, and it's a different world to that of buying – let alone selling – 45s back in the 70s. Today, mobile apps are a storefront, with the music advertising a whole lifestyle choice, not just in the music but clothes and other products.

This is the more subtle face of m-commerce: using mobile as the channel into a richer and wider commercial experience and that all important brand-consumer relationship.

Case study

Ministry of Sound

Über club and record label Ministry of Sound was the first major music brand in the world to use mobile to allow music lovers to purchase club tickets and have them delivered to their phones via an app, in partnership with solutions company Trinity Mobile. Downloadable for free over the air and online via iTunes and Zune Marketplace, the app lets fans across the world keep up to date with the latest club and tour dates, radio shows and album releases at the touch of a button – all at a time and location that is convenient to them, and all available to share on Facebook, Twitter and e-mail.

Whether it's the latest interviews from the club's Saturday Sessions artists or free streaming of a DJ mix, the app keeps users posted with the latest content from Ministry of Sound online, and brings them up to speed with acts such as Joris Voorn, Mark Knight, Laidback Luke, Sebastien Leger and other international DJs of repute.

But it is the way MoS is using the app to grow its business that makes it really stand out. With events selling out week in, week out, the safe and secure booking option allows users to prepay for an unlimited number of tickets, ensuring entry on both Friday and Saturday nights.

Big clubs aren't everybody's thing, so the app has a built-in radio section, allowing for more intimate listening with guest mixes from some of the biggest artists around. With 45 shows each week, each one individually tailored to a wide range of genres, users get to listen to and – more importantly – buy their favorite tracks. Users can also browse and buy albums, compilations and singles from the immense collection of music brought out by Ministry of Sound Recordings.

This also essentially extends MoS from being a London-based nightclub brand to something that can be enjoyed by a global audience - and significantly extend the reach and money-making potential of the brand using mobile and apps stores.

Games and gambling

While music has taken an early lead, and where retail is clearly going to be mobile commerce's big money, games – and to a lesser extent gambling – have become a surprise hit on mobile. In a marketplace that was dominated by Nintendo and Sony PlayStation in terms of portable games players, no one saw the fact that phones were going to become a serious contender.

Games

While early phones started to ship in the mid-1990s with simple games such as Worms built in, it wasn't until the advent of the smartphone – in particular, the iPhone's accelerometer – that people realized that what applied to music (over-the-air downloading and a nice screen to play on) could apply to games. Couple this with the fact that, thanks to Internet connectivity, you can play games live against other people anywhere in the world, and suddenly mobile gaming has become a huge money spinner.

In fact, it is estimated that around 60% of the apps downloaded from the apps store are games. On current apps store figures of 500 billion downloads, that's a staggering 300 billion games downloaded since 2008 when the apps store opened. And bearing in mind that most games apps are charged for, that is a lot of money. If you assume an average price of $0.59, then that's $177bn – currently by far and away the most lucrative part of the mobile commerce ecosystem.

Funnily enough, games are the most popular apps on the Apple apps store, but the least popular on BlackBerry. Make of that what you will.

In China, mobile games downloads are now outstripping western markets, with a study by Canalys showing that 51% of Chinese end users downloaded applications or games on their mobile phones – 29% more than their Western European counterparts. A similar Canalys survey carried out in France, Germany and the UK found that only 22% of respondents downloaded applications or games on their mobile phones.

India, as we have seen in earlier chapters, is also starting to look like an increasingly attractive market for mobile games. Right now it is nascent, but already in 2010 Analysys Mason found that the mobile gaming market in India generated $54.7m, with nine million active users.

The US offers a strangely contrary view, however, that is perhaps more indicative of how the mobile gaming market in the developed world will play out. In the US the number of mobile games players has, according to research by comScore, fallen 13% between 2009 and 2010. This has been driven by a 35% drop in mobile gaming on non-smartphones, which still represent half or more of the mobile phone market.

But, at the same time, smartphone gaming in the US has grown by 60% over the same period. And these gamers are much heavier users, the games are more expensive – reflecting their greater richness and interactivity – and each smartphone gamer is more likely to install and play multiple games on his device. So while overall gaming numbers on mobile have dropped – and it is widely considered to be a temporary decline, picking up in 2011 and 2012 as smartphone penetration increases – the revenues and potential revenues from mobile gaming in the US are still huge.

While gaming is indeed pulling in the revenues – and largely at the expense of the more traditional games consoles – the arrival of tablets, the combination of these devices, and the exponential growth of social media on mobile is producing huge developments and starting to attract interest. In fact, the two things together – social and gaming – is a powerful force. Research by Interpret, an entertainment, media and technology market research firm, finds that more than half (52%) of tablet owners, including the iPad users, are playing games on their device. Gaming is the second most popular activity on these devices, behind only surfing the Internet (58%). Furthermore, active gamers are more likely than the average consumer to plan on purchasing an iPad or other tablet in the next three months. This shows how these devices and smartphones are becoming the gaming platforms of choice for many gamers. Moreover, these devices and smartphones are creating new gamers who wouldn't normally have been into game playing.

This boom in gaming is seeing another revenue opportunity take shape: in-game advertising. Juniper Research forecasts that spending on advertising on mobile games will increase tenfold over the next five years, hitting $894m by 2015, up from $87m in 2010. This increase will be fueled by increasing brand interest in mobile as an advertising channel, and apps – which, as we've seen, are dominant in games.

Games such as Rovio's Angry Birds are making a significant impact by offering full versions of their games free to end-users, and funding them through in-game advertising. Opportunities in this area have been strengthened by the launch of key platforms designed to optimize the deployment of ads within applications, most notably Apple's iAd in July 2010. Similarly, Juniper Research finds that games are being successfully deployed as marketing tools by brands, such as Barclaycard and Volkswagen, which provides new revenue opportunities for developers, such as Fishlabs and Firemint.

According to Juniper Research's Mobile Games report written by Juniper analyst, Daniel Ashdown, in November 2010, "Angry Birds has been a huge hit over the last year on the iPhone since its launch; but arguably its relative impact, in terms of downloads, has been bigger on GetJar and, more recently, on Android Market, as a result of offering the game free with ads. Users get a great game for free, but advertisers get significant product/brand exposure; the same is true of mobile games as marketing tools."

Nevertheless, the report forecasts that, while growth in advertising spending on mobile games will be higher than end-user revenues, this latter business model will continue to be the primary source of revenue for players in the industry. By 2015, end-user revenues, which comprise those from pay-per-download and in-game purchases, will still be 10 times higher than advertising spending.

Gambling

Gambling services on mobile, meanwhile, have long been tipped to be a big banker. However, until recently they have failed to live up to that promise. That said, 2011 has been the year of mobile gambling, fueled by, surprise, surprise, the iPhone.

The iPhone, as we have seen, has got mass-market numbers of people involved in using mobile data services. It has also got them playing games, and this has not gone unnoticed in the realms of bookmakers and casino operators. In the US, mobile sports book betting – betting on sporting event outcomes, not to mention events within the game – has been a surprising hit with consumers. The ability to place bets instantly, usually on account, is really driving the market, not just among people at sporting events, but everywhere else. These days a gentleman can escort his lady to the shopping mall and still have a crafty bet riding on the horses, football, basketball, and even the javelin or other Olympic sports (something that will also see a surge in mobile gambling in 2012 in the UK).

US laws on mobile gambling, however, like their online counterpart, are confused. The typical rule of thumb is that the gambling happens wherever the server that the gambling takes place on is located. So it should be okay so long as the services you are using are in a state that allows gambling. But this is a very fluid situation, so it pays to check regularly online as to what is required to meet gaming laws in the US.

China has also been a huge powerhouse of mobile gambling growth, and will continue to be so over the coming decade as the country's billion-strong population gets smartphone-enabled.

Again, research by our friends at Juniper Research suggests that increasing numbers of mobile casino, lottery and betting services, along with the liberalization of remote gambling legislation, will see the scale of annual wagers on mobile gambling exceed $48bn by 2015.

In recent years, Japan Racing Association's IPAT service had been responsible for the bulk of global mobile gambling transactions, with UK's casino and betting services accounting for much of the remainder. However, China is the market worth looking at, as proved by the sharp surge in adoption of the mobile lottery service launched by VODone. At the same time, the US market is also poised to see the introduction of its first mobile lottery services to augment its healthy mobile sports book market.

Studies of the mobile gambling market find, interestingly, that users have eschewed multiplayer gambling apps – where you can play, say, poker against a collection of other players, a hugely successful segment of online gambling. Mobile gamblers prefer to multitask while playing "snacking" applications, as is often the case when people use mobile as an entertainment device.

One of the drawbacks with mobile gambling is that it is very well suited to the app environment, but apps store owners such as Apple and Android both exercise caution over gambling apps. Android is more open, but still has rules, and Apple has only just started to allow gambling apps to appear in its store. Getting gambling apps accepted on both these – and other stores – requires patience and can, it is claimed, result in less effective gambling games.

The answer is to perhaps eschew the apps approach and look to create browser-based games for the gambling sector. However, until HTML5 becomes a dominant force, the browser approach to casino games is often found wanting, since much of the functionality needed to generate a compelling experience can be hampered by network issues and other constraints, as we have discussed.

Brands

Like retailers, brands are getting rapidly attuned to the fact that mobile offers them a wealth of opportunities to market, promote and sell their goods, as well as offering a channel that allows them to engage with their customers and for those customers to engage with them. Much of how brands use mobile straddles the previous chapter on retail and the next chapter on marketing, but between these two pillars lies a wealth of opportunities for brands to use mobile to directly generate revenue; and perhaps more powerfully, to use mobile to indirectly generate sales, through that most elusive of phantoms – brand identity.

As we have seen in earlier chapters, mobile commerce is a complicated beast, being not just a channel to sell things through, but a way of driving people to your products, stores, websites and more. What we haven't touched on – and what makes up the bulk of this chapter – is that mobile is a great tool for promoting interaction between brands and their customers, either to create revenue through charging for that interaction, or in using it to get people to go to a store or website and buy goods and services. It is also an effective way to get people thinking about your brand, telling other people they know about your brand and creating what is becoming known as advocacy marketing.

But that's for the next chapter on mobile marketing. Here I want to look at how mobile can be used by brands to create a brand image and get consumers interacting with the brand.

Much of what mobile brings to brands is in developing interaction services, the same as with media and TV as discussed already in this chapter. Mobile offers a uniquely personal way to engage with consumers and to get them to engage with brands. The data that these interactions produce are in themselves valuable to the brands.

FMCG (fast moving consumer goods) brands are starting to look at the wider engagement of their consumers, offering everything from chat and dating to psychic and horoscope services to shoppers — especially, sad as it is to admit, around brands and supermarkets aimed at women. Bingo and dating services run by brands such as the supermarket chain Asda (part of Walmart) are already proving to be a hit on mobile in the UK, and are generating customer relationship management (CRM) tools, such as ways to improve loyalty. They also generate data about shoppers, their likes and dislikes, that the store can use to great effect or even sell on (assuming the customer has ticked the box saying they can, of course).

This is one of the key roles mobile has to play in any business, especially brands and retailers, but also for other content services that demand some degree of loyalty. The handset is a very personal tool which, as we have seen, can be used to generate interaction between consumers on an individual level and brands, retailers, TV programs and the media. This is where mobile's true strength lies: it inhabits the pockets of consumers, it is often, quite literally, next to their hearts in their jacket pockets, and the reach that gives brands is extraordinary.

The key thing is working out how to target these consumers most effectively. The interaction you are getting them to partake in has to be fun, enlightening and has to have something in it for them. The fact that the brand gets some useful data or gets a consumer to buy something he or she wouldn't normally have gone for needs to be obscured. The interaction needs to be enjoyable – which not only gets people to engage, but also prompts them to pass it on virally to their friends.

Much of this falls into mobile marketing, but at this stage it is worth looking at how brands can achieve this.

One way is to offer competitions over mobile (and usually online as well – you don't want to preclude anyone from joining in), or to cleverly turn the brand or its values into a game (so-called gamification – something we are going to see a lot more of in the coming months).

Competitions, such as those famously run by Walkers Crisps (see case study opposite) and Coca-Cola, to name just two, have seen consumers willingly divulging their mobile numbers and other data about themselves – and spending money – to either create a flavor of potato chips or to get some free credit on their mobile, as given away by Coca-Cola.

The Coca-Cola example is very interesting. The soft drinks giant put a shortcode on cans of Coca-Cola, Fanta and other youth-oriented sodas and got consumers to text it to get 50p worth of credit on their phone bill or prepaid phone. The campaign generated tens of thousands of responses and a massive mobile marketing database for Coke, all for just 50p per name. What is particularly interesting about the campaign was that it required mobile operators to figure out how to credit money, across all networks, onto phones – something hitherto they had shied away from. The move, prompted by the massive brand appeal of Coke and the gains set to be made in network traffic – plus whatever Coca-Cola paid them to do it in the first place – clearly made them rethink.

Not only did this lead to a fantastic promotion for Coca-Cola, but it has also ushered in the possibility of refunding money to handsets — something that neatly gets around the issues with using text to let people vote on TV shows (see the TV interaction section early in this chapter). This has prompted a wholesale rethinking of how mobile can be used around these services, as well as around brands, and is likely to kick-start a whole new wave of mobile interaction in the coming months.

Case study

Walkers Crisps

Walkers, UK purveyors of fine potato chips (or crisps, in the UK) was one of the early brand adopters of mobile in its commercial sphere. Back in 2008 it rolled out the innovative multimedia campaign called "Do us a Flavour, Win a Packet," created by digital agency Jigsaw, which delivered all their digital interactivity. The campaign invited the public to create the next great flavor of Walkers Crisps, with Jigsaw's creative and technical expertise providing integrated mobile and online interactivity to power engagement.

The Walkers competition was designed to encourage consumers to submit their ideas for a new Walkers crisp flavor, along with images or pictures illustrating the creative thinking behind their idea, using the web and mobile. This was where Jigsaw's technological expertise and knowledge in delivering and building WAP (Wireless Application Protocol) and online solutions came into play.

Digital interactivity played a key part in all three stages of the nine-month campaign, in which the winning consumer pocketed £50,000 ($80,695) plus 1% of future sales in prize money. The five runners-up received a not-insubstantial £10,000 ($16,140).

The interactive competition was run in three stages.

Stage 1: Walkers engaged the nation to send in ideas by asking what "tickles your taste buds," and inviting people to submit flavor ideas via mobile or web. Jigsaw powered web and mobile mechanics.

To enter via the Walkers website, consumers entered their flavor idea and contact details, and uploaded the image of what inspired them. To enter via mobile, consumers simply sent an MMS (picture message) with their name, postcode, suggested flavor and a picture of what inspired them to shortcode 60001. All images were checked, and participants received a WAP link to view their entry. They were also given the opportunity to forward the link to a friend and for others to vote on their flavor. Participants could also enter via post.

Stage 2: Six finalists were selected by five judges, including celebrity chef Heston Blumenthal.

Stage 3: Walkers launched all six flavors and the nation decided the winner, using cutting-edge technology provided by Jigsaw via SMS, IVR (Interactive Voice Response), WAP and on the Walkers Do Us a Flavour website. The winning flavor – the all-day breakfast – was then announced live on TV.

The campaign was designed to be fun and inventive, and to get consumers used to using mobile and the web – and increasingly the mobile web – to interact with Walkers. The campaign wasn't as such a mobile commerce play, but did use mobile to engage consumers with the brand and to use mobile to create content and vote – something we will be seeing more of from brands in the coming months and years.

Gamification

Gamification – or using games to create compelling, often branded services in place of a more traditional advertisement online and on mobile – has become something of a phenomenon in the modern multichannel interaction market. Much of it has been added around TV shows, but brands are also starting to do it, particularly as an extension of loyalty programs (see next page).

Many of them involve gathering points to redeem for rewards – much as businesses have done with loyalty schemes, coupons and vouchers – but have added an element of game play to the process, which offers more engagement and that all important fun factor. And when it's done well, the rewards to the business can be impressive: boosting engagement and brand awareness, as well as vastly increasing direct conversion, shareability and repeat business.

A few big brands have dipped their toes into the water. McDonald's sponsored farms on Farmville, and Entertainment Weekly has joined a variety of networks and studios that offer stickers on GetGlue. Now it's time to go further. Look at it this way: marketing has always been a competitive game, only now it has bonus levels, score cards and rewards for spending time playing when you should be doing something else.

There are of course many hurdles to gamification, not least asking yourself, "Does it add anything?" It is also worth looking at what you want to gain from doing this, how to get users to sign up and create a user profile – the all-important data that you are doing this for – and how you give points, and what those points mean and what they can be redeemed against.

As we have seen, the mobile games market is massive, and consumers increasingly want to play games. Tying them up with brands and marketing on mobile becomes a compelling offering, if the kind of brand you are has the kind of consumers coming to it that are gamers. Working that out is perhaps the toughest part of all.

Loyalty

The other area where mobile is starting to see some traction is loyalty programs. The logic is simple: rather than carry a plastic card around that you can accrue points on, why not use the phone? The phone, thanks to bar code scanning and NFC (see Chapter 9), can be swiped or scanned to put points on or redeem points from the program, just like a card. But being mobile and connected, it can be used to create much more. The loyalty program can be built into the workings of an app or m-web site. It can be used to contact consumers and can be turned from a simple loyalty scheme into a game, as we have seen above.

In many ways, mobile for retailers or brands, TV programs or anything else, is an extension of loyalty – either just plain brand loyalty or loyalty schemes. If you look at mobile like this, you can see that the inherent advantages of mobile are really what you want from a loyalty scheme.

Mobile is always on, it can deliver information to the customer, it can tell you where a customer is and what he is doing and, if you create your app or m-web service based around this idea of loyalty and reward, you can garner all manner of useful consumer information when people sign up to use your app or m-web site.

A prime example in the UK has been the pet store Pets at Home. Its app lets users sign up with the usual personal information about themselves, but it also lets them add in a whole load of data about their pets – species, breed, age, inoculation and medical history, insurance details and vet appointments – and seemingly lets pet owners manage their lives and that of their pets much more efficiently.

What it gives Pets at Home is a unique and specific insight into that person and his pet, so that they can target that customer with the right information — for instance, if he is a cat owner, facts and useful things about cats and deals for cat-related goods.

Mobile loyalty thus allows for much better marketing, which lies behind the carapace of the brand being interested in the customer and his pet on an individual basis. Like gamification, this personalization that m-loyalty can deliver is beginning to show brands and retailers that treating people on a one-to-one basis can increase yield per customer.

Extending this engagement into the location of the consumer, what they have looked at but not bought, and even what other stores they might have been in, especially through social location services such as foursquare and now Facebook, means that this loyalty program idea can start to deliver an unprecedented view of consumers, their habits, likes and dislikes — all of which allows you to deliver an even more personally targeted experience.

Of course, the downside is that the consumer has to opt in to let you do this and, as mobile loyalty becomes widespread, you will face massive competition from all other retailers. But right now, for those early adopters who can get in on the ground floor and deliver this sort of experience, the rewards are high.

General businesses

As the example of using your mobile app or site as a loyalty service, rather than just as a way of getting your store on the mobile phone, shows, mobile is all about delivering things that you can already do in other ways, but with some seriously interesting bells and whistles attached. And this idea translates into all manner of other businesses. In fact, you could argue that it works in any business in any market, so long as the consumers you are targeting have mobile phones. Here are some prime areas where mobile commerce is becoming the key play.

Ticketing and travel

One in every eight mobile users worldwide will either have a ticket delivered to his mobile phone, or buy a ticket with his phone, by 2015, with bar-coded boarding passes for airlines leading the way, claims a new study by Juniper Research. If this comes to pass, then more than 750 million users worldwide will be using mobile ticketing. This compares with approximately 1 in 20 currently, or around 230 million users globally.

Ticket delivery will be by SMS, bar codes, mobile web, smartphone apps or NFC, and will see people using mobile as a ticketing tool for everything from buses, to trains, to planes and all other transport services, as well as for everyday things, such as cinema, sports and other entertainment offerings.

The penetration of mobile tickets is predicted to be so high because, once again, it is a natural link between the mobile device, the web and the brand. As with all other brand uses of mobile, not only does it make for a handy and low-cost way to distribute tickets, but also it allows the company selling the tickets to learn a lot more about the ticket buyer. Further, it offers the opportunity to create loyalty and increase interaction, and up- and cross-sell, with them.

It also promises to cut down on the use – and waste – of paper, so there is also a nice green angle to it.

However, this level of penetration could be at risk if user experience isn't developed correctly at rollout, and could be threatened further if the mobile ticketing redemption infrastructure doesn't keep pace with user demand.

While mobile ticketing users are currently con[...]
of early adopting transport schemes in Japan, [...]
Europe and Scandinavia, the opportunities for mob[...]
spread right across the transport, sport, entertainmen[...]
sectors. It is expected to become mainstream in 2013, altho[...]
are high hopes that the London 2012 Olympics will usher in a[...]
mobile ticketing examples to a global audience.

Transport is obviously a key market for mobile ticketing services, and already train services in Japan are using it, as well as some trials happening in the UK (see the case study below). But it is not just limited to areas of travel such as rail, when reducing long lines forms an important driver for implementing mobile ticketing.

Case study

Contactless ticketing is making tracks in Russia and the UK

The St. Petersburg Metro in Russia is in the middle of a very successfully mobile-based contactless ticketing trial, which allows customers to tap in and out with their phones – all thanks to a clever gadget and some sticky tape. No really.

The trial uses SIM overlay chips and flexible antennas mounted on plastic film, which users simply wrap around their phone batteries. This converts their phones – smart, feature or run-of-the-mill – into contactless ticketing devices. The trial – being run by US company Ambiq Technology – adopted this seemingly unconventional and low-tech approach to NFC enabling phones, after testing many other devices and readers, including NFC-enabled handsets. Ambiq found that this option worked best and had the most traction with users. In fact, much of the high-end equipment it tested before the trials launch simply wasn't up to the job.

Mobile business **Chapter 5**

...he St. Petersburg Metro
...ustomers to top up cash
...and in the bank. While
...network operators are
...trial.

...1, so no results as yet.
...he UK, where Chiltern
...s mobile ticketing trial

The train company is testing an integrated mobile ticketing system that will finally solve the age-old problem of long lines at the ticket office. Well, that's the theory.

Under the trial, a free iPhone application provides passengers with details of the cheapest prices and train times, and then delivers the ticket as a 2D bar code within the application. Special scanners on gates at stations will read the iPhone screen to enable passengers to "touch in" and "touch out" of stations.

For the first time, passengers arriving at a station without a ticket will be able to get through the barrier, without needing to line up at ticket offices, call contact centers or negotiate ticket machines. The iPhone application will remember favorite journeys and debit card details, so that travel can be made with just a few touches of the screen.

This innovation marks the first time that any rail passengers anywhere in the world have been able to use smartphones to buy and receive rail tickets through one transaction. Unlike most commercial booking services, the Chiltern Railways iPhone application will not charge a booking fee, and the application will be free to download.

Soon the mobile phone won't just be for commuters to yell "I am on the train" into. It could also be their ticket, if these and other pilots around the world prove a hit with consumers.

Airlines have become one of the early adopters of mobile as a ticketing solution, with many now using it as a way of issuing online check-in customers with their boarding pass.

The trouble with online check-in is often that the traveler hasn't got access to a printer, so he has to check in online and then queue up at the airport anyway to get a boarding pass — negating for both traveler and airline the advantages of checking in online. Having the web-based check-in on the phone, and resulting in an electronic boarding pass, overcomes this problem neatly.

Many airlines are also now looking at the use of mobile on the plane itself. Although hampered by the fact that you generally can't have the GSM/3G running while in flight, as the devices' network scanning every 90 seconds is picked up by the headsets of the pilot, using in-plane Wi-Fi or even, in the case of Virgin America first class, iPads can offer the passengers entertainment and, more importantly, in-flight shopping facilities.

Indian airline Jet Airways is plastering 2D QR codes on its website, Facebook page and in its in-flight magazine to give its customers what it considers faster and better access to its online content on mobile. Phase two of the project will have the codes appearing on boarding passes and tickets too. The codes are supplied by 3GVision, and passengers need to download the mobile company's i-nigma 2D mobile bar code scanner onto their phone to take advantage of the offer.

Once the bar code is scanned by the individual's handset, the technology automatically directs the user to the mobile Internet site, making it easy to navigate through the airline's editorial content and promotional offers and services.

The US Federal Aviation Authority (FAA) has even granted an executive airline permission for aircrew to use iPads instead of paper maps and airport layout charts on some flights.

Travel agents and travelers

Travel agents and travelers are also benefiting from mobile in new and extraordinary ways. Travel agencies have been slow to adopt the mobile web, but Abacus International has put the power of mobile directly into travel agents' hands. The company partnered with Dublin-based Mobile Travel Technologies (MTT) to develop Abacus Mobile, a solution that allows travel agents to provide professional service to their customers even when they are out of the office.

Services such as Abacus Mobile, available to travel agents on smartphones, emulate the familiar "green screen" style of the Abacus Point of Sale system, allowing agents with the app to operate just as if they were at their desk, and so make their small operations more competitive.

Travelers too can benefit from mobile, with apps aplenty to aid foreign travel and ease the pain of currency conversion, provide maps, booking services, holiday ratings, holiday deals, and tables of inoculations and more. There is even an augmented reality app that, if you hold your phone over a sign, it will translate it for you.

In fact, the Apple Apps Store has a whole section devoted just to travel apps, with many hundreds of apps offering everything from taxi services to finding a toilet in whatever foreign town you happen to be in. (Fans of the TV shows *Seinfeld* and *Curb Your Enthusiasm* will note that George Costanza comes up with the idea for a toilet finder app, makes a fortune and then loses it all in a divorce settlement. Art truly imitates mobile life).

Case study

Lonely Planet adds augmented reality

Lonely Planet became the first travel company in the world to create augmented reality products for travelers with Android handsets, launching a series of 25 Compass Guides for popular European, US and Asian cities.

The application pinpoints the user's exact location, so that when in a new city you can find out what is around you – from the practical to the sublime – just by looking through the camera. The data that appear overlaid on the real world come from Lonely Planet information on the best destinations, accommodation, sites, bars and restaurants, and appear like post-it notes to points of interest. Key features of the Compass Guides include GPS-enabled maps and location-based information for hundreds of points of interest for every city, while the phone's built-in compass allows users to see their current location and how far or near they are to destinations and sites. Significantly, the service is designed to work where possible off-line, so that data roaming fees are minimized.

Lonely Planet worked with Austrian developer Mobilizy, which also developed the augmented reality features for the Wikitude app, to make points of interest in city guides compatible with AR technology. Partnerships are a natural way to speed up the pace of development, and Mobilizy was a good fit for Lonely Planet in this latest stage of its mobile development.

Live events

While ticketing touches on live events, there is much that mobile can bring to this important part of the entertainment and commerce mix. Premier League football clubs and the London Olympic Committee are among the front-runners in exploring how mobile can work at live events. It covers everything from information to fans between games to ticketing, merchandising, and more esoteric services such as fan-to-fan instant messaging, live betting and even layering extra web-based information onto the live event, through augmented reality (AR).

Many Premier League football clubs in the UK and other sports teams around the world are already looking at using mobile to deliver content to fans. Real Madrid has been one of the leading players, scoring a hit and a huge revenue goal with its mobile fan site that offers statistics, inside information, footage from the club, merchandise and more, all through a mobile portal. Everton Football Club has a BlackBerry app and an iPhone app that offer fans similar content and services. Fulham and Chelsea are also on the mobile map with mobile fan offerings. Before the year is out, most major sporting teams in Europe and the US will have some sort of mobile presence.

In the US, all major sporting leagues — be they football, baseball, basketball, hockey and more — have adopted mobile as a means of keeping fans connected and engaged with teams and events between actual games. The NFL (National Football League), for instance, runs a mobile news service that keeps fans informed 24/7 of news and scores in the league, features interviews and videos, and offers an immersive experience around games. The NFL also offers a range of apps for iOS and Android that deliver the same rich content for fans sitting at home, and extend the reach of the NFL's websites and other services into the mobile environment. The NFL features games that can be played with players and teams from the league, generating extra interest and revenues for the league.

The National Basketball Association (NBA) in the US has also seen significant traction on mobile, with the 2011 playoffs generating an 87% increase in mobile app downloads for the NBA's app, compared to those in May 2010.

This, along with the NFL's successful forays into mobile, show that the US market is eagerly embracing mobile services around the sports and live events arena. As with apps and m-web properties involving TV programs, these services do a great job of keeping the sports brand and the teams in the consumers' minds between games — something that proves lucrative to both the teams and the leagues, as well as their sponsors and advertisers.

This is one of the key powers of mobile. Even if the app or m-web property doesn't deliver revenue through its download, it gives sponsors more visibility, and it increasingly drives traffic to merchandise and other content, which in turn produces more eyeballs for sponsors and on it goes.

In stadia

It is what clubs and stadium owners can do with the plethora of mobile users in the stadium — or realistically, on their way to, in and away from the stadium — on game days that is piquing the interest of some of the best known clubs in the world.

Mobile is key when looking at the best times to interact with fans. Fans are at their most passionate when on the way to the match, at the match (or watching in the bar), and on the way home. The only personal device they are carrying with them at that point is their phone. They can check the website, but they won't have a great experience. Of course, they can watch Sky or ESPN, but this doesn't give a personal experience from their own club. Mobile and wireless devices are invaluable for connecting with fans at this very important time.

Work is underway at many clubs to make the most of this time. Many clubs, such as the top UK Premier League teams, have an iPhone app that offers the team sheet information as soon as it comes out, news updates, text commentary, etc, as well as a WAP site, which offers up-to-the-minute information. These clubs also heavily advertise shortcodes and keywords in the stadium, which link people straight through to products and services on their phone.

Gambling operators such as Betfair, William Hill and Ladbrokes are also keenly eyeing the potential of mobile within the stadium, looking to build on the massive success they saw in 2010 with mobile sports books. They want to offer services where fans can bet on events within the game as it unfolds before them – who will get the next corner, foul, penalty, sending off, goal or free kick.

To make any of this happen requires connectivity and nice fat broadband – something that networks in the UK at least are currently striving to deliver. Fans struggle to make a phone call or send a text, let alone have any meaningful interaction with anything, while they're at the stadium, as the networks are just saturated. With 50,000 people all in one place, the networks simply can't cope.

Ironically, the Premier League has recently given clubs the right to send replays to the fans' handsets in the stadium straight after they happen. This is a massive opportunity, as previously the earliest a club could show any footage was 12 hours after the final whistle, when, you could argue, the moment had passed.

Similarly in the US, sports clubs, through the leagues, can use replays on mobile almost as soon as they happen, and they certainly use them in the aftermath of games, keeping user interest in the whole event going. This again presents an ideal opportunity to engage fans within the stadium as the game unfolds, offering all manner of revenue and loyalty-generating opportunities.

But very few clubs in the UK and in the US will have the infrastructure in place to make the most of these new rights straightaway. It requires a complete reworking of mobile connectivity in any older venue.

One solution is to look at how to build out wiMAX – a sort of Wi-Fi on steroids – networks within the stadium through companies such as IMT, but again cost is an issue. Network operators are struggling with how to overcome the saturation their networks are seeing, with O2 announcing that it is going to build a free national Wi-Fi network that will offer proper broadband mobile capabilities. But that is two years away.

Whatever the network issues, mobile interaction at events and around events will become commonplace, first in football and then eventually everywhere.

There is also a lot of mobile commerce action around music festivals, where mobile is being used not just for ticketing, but also to provide extra content and services, a chance for third parties to make money from consumers at festivals. One prime example is the use of Shazam to recognize live tunes and let consumers buy the artist's work. There is nothing like getting someone to buy while in the throes of enjoying the music being played live.

Similarly, there is the chance to get user information and to interact with those users after the event to keep the relationship alive, by selling them video and audio of the live event they attended, and offering deals on merchandise, other festivals and tickets for the next year at a discount.

In fact, all that applies to brands, media and TV companies and anyone else, also applies here in the live arena.

The problem, as ever, is network connectivity, but there are ways around this. As the concept of mobile at live events becomes an integral part of the event experience, these solutions will be deemed financially viable enough to become the norm.

Case study

The Connecticut Sun team brings mobile marketing to the WNBA

The Connecticut Sun WNBA (Women's National Basketball Association) team has become the first US sports team to use proximity marketing to engage home crowds at its Mohegan Sun Arena. The service gives fans in the stadium access to pictures, videos, ringtones and other team information via their mobile phones, in a trial with proximity marketing company ACE.

The content will be delivered to fans using Bluetooth and Wi-Fi installed in the stadium, to push marketing at the assembled throng. The logic is that, WNBA games attract large audiences on a regular basis, but over time, traditional marketing on posters, signage and other advertising become invisible to the crowd. Mobile, however, allows messaging to be popped straight to the consumer.

Connecting the content with the team and the games makes it even more likely that the consumer will open a message and will see any advertising and sponsorship messaging.

Everyone else

In fact, all businesses can utilize mobile in some way, shape or form to enhance their interaction with their customers – be it a simple text message to confirm appointments, right up to engaging people on a personal level with a medical diagnosis via an iPad.

All the lessons that you can learn from the sectors detailed above (and in the previous chapter on retail) apply to almost any business that has any sort of customer. As we shall see in Chapter 7, it can also apply within the company itself. Mobile can also become an integral part of everything, from charity donations to the work of real estate agents, from market research firms to farmers' markets, from car dealerships to shipbuilding.

Case study

Bringing it *all* to the phone

Mobile is not just about payments or social media or content. It's about all those things, and what makes it such a powerful tool is that it can help users share not only their thoughts and feelings, but also now their stuff - while they are talking to each other.

Scientists and engineers out in Palo Alto, California, have developed an app called Thrutu that lets users send stuff phone-to-phone to people they are talking to (voice calls: remember those?) in order to share things. The app has 11 buttons that let users quickly share stuff, be it photos, location, sketches, even the weather. Oh, and you can give the caller on the other end of the line money too.

Thrutu offers callers the chance to share, without interrupting their call:

- **PayPal:** Send money over a phone call, instantly and securely. For example, when you call someone with a friendly reminder to pay you back, they can immediately transfer the funds into your account.
- **Meet Me:** Quickly find the best place to meet in person. Meet Me suggests venues, such as cafés or cinemas, that are located halfway between the two callers. You can also instantly discuss your options and agree upon the destination.

- **Shared Search:** Search and browse the web together. Either caller enters a word, and both can see and click on the results.
- **Doodle:** Share sketches. If you want. Doodle is also integrated with sharing locations and photos in Thrutu, so users can add a personal touch, such as an arrow on a map, or a heart or smiley face to a shared photo.
- **Coin Flip:** Make decisions or settle arguments with the toss of a coin. Collaboratively.
- **Mood Ring:** A cute way to let the other caller know how you're feeling – without having to use words. This is, after all, aimed at tweens and teens. It's not a business app. Yet.
- **15 Together and Tic Tac Toe:** Play classic games across the Thrutu platform, all while continuing conversations, encouraging competitive banter.
- **My Flickr and My Twitter:** View pictures or read tweets together, with instant, shared access to Flickr and Twitter streams.
- **Wish You Were Here?:** Share your local weather forecast. Whether on a tropical vacation or snowed in at home, callers can gloat (or complain) about their current weather while on the phone.

ACTION POINTS

- **Select your mobile features with care.** Mobile is a highly engaging tool for getting businesses in front of consumers, but select carefully from SMS, WAP, mobile websites, apps, MMS messaging, bar code scanning and more.
- **Survey your customer base.** As with all things mobile, as a business you need to look very closely at what you are trying to achieve with mobile and who your

customers are, and tailor the medium and the message to suit.

- **Don't bombard customers.** Even if you hit the sweet spot of the right kind of messaging delivered in the right way at the right time to exactly the right people, the rule of thumb is once a week. Twice for a really loyal customer.
- **Build your offering around timeliness, relevance and location – in that order.** If you are using mobile so that consumers come to you, then look at who they are and why they will be interacting with you via mobile. This is crucial.
- **Remember your manners.** Any form of interaction you initiate, especially anything that requires the customer to text or message you (and even more so if that carries a cost), should be acknowledged with an instant reply to say thank you.
- **Use the subsequent interaction wisely.** If manners maketh the man, then the reply channel can also be used to prompt another text and double the ARPU (Average Revenue per User) from that person.
- **Technology isn't for everyone.** Don't think that by having a mobile offering – especially one dripping in the latest augmented reality, location-based 3D bells and whistles – that everyone will love it (and your company). Make it seamless.
- **Technology isn't for every business.** Just because you can, doesn't mean you should. It might not be right for your business to use all the latest mobile technology. In many cases, a simple text-based service is all you need.
- **Check what's legal.** Know what you can and can't do when connecting with the public. This means the data you collect on them or data you purchase. Most services on mobile are opt-in. Check with your local communications commission and take legal advice.

- **Get outside help.** Find a good third party to handle not only the technical setup, but also the legal and regulatory side of things. There are many, many companies out there that handle this while developing services. Use them.
- **Grow with the flow.** Pick a third-party provider to help you, not based just on what you want to do right now, but one that can understand your roadmap of where you want to be on mobile in the months and years ahead.
- **Don't jump in too deep, too fast.** It's your call. That said, don't let them talk you up into things you don't need. Take a moment and think what you are looking to achieve.

CHAPTER 6

Mobile advertising

🔊 How can "push" communications target consumers based on who they are, what they like and where they are – and what are the risks?

🔊 What other methods – such as ads in apps, ads in content and on m-websites, social media, and augmented reality – are worth exploring?

🔊 How can advertising play a part in search and price comparison sites and on billboards and posters?

One of mobile's key strengths is that it occupies a personal position in the users' lives: it is typically there when then go about their daily business, nestled in their pocket or purse while they are at work or at the store. They have it with them while they relax over dinner; it sits on the sofa while they are watching TV; and, increasingly, it is on the nightstand next to them while they sleep. It is a constant companion.

And this, potentially, gives brands an unprecedented reach into every waking – not to mention sleeping – moment of a vast number of consumers' lives.

The idea of using the mobile device as a marketing and advertising channel has been with us since the early days of mobile. While mobile network operators charged users a premium for using a mobile to make and receive calls, young turks looking for new business models looked at how to offer mobile users free calls and texts in return for advertising messages. The most famous of these, Blyk, launched by two Finns (Pekka Ala-Pietilä, formerly president of Nokia, and Antti Öhrling, ex-chairman and founder of the Contra advertising group) arrived in the UK in 2007 and offered free calls in return for "connecting people to brands." Aimed at the 18–24 age group, the idea was that in return for receiving and passing on brand messaging via mobile – typically text, but not exclusively – users got free calls and texts.

Hailed at the time as the future of mobile, Blyk failed to take off to the degree that many industry watchers predicted – although it does still operate in Finland, India and a number of other markets – as advertising on mobile has long been treated warily by consumers.

This, however, isn't to say that it can't and won't work. Part of m-commerce's success and widespread acceptance will, nay does, hinge on the link between the device being used as a marketing tool, and then that marketing directing users to buy something – be it on the phone, with the phone or in a more traditional store (with or without the phone).

What is interesting is that this is a much more sophisticated play than merely using advertising to subsidize calls and texts. As you may be getting the idea from the previous chapters, mobile is one of those technologies that doesn't necessarily create or replace something else, it adds to it. And so it is with advertising and marketing. All the rules that apply to advertising and marketing through any channel – bar perhaps print media – still apply. Consumers need to be treated respectfully and not bombarded. Ads now have to be targeted and offer something of value, rather than just a message to go buy something. What mobile brings to this new world of advertising is better targeting of individuals based on their tastes, their social connections, their preference and their previous buying history – but all tied to where they are at any given time.

This, combined with the fact that the phone can be transactional, combines to give a powerful offering to brands, advertising agencies, network operators and retailers to build that all important relationship with their customer base, as well as attracting new customers. Through this, and the power of mobile social media, there is also the chance to let your loyal customers influence your prospective customers for you, as we shall see.

Here it is important, I believe, to distinguish between mobile marketing and mobile advertising. In the non-mobile world there is a distinct difference between marketing and advertising, and this carries through to the mobile channel. There is, of course, an overlap, but in essence they are two different disciplines that have two distinct aims in mind. As such I shall be looking at them separately in this chapter.

Advertising is defined as "the paid, public, non-personal announcement of a persuasive message by an identified sponsor; the non-personal presentation or promotion by a firm of its products to its existing and potential customers." Marketing, meanwhile, is regarded as "the systematic planning, implementation and control of a mix of business activities intended to bring together buyers and sellers for the mutually advantageous exchange or transfer of products" (about. com).

Advertising is, in theory, a subset of marketing, but they are both used within the mobile commerce sphere to influence and persuade people to part with their money. And there are many different ways that they can use the mobile channel to attain this goal.

What is mobile advertising?

Mobile advertising can take many forms and, I suspect, between the time of me writing this book and you reading it, there will be more ways of using it than I have covered here. Basically, however, it all depends on whom you want to reach, with text being the simplest way to reach the maximum number of mobile users. More sophisticated image- or video-based marketing is more the preserve of the well-heeled smartphone user.

Typically, early forays into mobile advertising focused, as we have seen, on simple text-based messaging – often appended to the end of a text or sent in an immediate but separate follow-on text – to subsidize the cost of calls or text messages. But soon, early adopters of advertising in mobile started to look at how they could learn from the online world and serve up display ads. So, as the mobile content marketplace grew more sophisticated and companies from operators downward created mobile portals to sell things on, so small banner ads started to appear.

This was, to all intents and purposes, just online advertising on a different screen. While it adopted some of the targeting that would make mobile advertising the hit it is set to become, much of it was fairly unsophisticated in its reach or function.

As handsets have become more sophisticated, and as the mobile web and apps have become a more commonplace means of accessing content on mobile, so the mobile display advertising market has moved on.

While this form of display advertising is a lucrative and potentially huge market (and one that we will come to anon), there is another strand to mobile advertising that seeks to target on a more individual basis, using the device as a two-way communications tool to build a relationship with consumers. This form of mobile advertising is where marketing and advertising overlap: it is the pushing of a paid-for public message, as per advertising, but it's personal and targeted, as per marketing. And this, to my mind, is where mobile as a marketing tool gets interesting.

SMS and MMS get personal

There is an unwritten rule that suggests, based on an average of all the research done on this, that 70% of people will open a text message sent to them within an hour of receiving it, regardless of whom it is from. Of course, most of us with mobile phones have an almost Pavlovian response to message alerts, since they are usually from someone we know. As marketeers and advertisers have sought to exploit this, so we have slowly – thanks to their careful introduction to us – started to accept that if we have a new message, it's probably something interesting, even if it's from a brand.

This is why this level of engagement is unheard of in all other areas of marketing. Direct mail – stuff rammed through the real-world mailbox in your front door – has an opening rate of around 0.1%. Text already appears to be some 700 times more potent as a marketing tool.

However, simply opening a text is pretty much akin to picking the direct mailer up off the doormat. There is still ample opportunity for the recipient to stick it in the bin. In text terms, the message is simply opened and unread, or read and trashed. Unless well targeted, many text-based marketing messages do end up not being acted upon.

However, with brands, agencies, telecoms and regulators all keenly aware that most people view their phones as personal, marketing messages to mobile starts from the premise of being targeted. Where paper-based direct mail relies on that 0.1% of a simply enormous and random number of people acting on their message, mobile marketing is predicated on being sent to relatively small numbers of people who marketeers know will more than likely be interested in what they receive.

It's a virtuous, as opposed to a vicious, circle: you send a relevant marketing message to a group of people who are likely to be interested in receiving it, and you do it on a device that is very personal to them. For this reason we see text-based marketing messages being acted on by between 10–15% of the 70% of recipients who open them within an hour. Get it right and it yields vast returns. Get it wrong, however, and your brand can rapidly become toast.

Case study

Faith Shoes uses SMS campaigns to drive footfall

Back in 2010, UK footwear store Faith dipped its toe, if you'll pardon the pun, in mobile marketing with an SMS marketing campaign. The campaign generated an astonishing 47%

increase in revenues, and led to a further 30% increase in revenues through fashion magazines, which also ran a campaign to get users to text a shortcode from Faith advertisements. Since then the company has rolled out numerous SMS campaigns. The purpose of each SMS campaign is to provide new product information and promotional offers to drive foot traffic into stores and to build brand loyalty.

Faith's activity commenced with two campaigns. First, a Friends and Family promotion offered 25% off full-price products which ran over a three-day period; and second, a promotion in conjunction with a high-circulation fashion magazine offered 20% off full-price products, which ran over a six-day period. Talin Vartevanian, head of e-commerce at Faith, went for SMS marketing for its simplicity. She explains: "SMS marketing has proven to be an extremely successful revenue generation tool for us. It is quick to set up and once launched, the message is instantly communicated to the customer, which is especially beneficial if they are already out shopping. This makes SMS particularly strong at driving footfall in-store, but has also proved to be very effective in increasing online traffic."

Similar levels are claimed for MMS – picture messaging – and the rise of smartphones is delivering a growing number of MMS interactions too, as brands seek to build on the success they have seen with text-based marketing messaging.

Where text has proved the concept, the ever competitive marketplace is seeing more and more rich media content being used in mobile advertising campaigns. The content is an advertisement, but also something that people want to watch and, ideally, pass on from mobile to mobile, virally spreading the ad but bringing entertainment to many.

The adoption of smartphones has in fact caused a surge in spending on mobile advertising. While the advertising industry has largely ignored the hyperbole around the channel, there was nevertheless a 32% growth spurt between 2009 and 2010 in Europe and the US, with similar levels of growth or better expected for 2011 and 2012.

This has been driven by executives in ad companies getting iPhones and other smartphones and tablets, and seeing the potential. Consumers also are leading them on, with their increased consumption of rich media and a hunger for smartphone content that embraces what would traditionally have been classed as advertising.

If proof is needed that mobile is becoming a sought-after advertising medium, then research by the Internet Advertising Bureau in the US and UK finds that the growth in mobile advertising expenditures is coming not from the traditionally mobile savvy areas of content and media companies, but from financial services companies, telecoms and high-end electronics brands, as a wider group of businesses start to see mobile's potential to reach people. It won't be long before all retailers are looking at how to leverage the power of mobile.

On location

One of the main reasons why advertisers want to make use of mobile is that it can target consumers on a personal level, based not only on what they like, what they have agreed to respond to and what they have clicked on in the past, but also where they are. Location, as we have seen already in this book, is one of mobile's main attractions to commerce: knowing where someone is when you try to sell them (or tell them) something adds a whole new level of relevance.

And it is working. A study in the US by JiWire, a location-based media company, has found that location-based mobile ads are driving 17% of consumers to make purchases while mobile, and 20% to visit physical store locations after seeing a relevant ad. Additionally, the greater the discount offered, the farther the mobile audience is willing to travel to redeem a promotion.

How the figures break down:

- 78% use location-based apps on their phone.
- 29% use them multiple times a day.
- 34% clicked on an ad in response to a location-specific message.
- 57% are more likely to engage with an ad that is relevant to their location – an increase from 46% in Q1.
- 17% have made a purchase in response to a location-based advertisement.
- 84% of people who use app-enabled phones have participated in a shopping activity.
- On average, the mobile audience uses 1.6 devices to connect while on the go.
- 20% of the on-the-go audience visited a store in response to a location-based ad.
- 42% said they are most likely to use location-based services for finding store locations.
- As the discount in the ad increases, the more distance a customer is willing to travel to redeem the offer. This provides new opportunities for brands to attract new customers across a broader distance and to drive in-store traffic and sales (as we shall see in the section on mobile marketing).

Some dos and don'ts

There are some important rules to bear in mind when trying to target consumers with any sort of messaging, particularly advertising content. To the retailer or brand, the message may seem totally pertinent and their location ideal, so how could the targeted customer not be pleased to get 20% off? You'd be surprised.

The key thing to remember is that users have to opt in to receive a message from you. Under data protection laws in most developed markets – certainly in the US and EU – you can't send unsolicited electronic messaging of any sort to anyone.

With mobile you need to have the phone's number to send a text or MMS to the consumer, so there is a good chance that, in order to get that number, you have to get the consumer to sign up to something. Here the small print is everything.

With other forms of location-based services that ping consumers with a message, an offer or other text as they pass your store or enter a geo-fenced area, you also have to have their agreement to do this. Again, the sensible and easiest way to do this is to get people to sign up for such services online or on the device, and give them the power to say yes to receiving these messages.

But even with that sort of approval in place, common sense is really the key here. While consumers may well have signed up to your service to say "Yes, send me marketing messages relevant to what I like and where I am," this doesn't mean that they want you to bombard them with said ads and offers.

The phone, as said, is a hugely personal possession and people don't want it abused. As a business it will do you no good whatsoever to deluge someone with messages – relevant or not – as they will very soon get tired of them. You have to also assume that, just because they are signed up to get messages from you, it doesn't mean that they aren't getting messages from your competitors, and other vendors and brands too. You may only be sending out one message a day, but they could be getting a dozen.

Similarly, I walk past Starbucks every morning on my way to the office: do I want to get a deal every time? Sometimes I do, sometimes I don't.

This raises something of conundrum for marketeers: how do I keep my brand visible, make a good ROI (return on investment) on my mobile marketing investment, keep ahead of my competitors, but all without really annoying my customers by giving them too much or too little?

The key, I believe, is to err very much on the side of caution. Even if someone has opted in to receive messages from you, only send them one, perhaps two, a week. If you are lucky enough to be able to run a geo-location marketing service, then, as I walk past Starbucks every day, only send me offers occasionally (or get really sophisticated and let me search them out as I walk past if I want one).

Most of all, you must offer all users, on every message, a clear way to stop this. At this nascent stage in the use of mobile as a marketing tool, it pays to let people try it and, if they wish, stop it.

Early mobile content subscription services suffered horrendous publicity meltdown on both sides of the Atlantic when no stop processes were built into the ringtone offer. This has since been regulated, and now it is unusual not to have a stop message. Still, it is worth stating that this is crucial.

It is also crucial to manage who gets what. In the UK, O2 More's location-based mobile advertising offering allows the user to sign up for multiple categories of offers online through an interface that also allows them to go back and adjust and manage what they are doing and what offers they get. Once out and about, O2 users then get relevant offers pertaining to where they are and things that they have expressed an interest in online. In theory, it offers the marketing nirvana of the user telling O2 what ads it wants. O2 can then send those ads – which it has sold to brands, let's not forget – to the user at the most compelling time to act on them.

But each has to have a stop command. As a user myself, I find it can get a bit wearing if I am in a busy commercial district that happens to have several brands that I have signed up to receive messages from.

Other forms of mobile advertising

While I have so far focused on how to use mobile as a channel for sending out marketing and promotional materials – push marketing – there is another strand to mobile as an advertising medium that can be used to drive commerce: in-content advertising.

Much like the display advertising in print publications, or even advertising on TV, digital media offer an ideal platform for display advertising. Online this has become a lucrative market for banner ads on websites, search advertising and pre, post and interstitial video ads in video content.

On mobile, these online advertising models have been replicated – with varying degrees of success – and have morphed to produce new forms of advertising that exploit the personal and private nature of the mobile device. Technological developments around mobile have also created a whole new range of advertising. Broadly, these can be broken down into several areas, with some ideas from the early days of mobile, and others with more longevity in our smartphone world, but each with its own merits.

In-content advertising

Many may accuse marketeers and brands of incontinent advertising, but in-content ads are simply those that sit within the content being watched or looked at, and are really just an extension of banners and other small ads found online.

The in-content advertising market started when mobile network operators thought they could corner the whole mobile content world with portals (you go to the operator's mobile web portal and from there buy content, music, etc, and the operator sells ads around this). This model was always tenuous, but the arrival of iTunes on mobile put paid to these ambitions in many markets (although the operators and I agree to differ on this).

But I digress. In-content advertising is essentially banner display advertising that appears within mobile websites, or is served up within web-enabled apps. It works, because if the consumer has gone to that site or downloaded and then fired up that app, then they are interested in that sort of content. You can therefore serve up relevant ads. (Where do these ads come from? Ad networks. See a bit farther on.)

These display ads usually take the form of banners on m-web sites or within apps and games. They are typically clickable, taking the user off to a mobile website, presumably a transactional one if people have done their homework. However, with the lack of multiscreen capability on all mobiles and tablets, this means leaving the site or application that the user is currently in: a massive flaw.

In-content ads have worked well in mobile games – and in fact have helped grow the revenues generated in mobile games – but they do have the problem of interrupting the game play. One result of this has been the use of in-game collateral to carry simple brand awareness advertising, much as can be found in the real world. Funny how the real world still has things to offer our digital consumers.

Despite these shortcomings, the market for in-content advertising makes up the lion's share of the mobile advertising market value. However, it is widely expected that, thanks to the retail industry, coupons and other messaging-based advertising is likely to surpass this as mobile advertising grows.

For a business, this is a good way of cheaply getting some targeted advertising out there, especially if you are looking to drive traffic to a mobile site or start an engagement with consumers. It's not particularly targeted.

Case study

Flirtomatic global ads serving

Flirtomatic, the fast-growing online and mobile dating and social network service, with some 4.5 million users worldwide, augments its income by serving up ads to its users, tailored to where they are geographically, who they are and what they are interested in. To do this effectively – and to allow it to concentrate on its own core business – it works with Mocean Mobile, a global mobile and online ad serving company.

Flirtomatic currently serves more than 600 million advertisements per month globally, so this is a big and complex task for the company. Mocean's platform allows for a massive assortment of advertising options to be dealt with, including user-generated and house ads, premium placements, performance campaigns, mobile-specific targeting and gender targeting, among others – all of which chime with Flirtomatic's varied demographic.

Furthermore, the mobile social networking company chose Mocean Mobile as its technology partner for its flexible support of rich media formats. This allows Flirtomatic to serve ads that are not only tailored to the device that is viewing it, but also to the person, their location and their circumstances, in order to maximize the revenue it gets from click-throughs on the ads.

Flirtomatic says it chose Mocean because it needed a platform that could support the high frequencies of visitors, each needing an ad, that the company was attracting, especially during peak hours in different regions.

Search advertising

Alongside in-content display advertising, the online world has also delivered to mobile the concept of search advertising. Pioneered by Google, search advertising works the same on mobile as it does online: companies bid to be the highest ranking paid-for result when certain searches are carried out in a search engine. The highest bidder on certain keywords and phrases comes out on top of the list of search results that are denoted as paid for.

As with the online model, this brings totally relevant content and services to the top of the list when a consumer searches for something, and is about as relevant as you can get. However, mobile does offer some challenges – and some opportunities – not found with search advertising online. First up, the smaller screen and lack of multiscreens means that the ability to display an array of paid-for and non-paid-for results, along with other relevant ads as found online, doesn't translate well.

On mobile, Google's search results throws up one paid-for search ad at the top and then the usual meta-data driven search results. This cuts the potential advertising slots on mobile search down from around six to one. However, for the advertiser and ad server (in this instance, Google), which gets paid on a per click basis, the thinking is that the searches can be so relevant – what with location being added in where appropriate – that each single ad will yield more clicks and have more impact. Well, that's the theory. Mobile advertising is at an early stage, so this is largely untested.

Search advertising on mobile, especially where you can work location into the equation, offers a much more targeted way of reaching consumers who are looking for specific things. Coming out on top on a search has a strong click-through rate online, and there is no reason to assume it won't work on mobile too. What it offers a business — especially physical retailers — is a chance to grab a shopper while she is out looking for something specific. Team this with a coupon or offer, and you have the makings of a great foot traffic generator.

For online-only retailers, mobile search offers a great way of getting people to discover your mobile website. It's not so good for apps, as they don't have a search environment. Yet. To market apps, you need to look at how to use mobile marketing in its fullest way. As we shall see.

Apps and m-web

Applications and mobile websites, as we have seen, offer marketing opportunities aplenty, being ripe real estate for the display of ads, links and even content advertisements.

With m-web sites, many of the rules around in-content advertising and online advertising apply, only constrained by the screen dimensions and the reliance on connectivity to download and stream content.

Where m-web sites differ from their online companions is that the psychology of how they are used is perhaps subtly different. Consumers are on the move, and they treat mobile data access as expensive and a premium service and their device as personal. All of these things suggest that advertising appearing within things they are doing should be as unobtrusive as possible and easily turned off. Where pop-ups within online websites are really quite annoying, having them happen to you while you are hurriedly using your mobile to find something is totally counterproductive.

If you want to use advertising to give your brand a bad name, putting a massive ad on an m-web site so that it slows down the loading of the site is a great way to do that.

Apps present two challenges when it comes to advertising and marketing: how to use them to advertise and market things, and how to use mobile to advertise and market the apps themselves.

The former is reasonably straightforward to address. If you want to make extra money from your app, then sell ads in it as in-content advertising. Try to check the relevance and deal with an ad-serving platform to get the ads, so that someone else takes the management of this process off your hands. But think carefully: do you really need ads in the app and will they deflect from the app's loveliness?

The second aspect of mobile app advertising – how to actually get people to find and buy or download your app – is a harder one to tackle. Apps stores have at best tens of thousands or, at worst, hundreds of thousands of apps on them. How do consumers find yours?

The key seems to be to advertise them through traditional advertising channels, rather than relying on the apps stores' own search and recommendation functions (although these are a must too, to capture those searching within the apps stores). How do you use mobile to create awareness of your app? Well, first of all, if you have a mobile website, plug an ad for the app into it. Short of that, start using in-content ads on other sites and in other apps to create awareness of your app.

Market it where possible through any channel you can, is the simple advice.

This is the shortcoming with all apps – getting people to find them. It is why I would always advocate that any putative move into mobile is done using mobile web: it comes up on search engines so people can find you. Once you have people on your site, then you can point them to your app. Similarly, by advertising on other sites and using search ads, TV, radio and newspaper ads and in-store ads, you can also send people to your app.

Rule of thumb: people will go for apps then and there when it's in front of them. They will search you out on the web if they are just looking.

Coupons and vouchers

Coupons and vouchers, as we see in other parts of this book, are becoming key drivers for getting people into stores to spend money. The idea is simple. You send consumers a voucher that gives them a 20% discount (or a percentage of your choice; you have to work out the economics of this around your business) if they come into your store and buy something.

The model is well proven with paper-based coupons you cut out of the newspaper, and has worked for years. It is a great way of clearing stock, promoting specials and getting people to come to your store, bar, restaurant or whatever your business is in times that are usually dead: Tuesday afternoons, typically, in retail.

Mobile does the same thing, bringing people into the store to redeem vouchers sent to their handsets. The twist? It can be done at any time to get them to come in, or it can be done as they draw near to your location, or as they search online for your kind of business. This is why I have decided to write about them here, after SMS/MMS advertising and in-content and in-app advertising, as they straddle both. Mobile coupons can be discovered on the mobile web, through search advertising, or from ads that are in content, as well as being pushed out to signed-up consumers based on location, or the fact that they are searching.

They are also delivered through social media, which is increasingly filling the gap between mobile social networking and mobile advertising, at least in retail. Facebook Deals – as we shall see later in this book – uses the fact that users have checked in at a certain store to then send them money-off deals if they get their friends to check in also.

Whether delivered via social media, mobile push messaging, downloaded from websites or, indeed, cut out of the newspaper, coupons and vouchers are still an excellent marketing tool that drives people into your store to buy things. As with all things mobile, the mobile aspect tends to yield much greater conversion – and therefore better ROI – than the paper-based version. And again, when location driven, it can be really quite profitable.

One downside of this kind of marketing, however, is that it doesn't necessarily result in organic growth of your business. One complaint about vouchering is that it can drive many people to come through the door, buy something cheap, leave and never come back. As a business, you haven't really gained much.

Take a restaurant, for example. A Groupon offer for two meals for the price of one on a Monday night in May, say, brings in 100 extra covers, each essentially at half price. That makes for a lot of work for half the profit, and little chance for repeat business at full price in the future. You may get them back if you do another offer, but again you are cutting profits.

While there is a growing excitement around vouchers and coupons, many businesses – especially smaller ones – are starting to see them as more of a hindrance than a help.

Case study

US local government uses mobile to aid small businesses

All across the United States, a growing number of local governments and organizations established to promote their communities are rapidly turning to mobile to drive traffic – and sales – in small businesses.

A great example of this is Evanston, Illinois, a suburban municipality 10 miles north of Chicago. It has set up a small non-profit organization called Downtown Evanston, that provides marketing and management services to downtown Evanston's small business. Made up of commercial and residential property and business owners, the organization has teamed up with some Northwestern University students to push a new mobile app, which the partners hope will increase the exposure of small businesses in the Evanston community. Shoppers strolling the streets of downtown Evanston will be able to find, sort and use digital coupons for nearby businesses at the push of a button, thanks to the app that replicates and promotes the popular paper-based couponing that the local area has been using for years.

It keeps people loyal - and informed about - their locale, as well as making businesses greener by not having to print so many coupons.

Price comparison sites

Another, slightly left-field approach to marketing that many retailers are adopting is to get themselves on third-party price-comparison websites and mobile websites. These services have grown up online to help online shopping, and have made a fruitful transition to mobile.

The principle is simple. These third parties take a small cut of each transaction to build comparative databases of services and how much they cost, allowing users to add various criteria to find the best deal available. The technique was pioneered online with car insurance, and has since expanded to everything from home insurance to utilities to mobile phone tariffs.

On mobile all these things are available, but the technology has extended to encompass using the handset and its location to let consumers search for particular goods. The price comparison service sends back not only the cheapest option, but also the cheapest relative to where the user actually is at that time.

Many of these sites are also starting to incorporate bar code scanners, so that consumers can go into a shop, scan the bar code of the item they are interested in and find where else – in both the real world and online – that item can be found and at what price. It is, sadly, becoming something that many people do in bookstores: scanning a book's bar code to then order it more cheaply online for next day delivery.

The cost of price-comparison sites depends on what you are selling, how many clicks you get and the total value of what you are selling, but again needs careful consideration as to the cost versus how much you want to make. It is also making the physical store a very cut-throat place for retailers.

Idle screen ads

This is an early mobile advertising technique pioneered before the smartphone revolution, but one that still hangs around at the ends of the mobile advertising market, neither succeeding nor failing. The principle is simple: software that sits on the connected phone and puts ads onto the home screen of the phone, so that when the user wakes the phone up, there is an ad.

Pioneered by Celltick in the mid-2000s, idle screen advertising looks on the face of it like a surefire hit, but it doesn't account for how people view their phones. Typically, most people reserve this prime bit of phone real estate for photos of their loved ones – my cat Nelson takes pride of place on my iPhone, much to the chagrin of my wife and kids – and so the idea of filling it with ads, relevant or not, hasn't really taken off.

That said, Celltick still runs its platform. It has recently won an award for being an innovative marketing platform, and claims to work with

50 operators worldwide, reaching 100 million people. It is a potential area for advertising on mobile and, being dynamic, it does lend itself to localized updates and can offer a nice way to use mobile to advertise. I will be sticking with Nelson.

Augmented reality advertising

At the cutting edge of mobile technology – and pretty much the preserve of the smartphone – augmented reality (where, using your phone's camera, web-connected software overlays stuff onto the real world on the screen) is still a technology looking for a use. One of the areas where it is being assessed with interest is in how it can be used to overlay advertising onto the real world when a user holds his phone up.

As discussed elsewhere in this book, one early use is yell.com's app which lets the user see who, of those that have paid to advertise on yell.com, is located around them. A sort of advertising overlay on the real world. The potential for this is huge, but still to be realized in monetary terms. Further, it only works with high-powered smartphones in well-connected areas, so is currently limited to a few select places.

In theory, it offers a rather neat and practical application of mobile advertising, where users can actually find what they are looking for without typing in search terms or clicking on ads. They just hold up their phones where they are and see what's around them. Definitely one to watch for in the coming years in developed markets.

Smart posters

From the sublimely modern idea of augmented reality to the seemingly prosaic world of billboards and advertising hoardings. Yes, posters are part of the mobile advertising mix.

The poster used to be a fairly static piece of advertising real estate, but with the advent of mobile connectivity, Bluetooth and, eventually,

NFC, posters are becoming interactive. There is now a move to make posters on bus stops, in shop windows and the like, through to massive billboards and even buses, communicate with phones and their users.

The simplest, and currently most prevalent, form of smart posters that interact with phones are those that feature QR (Quick Response) or 2D bar codes. If your phone has a QR code reader, these can be scanned by the phone's camera. They usually fire up a website relating to the company on the poster, though sometimes they can fire up other apps on the phone, such as e-mail or SMS, in order to instigate a conversation with the brand; or they can ping a voucher.

Similar technology is being seen in action on newspaper and magazine articles, and is starting to make print advertising more interactive.

More ambitiously, and covered elsewhere in this book, some are getting Bluetooth and even NFC, and can "talk" directly to the phone, sending content, messages or offers and vouchers.

This kind of mobile advertising is more associated with bigger brands and companies who can afford (a) the big posters, and (b) the technology to do this sort of thing. But there is no reason why QR codes can't be applied to homemade posters in a small shop or on a market stall to help engage consumers and extend the mobile commerce dream to these smaller retailers.

QR-code software is available for free, online, and I believe that we are on the cusp of an e-commerce revolution, with the millions of small businesses worldwide driven by this sort of mobile marketing technology.

Social marketing

A lot has been said in this book and elsewhere on how powerful social media has become. Now that more than half of Facebook users regularly use the site on mobile – not to mention Twitter, foursquare and numerous other social networks – mobile social networking is pretty much tautological. What this means is that social sites now offer an unprecedented platform to run m-commerce, but also to help engage people in m-commerce, market services and market real-world businesses.

As we have seen in previous chapters and in this chapter, networks such as Facebook already use the location element to deliver business deals, vouchers, coupons and publicity. These sites also carry display advertising, posts and input – with links – to commercial sites, as well as recommendations and personal endorsements from friends and "brand champions," making social networking almost akin to a mobile system for commerce.

But while much attention is focused on how big brands can use a big site like Facebook to market and transact on mobile, social media also offers small businesses an ideal platform to cheaply market to, engage with and even sell to consumers.

Case study

Whatser, the story for local businesses?

There are a proliferation of social network sites out there on mobile. None have the critical mass of Facebook, Twitter or even foursquare, but sometimes that can be a good thing. One example of this is a Dutch start-up called Whatser, which is using the idea of signing into places and collecting them, not only as a way of giving people something to do, but also as a marketing tool for small, independent and local businesses.

Combining recommendation, location-based services and social networking, all on mobile, the Whatser app lets local businesses and global brands gather and reward loyal customers based on where they are. When a user adds a place to his collection, he receives relevant offers, promotions and updates from that business.

For businesses, Whatser offers a meaningful way to communicate with and reward regular customers in order to build loyalty, drive foot traffic and increase sales. The merchants pay Whatser €8.33 ($11.80) per month, and this gives them access to a simple dashboard that lets them message their fans about deals, offers, events and more. The first global brand to sign up to use the platform was G-Star RAW.

Whatser also plans to add a range of features to the platform to extend this symbiotic relationship further with:

- **Push notifications:** Merchants can send updates and promotions to customers who live in their city. These messages will appear as push notifications and in the user's activity stream.
- **Peer-to-peer sharing:** Users can share the updates they receive with their friends. Updates go viral, and a merchant's circle of regular customers grows organically.
- **QR codes:** Merchants can send out specials that can be redeemed in-store. Coupon redemption will be tracked within the Whatser dashboard.

Mobile ad-serving networks

This rich mobile advertising marketplace, be it message based or display based, has, as in the online world, created a massive advertising-serving marketplace. Google, Apple and many others seek to act as brokers for relevant advertising, charging, as they do in the online world, on a cost-per-click basis, as we shall see shortly.

In fact, if you are looking to monetize your app or site with ads on mobile, then the best way to do it is to pay an ad-serving network to serve up relevant ads to your content, and get paid on a per-click basis by the advertisers via the network.

Google pretty much owns this space, but in 2010 Apple launched iAds, when the company bought mobile ad company Quattro Wireless Network. Google, as it has done online, is targeting serving up ads into search results, while Steve Jobs claims iAds is revolutionizing the mobile advertising game by targeting app advertising.

That's not to say that Google isn't serving up ads to mobile websites. Its AdSense platform – now available in 15 countries worldwide – can match the content of the ad to the content of the m-website being viewed to get even greater relevance.

Either way, these two giants offer the opportunity to get ultra-relevant ads – and all the accompanying stats – served up either to your apps, or for you to appear in search results.

For all the other forms of advertising, there are an array of advertising platforms that target apps, content, portals, platforms and m-websites with ads, also with the accompanying stats and feedback. There are hundreds of them (too numerous to mention here, and I am not in the mood to be partisan) but Googling "mobile ad networks" brings up many of them. Paradoxically, all in the paid-for ads section.

ACTION POINTS

- **Make the most of mobile for marketing.** Mobile is the ideal tool for marketing and advertising. It offers a means of finding your mobile commerce presence – be it app, m-website, your online shop or even real-world premises.
- **Start with text.** There are numerous ways of doing mobile marketing and advertising. To reach the maximum number of mobile users, text is the easiest way to get in front of people on their home screen.
- **Target smartphone users with richer offerings.** If you want to target smartphone users, you can make much richer push marketing offerings, featuring images, video and interaction.
- **Get permission.** But whether sending text-based marketing or something much more complex, you still have to make sure that you have the recipients' permission to send it to them.
- **Limit your messaging.** Make sure not to bother them too frequently – something that requires a careful balancing act. Contact targets enough so that they keep you in mind, but not so much as to be intrusive.
- **Drive foot traffic.** Mobile is an ideal way to drive traffic into your shop, whether you are a multinational chain or a small independent store; and there are platforms to help you do it that suit almost all budgets.
- **Consider off-the-shelf packages.** If you really don't have the money, you can build a mobile messaging platform yourself using off-the-shelf software such as MarketingPilot or marketingQED

- **Don't rely on one channel to market your m-web offering.** Mobile advertising through push is one thing, but mobile advertising within other sites, on search results or elsewhere in traditional media can help users find you – and your products.
- **Keep it targeted.** The software and ad-serving platforms can all help – with amazing accuracy – get your ads in front of the right people and, thanks to location technology, at the right time and place to maximize the chances of them buying from you.
- **Plan the user journey.** But you must understand who you are trying to sell to, how the mobile ads will start that journey, and make sure that they can actually get from the ad to your app or m-web service.
- **Keep on top of stats.** Budget for various levels of pay-per-click and regularly assess all the stats that you can, not just on how many people are engaging with your ads, but where they come from, when and where they go, and when they buy and when they don't.
- **Use analytics to keep improving.** Analytics around advertising on mobile can be enlightening and can help you shape your business, hone your site, help you decide whether you need an app, and how to best message your customers and prospective customers.

CHAPTER 7
Mobile health care

🔊 How can mobile deliver services which provide doctors and patients with better information, monitoring and education?

🔊 What impact will text-based services have on efficiency levels in the sector?

🔊 Why are developing countries likely to benefit most from mobile health care?

In 2010, 13.5% of the world's population (that's 980 million people) will be over 65, and 60% of them will suffer from chronic and degenerative illnesses. This situation, combined with the current shortfall of specialists in key medical assistance sectors, and the fact that these specialists must spend between 30%–50% of their time on administrative tasks instead of health care activities, are putting additional pressure on public health care budgets.

Consider this alongside the fact that there are 2.3 billion mobile subscriptions in the developing world and 300 million computers, while there are only 11 million hospital beds.

So one area where mobile is quite literally a life saver is in its role in health care, offering everything from a way to remind people to take their medication, to helping in remote diagnosis, to letting doctors share medical data globally on the fly and in training and by informing, educating and helping health care professionals the world over. It is attracting particular attention in the developing world, where mobile is offering to lift people out of Internet poverty and into the 21st century. What mobile can do for communications and commerce, it can also do for health care – which too has a revenue element attached.

Consumers and professionals are increasingly using their mobile devices for health care information. They are also interacting with health care providers and colleagues on their mobile phones. Of US consumers, 85% have cell phones – and growing – versus only 65% having broadband access. The divide between mobile use and broadband Internet access is increasing. Additionally, it is not just a consumer-focused trend, as Manhattan Research reports that 70% of physicians say PDAs and smartphones are "essential" to their practice.

Although the potential benefits of mHealth solutions have been widely discussed for over a decade, the market never emerged from the trial phase. According to the new Global Mobile Health Market Report 2010–2015 by research2guidance, smartphone applications will enable the mHealth industry to successfully reach out to 500 million of the total 1.4 billion smartphone users in 2015.

Not only are consumers taking advantage of smartphones to manage and improve their own health, a significant number (43%) of mHealth applications are primarily designed for health care professionals. These include CME (Continued Medical Education), remote monitoring and health care management applications.

Currently there are 17,000 mHealth applications in major app stores, 74% of them adhering to the paid business model. With more and more traditional health care providers joining the mobile applications market, the business models will broaden to include health care services, sensors, advertising and drug sales revenues. With the growing sophistication level of mHealth applications, only 14% of the total market revenue in the next five years will come from application download revenue, believes research2guidance. Some 76% of total mHealth application market revenue will come from related services and products such as sensors, and the other 10% from ancillary mHealth information services on mobile.

Other areas that will contribute to m-Health revenues include fitness and health care smartphone apps, and eventually advanced apps that link to sensors worn on the body.

Monitoring

According to Juniper Research, revenues from remote patient monitoring using mobile networks will rise to almost $1.9bn globally by 2014, with heart-based monitoring in the US accounting for the bulk of early mobile monitoring rollouts. Juniper's mHealth report further found that mobile health care monitoring will demonstrate substantial growth in the US and other developed markets. However, while mobile monitoring will contribute to health care cost savings in developed markets, national wealth and the structure of the health care market in a given geographical region will have an important bearing on the extent to which it is rolled out.

Remote monitoring is really mobile's forte in health care. Doctors can now continue to monitor acute cases from afar, without having to stay at the hospital or make frequent visits to the bedside.

AirStrip from GE Healthcare is taking the medical world by storm in the US, offering doctors the ability to stream in near real time patient stats, particularly the heart, to an iPhone app, so that they can continue to monitor those most at risk when doing other work or on their downtime. The app is proving invaluable, but comes at a price. To work, the hospital has to buy the AirStrip server and all the technology needed to hook up the monitors to it. This is something we are likely to see in countries where there is no state-run health care system.

But it doesn't have to be costly. In Africa, the opportunities for mHealth monitoring will be limited to SMS-based services, primarily putting doctors on call, but leveraging the often superior mobile networks to do it, rather than the old fixed-line phone networks.

African medics will also see a proliferation of SMS-based education programs that offer a cheap and widespread way of informing the population about good health care and hygiene, thus reducing the demand on the health care profession in these poorer countries.

Operations

I couldn't resist calling this section "Operations". Of course I mean to take a look at how mobile is used to help efficiency within the medical sector, rather than playing a role in surgery, but who knows. That might be just a snip and a stitch away.

Anyway, mobile, particularly text messaging, has a very important role to play in how health services operate worldwide. There are issues with wasted time and resources that hit profits. So how can mobile help?

Forgetting an appointment is all too easy, yet for health care providers it can be too expensive and impractical to devote administrative time to reminding and chasing patients. A far easier way to eliminate missed appointments is to automatically issue reminders via an SMS to the patient's mobile phone. This has numerous, significant advantages.

Physicians' own findings show that the worst culprits for missing appointments are 16–34 year-olds: the text generation. While they might ignore a voice call, or fail to open an e-mail, research confirms that the majority of people, particularly in this age group, will open and read a text message. Promptly too.

The reminder itself is enough to ensure that most will honor their appointments. Where this isn't possible, the health care provider has the chance to reschedule: to give the current appointment to someone else, thereby reducing waiting lists, while issuing a new date and time to the original patient.

Dedicated mobile health care applications exist now to automate as much of this process as possible, by integrating routine text reminders with existing hospitals'/clinics'/doctor's offices' diary and calendar systems. There is even the potential for the system to offer and book alternative dates and times, and to contact patients on the waiting list to offer them last-minute cancellations. And it isn't just doctors' offices or hospital departments that stand to benefit from such facilities. Dental practices, opticians and physiotherapists all suffer from the same issue of making the most of their billable time.

What's most exciting about all this is that adopting such practices is extremely affordable – particularly when contrasted with the huge losses that are incurred with every missed appointment. Where the effect of a no-show is extra administration, not to mention the waste of a consultant's valuable time, which in the UK adds up to a loss each time of £110 ($180), the most it will cost the health care provider to issue a text reminder is a few pence (less than 10 cents) per person.

Finding spare capital is particularly tough in the current climate, but use of a text service qualifies as operational expenditure, which is much easier to budget for – especially in the face of huge potential savings and the positive implications for reducing waiting lists and improving patient care.

Health service providers don't even have to manage the system themselves. It can be provided as a remotely-hosted, complete solution, requiring no investment in special hardware or software. The service uses the administrators' existing calendar and patient contact systems, and the recipient's own mobile phone.

The potential applications extend beyond missed appointments too. Automated text contact could also be used to bring greater consistency and reliability to staff scheduling. For example, for last-minute deployment of agency staff in response to an unforeseen absence, or a sudden spike in workload. Scheduling and coordination of community visits could be similarly managed.

Today, such processes rely heavily on voice messages and voice calls, without the benefit of diary integration. The result is a lot of chasing, and the costly penalty of lost time. With an integrated SMS solution, contact is made swiftly, and appointments confirmed or changed in a timely fashion. Best of all, virtually no manual intervention is needed, eliminating administration costs almost entirely.

The outcome is a win-win all around. Doctors' time is more fruitfully spent and can be reimbursed accordingly, waiting lists are significantly reduced as more appointment slots are filled, patient care is improved, and a potentially costly administrative burden is lifted.

Missed appointments and costly "dead" time is an issue for health care providers the world over. The opportunity is there to harness a commonplace, mainstream technology to transform fundamental patient administration in a way that's easy, natural and costs little more than a Band-Aid.

Physicians, this is a real chance to heal yourselves.

Case study

MAMA brings US baby care to the world

Because mobile phones are now pretty much global in their distribution, a US initiative to bring pregnancy and childcare information to the women of the world is using mobile to keep mothers everywhere informed on how best to look after themselves and their offspring.

The Mobile Alliance for Maternal Action (MAMA) is a partnership between the US Agency for International Development and pharmaceutical company Johnson & Johnson, with support from the UN Foundation, mHealth Alliance and BabyCenter, that will use mobile messaging to quickly and easily disseminate information that will inform women of ways to care for themselves during pregnancy, dispel myths and misconceptions, highlight warning signs, connect women with local health services, reinforce breast feeding practices, explain the benefits of family planning, and make new mothers aware of how best to care for their babies.

Over the next three years, the partnership will work across an initial set of three countries - Bangladesh, India and South Africa - and lessons learned there will be shared globally among similar initiatives in other countries, accelerating efforts to reach millions of women worldwide.

The scheme, which uses mobile's unique ability to reach so many people, even has the backing of US Secretary of State Hillary Clinton.

Patients

For the user, the mobile phone offers everything from the ability to call an ambulance or speak to a doctor, right up to being able to help self-diagnose and medicate (within very strict guidelines, of course). It also helps people share symptoms, or rather, share details of symptoms, not a contagion, among one another.

Of course, calling an ambulance or speaking to a doctor is no big deal in the developed world, but in the developing world, where mobile phones are suddenly connecting people – about 60% of the world's handsets sold each year are now being sold in the developing world – this suddenly opens up health care possibilities previously only dreamed of.

Improved network capabilities are, in both the developed and the developing world, allowing doctors and health care professionals to make remote diagnoses of patients. In the developed world, this can help cut down on doctors' waiting room times, improve efficiency and leave doctors more time to concentrate on other things. (Sadly, this is often paperwork, but it all helps.)

In the developing world, where people live geographically separated and transport infrastructure is poor, remote diagnostics can mean the difference between life and death, opening up the world of health care to people hitherto denied it. How you get the medication to them is another matter, but it's a start.

Patients are also taking advantage of mobile health care services through simple text reminders to take their medication or to keep doctor or hospital appointments, again saving time and money for the doctor in the developed world; and creating the ability to improve the health of people in the developing world without onerous costs, since it uses technology already in place.

Finally, mobile is also an ideal tool for the education of people about basic health care, first aid, hygiene, midwifery and more. Again, this is pertinent to both the developed and the developing world, where the same issues come into play.

Mobile, thanks to its ubiquity and familiarity in both the developed and the developing worlds, offers a real chance to help humanity – a grand claim, but among all this talk of commerce, it is worth noting that there is a very human reason to use communications for the good.

That said, there is money to be made from developing apps and m-web health care services in both the developed and the developing worlds. Revenues for network operators, developers and other third parties, not least medical companies, logistics companies and others, are significant long-term.

Looking to the future, the market for health and fitness mobile applications will thrive and eventually spawn a new market for advanced apps that integrate sensors worn on the body.

Case study

Project Masiluleke: using mobile to combat AIDS/HIV

Project Masiluleke in South Africa is using a low-cost, high-impact tool in the fight against HIV/AIDS. The project is sending one million text messages – written in the local language – per day throughout South Africa that encourage people to be tested and treated for HIV/AIDS. The idea is that upon receiving the text message, the person will then call a helpline, and counselors can advise them on where to get tested, offer advice on what the outcome might mean and follow up on any treatment.

In South Africa, a quarter of the population is estimated to be infected with HIV, but less than 3% know their status. The broader goal of the program is to have those infected receive treatment and to halt the spread of the disease. Initial results from a beta test of the project indicated that it helped to nearly triple call volume to the AIDS/HIV helpline in the three weeks during which it ran. The project partners are building in rigorous monitoring and evaluation of the project. For example, they are linking calls to the helpline to PCM text messages through the use of distinct phone numbers that allow organizers to verify the number of calls generated by the program. Once the project is operating successfully, the system will be expanded to provide information about TB resources and treatment.

The next phases of the project will be the use and extension of the Praekelt Foundation's TxtAlert program to remind HIV-positive patients to take their medication and keep medical appointments; the creation of virtual call centers staffed by highly adherent patients; and the deployment of easy-to-use home HIV test kits, since the social stigma attached to HIV often prevents people from going to public clinics for testing.

Challenges remain for scaling projects like Masiluleke. Working across multiple networks, developing relevant messaging, and utilizing resources to take the initiative further are all difficult. Yet the project's early achievements point to some factors that increase the likelihood of success.

Doctors

While patients have much to benefit from mobile, many people think that doctors have the most to gain. As seen above, mobile can do simple things like cut down on waiting times, avoid missed appointments and help doctors to diagnose without having to travel. But the mobile framework also allows doctors to interact with one another, to learn and educate remotely, and to share case loads and diagnostics.

In the field of diagnostics, services such as Drchrono in the US are taking the idea of patient charts and data to a new level. Utilizing the camera and other aspects of the iPad 2, Drchrono lets doctors (or rather, their assistants, I assume) input patient notes and case histories, photos and physical examinations into an app that allows for remote diagnosis, prescriptions and even claims to translate medical speech into "text."

This sort of thing, like patient records on steroids, will revolutionize the medical profession in the developed world, as it allows for not only easy access and digitization of patient data (including video and photos), but also the connectivity and ability to share and consult with other doctors and experts easily and remotely. Surely a win-win for patients and medical professionals alike.

On a more prosaic level, mobile can also help doctors find out how much of a particular drug or vaccine is being held in various locations, and can help in the fight against counterfeit drugs – especially in the third world – by allowing patients to text the reference information on the drug's packaging to the doctor or drugs administration for verification.

Mobile is also helping to track, in something approaching real time, the spread of disease and outbreaks of epidemics, aiding in quarantine and efficiently treating diseases before they get out of hand.

There is also the more mundane idea that the mobile phone can be used by medical professionals to take payment from patients using technology such as the app-and-sleeve card readers advocated in Chapter 4.

It is interesting to note as well that, in the years to come, mHealth apps will probably cease to be distributed primarily through apps stores. Participants in the research2guidance survey anticipate they will be distributed by doctors. At the moment, apps stores are still the distribution channel of choice, but in the future it is expected that traditional health care distribution channels, like hospitals and specialized health care product vendors, will become the predominant distribution channels.

This would represent a significant shift when compared to the market today, as the smartphone apps store model has been the key driver behind the initial success of mHealth applications over the last two years.

More than half of all respondents (53%) believe that currently apps stores are the best distribution channels, followed by health care websites (49%). Traditional health distribution channels like doctors (34%), hospitals (31%) and pharmacies (16%) are ranked as second and third tier distribution channels. Despite the fact that mobile operators are regarded as players who will help the mHealth market grow, they are not seen as appropriate distribution channels either now or in the future.

In five years' time, survey participants anticipate that the traditional distribution channels will have much higher percentages, with hospitals at 68%, doctors at 65% and traditional health care websites at 56%. These will become the main platforms on which to sell mHealth solutions. Generally speaking all distribution channels will grow in importance, but developers envision that in just five years the major distribution channel will be doctors prescribing or suggesting applications to patients as a component of treatment.

Home care

One of the greatest markets for mobile in health care is shaping up to be home monitoring. A wealth of equipment and apps now exist that allow a person to monitor his vital signs, check to see whether medication has been taken, and even indicate whether a person is upright or not.

All very handy if you have elderly relatives to monitor.

Many US health care consumers are finding that, as the baby boomer generation – that is, their parents – become older and more infirm, looking after them in residential care is very expensive indeed (often at the expense of a child's inheritance). With competition for places in assisted living and nursing homes increasing, and therefore forcing up prices, many people are turning to using mobile remote monitoring. This allows their parents and elderly relatives to continue living at home, and independently, while their offspring can still keep a close mobile eye on how they are doing. They can check if a parent has taken his medication, what his heart, blood pressure and other vital signs are, and whether or not he has fallen.

There are also mobile apps that can allow the "patient" to contact someone if they become incapacitated in some way.

These apps and services, which are becoming increasingly prevalent in the US, are not cheap. In fact, they are becoming quite a revenue generator for many health care companies. But compared to the cost of in-home help, nurses and, in particular, residential care, they are considered a bargain.

Case study

Orange brings eHealth expertise to UK with smartnumbers

Cutting down on the time it takes to get to the right person or people in a medical unit can not only save lives, it also saves money. Aiming to produce this kind of efficiency in UK health care services, mobile network operator Orange has launched Orange smartnumbers, a health care-specific service aimed at cutting the time it takes to contact health care professionals.

This new service gives callers instant access to the best-placed person or team available, providing patients and health care workers with the ability to reach the right person the first time, and every time, they call.

The launch signifies Orange's first activity in the UK health care industry, and the first service of its kind in the UK by any mobile operator. Orange has had a dedicated health care division in Europe for four years, and has a 10-year legacy in the health care sector. Recognizing the huge potential for mobile communications to improve efficiencies for health care professionals, and ultimately patient care, Orange is building on its experience to offer this new solution that will improve how health care professionals and patients communicate with one another.

Orange smartnumbers provides patients and health care workers instant access to the best person available to handle their call, improving accessibility to health care individuals and teams. For example, if a doctor on duty is unavailable to answer a call, it will be diverted to the appropriate colleague or team. The solution enables greater flexibility, control and monitoring of calls, thereby empowering employees and informing managers.

For community-based health care staff working on the move, such as midwives and nurses, 60% of ordinary calls to health care colleagues fail to reach the right person the first time. With time saved on locating colleagues, the efficiency of those people working outside doctors' offices or hospitals is increased, resulting in the health sector being better able to focus on providing first-class patient care.

Orange has partnered with Resilient Networks plc to provide this low-cost, easy-to-implement service that equips doctors' offices and primary and secondary care clinics with the tools to help meet their service quality and efficiency targets.

ACTION POINTS

- **Mobile health care boasts countless revenue opportunities.** App creators and developers can build for consumers wishing to use their phones for everything from diagnostics of simple things, to first-aid tips, to diets, to medication.

- **Target the health care industry.** There is a thirst to combine mobile ubiquity and connectivity with the needs for doctors to work remotely when off duty.
- **Research potential markets.** From a humanitarian point of view, mobile health care offers a rich potential for education, virology, disease awareness and basic health and lifestyle information in developing countries.
- **Beware the legal minefield.** From a business perspective, make sure you get any data you use in your apps and services from a recognized source. Misdiagnosis can be a legal minefield.
- **Always consult your doctor if your symptoms persist.**

CHAPTER 8

M-commerce within the business

🔊 Why should companies look to mobile for their communication, reporting, assessment and training processes?

🔊 How will mobile transform the tracking of goods, vehicles and people?

🔊 Where can mobile make a difference to customer service levels?

The bulk of the promise of mobile commerce lies in how it acts as a tool to get consumers engaged with brands, services, retailers and more, and how it turns that engagement into some sort of sale, through any of the sales channels open to a business. But mobile also has a role to play within the actual business itself, and I think it is worth, at this juncture, taking a brief detour into the world of B2B and internal mobile use within a business.

Of course, no business professional would leave her desk without a mobile phone (or two) in her pocket these days. It is, after all, a telephone and messaging device. Personally, I conduct virtually all my business calls using my mobile phone, and when without it – on those very, very rare occasions when I have forgotten to take it with me – I feel totally isolated from my professional (and increasingly my personal) life.

The mobile phone has already revolutionized the working man or woman's ability to work on the road or remotely. Mobile, in fact, came to prominence on the back of its use in the business world. Early mobile phones and the calls made on them were so costly, only corporate money could cover the expense, and only for the most important employees. As costs have fallen and technology has become more widespread, the mobile phone has become an essential business tool of the everyman. No stockbroker, politician, journalist, delivery man, plumber or social worker could do his or her job without one. But the richness that modern mobile commerce offers has thrown up some interesting opportunities within the business sector to employ mobile in streamlining business and offering much richer customer experience.

The business to business (B2B) market is almost as richly blessed with applications for mobile as the consumer market, and in all its forms, from calls to text to apps to mobile web, as well as things like geo-location and even augmented reality. All have a role to play in the marketplace, offering better ways to interact with business customers, better ways to run businesses, and better ways to safely and efficiently manage staff.

Tracking and customer relations

One thing that can be directly translated from the consumer world to the B2B space is the use of mobile as a customer relationship management tool — offering the chance to improve how your customers interact with you and access what you have to offer. This can simply take the form of delivering mobile websites or apps that make it easier for customers to purchase your goods or services, or to track orders or shipments.

Logistics companies like UPS and FedEx have been delivering this for some time now to customers, offering an app that lets a business track deliveries and shipments made through their firms, as well as placing orders and all the other aspects of interacting with these businesses. These services, lifted directly from the kind of thing that occurs in the consumer's world, are just the tip of the iceberg in terms of what mobile can deliver to businesses on a B2B front.

Productivity and workflow tools typically found as software on computers, along with accounting and database software, are starting to emerge as mobile apps. Or, at the very least, as mobile apps that let managers oversee from their phones how these things — and other automated processes — are progressing.

M-commerce Boost your business with the power of mobile commerce

One area of particular interest in the business community right now is an app for e-commerce managers. While they are on the road, they can keep on top of their e-commerce and multichannel commerce stats, and adjust marketing, keyword spending and search engine optimization parameters from their phones.

The model doesn't just apply to e-commerce practitioners, as it works equally well with accounts, databases, marketing, customer relationship management (CRM), call center management and direct marketing campaign management – simple apps that let the business professional in charge of that particular aspect of the business stay on top of what they are doing while on the road.

Sales force automation tools have long existed. Where they once were run on laptops and needed an Internet connection in a road warrior's hotel room to work, now a simple smartphone with the right apps and a 3G connection allows a sales manager to travel anywhere in the world and still stay on top of his or her teams, targets and results.

Furthermore, with the advent of tablets and smartphones has come a whole new way to deliver product demos and sales pitches. It won't be long now (fingers crossed) before PowerPoint is no longer the high point of a sophisticated sales pitch. With the rich graphics and capabilities of modern devices, and their inherent connectivity, interactive, highly tailored sales pitches on a dynamic device are set to revolutionize sales and marketing.

Richer display media make it much easier to inform prospective clients, and their connectivity means that data used can be as up to the minute as possible. All together, these make the use of mobile in the B2B environment the next wave of mobile commerce, and it will break in the next two to three years.

Case study

App lets e-commerce managers manage on the move

E-commerce is a 24/7 business, and so managing it requires herculean efforts on the part of e-commerce managers. Since many of them have homes - not to mention meetings - to go to, keeping on top of how their e-commerce systems are working while not at their desks is business critical.

Answering this need, e-commerce software vendor Tiger Commerce has created an iPhone app to complement its browser-based online shopping software, which allows merchants with e-commerce offerings to track how the site is performing without having to log on at a computer.

The company's free app allows order tracking and on-the-move updates, so shop owners can stay in touch with new orders and new customer registrations, as well as historical shop data - without needing to access a laptop or computer. Tiger Commerce clients can also use the app to log into their shop's Google Analytics account for up-to-date analysis of shop-visitor data.

Worker and vehicle tracking

The previous section offered some insight into how mobile can — and is — transforming the way many professionals work. But it is also having an impact in some of the toughest jobs out there, offering a whole other range of professional and consumer applications.

One particular area of the workforce that has benefited greatly from advances in mobile technology is lone and remote workers. The UK's

Health and Safety Executive defines lone workers as those who work by themselves without close or direct supervision. They are found in a wide range of situations, such as people working away from a fixed base – such as social care workers, sales teams, technical field staff, delivery personnel, health care workers, environmental inspectors or field engineers. It also includes people working separately or outside normal hours, such as security staff, bus drivers, prison officers, maintenance and repair staff, paramedics or cleaners.

People working alone from a fixed location, such as a shop, construction site, petrol station or kiosk, can also be considered remote and lone workers. Due to their vulnerability, not to mention the love of litigation of people today they, need protecting.

The Health and Safety (Offences) Act 2008, introduced in the UK in March 2009, raises the maximum penalties available to the courts in respect of certain health and safety offenses. This, combined with the Corporate Manslaughter and Corporate Homicide Act 2007, places even greater emphasis on organizations and management to ensure their employees are safe.

So what is available? The simple answer is to give each of these employees a mobile phone and pay for it, but that doesn't always fit the bill and can in itself be a risk.

One way around this is wireless tracking. Wi-Fi and 3G can enable a badge worn by the worker, which can then be tracked using the same location technology used in mobile marketing and other mobile tracking applications in the consumer world. Such systems use badges that are the same size and shape as typical ID badges, and fit easily on a lanyard with other credential cards.

The Wi-Fi badges enable easy two-way communication between staff members or personnel, such as contractors or site visitors. This helps organizations increase staff productivity and personnel safety.

Integrating with other back-end software, employee and contractor wireless tracking also provides information such as worker proximity – so you know who is nearest to what – as well as condition data from remote locations, such as temperature and other atmospheric data.

Many of these solutions also feature a text-messaging facility. Not only can the people monitoring the workers see where they are and what the weather's like there, but they can also message them if need be, or be messaged by the workers. This text-messaging capability combined with accurate real-time location provides a powerful way to remotely manage even a large area and numbers of people.

This small Wi-Fi badge device also provides an ideal way to improve staff and visitor security. This is because a badge wearer is able to send an alert if he is being attacked or if immediate help is needed. The alarm reveals the precise location of the badge at the time of the alert, and it can also be programmed to call security, re-point video cameras to the alert area, or control door locks and lighting, all customizable for your environment.

The badges use a high-energy rechargeable battery that works for weeks or months without recharging.

Such solutions also apply to company-operated vehicles that can be fitted, James Bond-like, with GPS tracking software to accurately track cars, heavy goods vehicles, off-road vehicles, plant equipment and any motorized machinery.

Not only does this let you keep an eye on where your vehicles are, what they are doing and if they have been stolen, it also means a business can more accurately schedule deliveries, can better allocate jobs to the nearest vehicle, see what time a delivery will arrive, locate drivers, view the whereabouts of high-value deliveries, and receive free tracking reports, all in real time. It can also see how a driver is behaving, journey details and fuel efficiency.

Thousands of vehicles have this solution in place because it reduces company costs, improves their administrative efficiency, increases security and enhances customer communication. It is intuitive and easy to use. Plus, it gives you a map of where all your vehicles are. Like I say, it's all very James Bond.

Borrowing from the consumer mobile marketing world, companies running vehicles can also set up geo-fences that alert them when a vehicle has arrived somewhere or passed a particular milestone on its journey – again aiding planning and logistics, which leads to improved customer service.

Stocks and shares

One specific area where mobile has a successful B2B track record to date is the corporate finance market, especially in terms of stocks and shares management. Many traders have been using apps and secure m-web feeds on mobiles to monitor their positions on trades whenever they leave their desks for a sandwich or the call of nature.

As mobile connectivity, security and device functionality improve, these services have escalated from being simple stock watchers to offering extremely rich analytical content in real time, right through to allowing for the actual trading of stocks, shares and commodities from the mobile device itself.

There are two main ways that the cut and thrust of trading has been moved on to the mobile platform: using mobile to browse and interact with a broker's website, or trading via apps that connect seamlessly through a broker. It's the old apps/m-web split again.

While share trading on mobile has become commonplace in the major western financial markets, it is in the developing markets such as India and China where it has the most potential. Already the

Bombay Stock Exchange has opened up trading via the mobile platform for traders in that city to deal, via mobile, across Asian markets. The service uses technology developed in the US in 2002 by Interactive Brokers, and will open up the Asian stock market to millions of potential traders, professional or otherwise. With 652.4 million users – and a further 17 million being added each month, according to the Telecom Regulatory Authority of India – this is potentially a huge opportunity for millions of people to benefit from share trading.

Across the developed world, share trading on mobile has been given a boost by the arrival of the iPad and other tablet computers. The large screen and improved interface mean that these portable devices can extend greatly the scope of what mobile trading has to offer, including live news feeds, more accurate and easy to interpret graphics, video and other content, all on a handheld device.

Improving network connectivity and security, ushered in by the mobile payments side of things (see Chapter 9), are also increasing people's confidence in undertaking these sorts of high-end financial transactions on a mobile device.

Other financial business services are also set to grow on mobile, as mobile banking in the consumer sector (again, see Chapter 9) starts to spill over into offerings for the "prosumer" (professional consumer) sector. The ability to check balances and payments is one thing, but for a financial director to be able to keep on top of often quite complex accounting via a smartphone or tablet also frees up how he can work.

The Internet was meant to see the end of people working in offices, but it never really happened that way. Mobile, on the other hand, does have the power to let people do complex tasks on the move, or at least away from the central office, without impeding productivity or anyone really noticing where a person is located. At the time of writing, I am doing this part on an iPad in a bucolic location in the UK – but no one reading this would know that. Most of the rest of it was written in my office on a desktop Mac, or in various places around the world on a laptop. This seamless ability to work anywhere – coupled with increasing fuel and transport costs – could usher in a whole new way of working for many office-bound employees.

The fact that city traders are doing it shows that even the most entrenched, location-bound jobs can change and adapt in a mobile world. We will see much more in the prosumer mobile business, and the rewards for companies offering the apps, m-web and other services to make this happen should have rich pickings. Corporations tend to have more money to spend than consumers, and if consumers are spending vast amounts on apps and m-commerce, pro-m-commerce is likely to be a huge revenue generator.

Case study

CNBC uses iPad app to fuel trading data

With stock and share trading becoming one of the early boomers in mobile in a business context, it is unsurprising that there are a growing array of trading data apps for phone and, increasingly, tablets. Business TV company CNBC has become one of the first B2B media companies to tap into this market, with the launch of an iPad-specific app that gives users access to live, real-time stock quotes - before, during and after market hours - from both the New York Stock Exchange and NASDAQ. The app also delivers breaking news alerts and access to top CNBC video clips, including the latest CEO interviews and market updates via CNBC's video-on-demand.

The CNBC Real-Time iPad app includes live, real-time stock quotes and charts, with real-time streaming stock quotes, accompanied by company-specific news, related video, profiles, returns and key metrics. It also delivers real-time and historical interactive charts that offer custom time frames from one day to five years, including pre- and post-market trading.

The app also offers "My Stocks," with which users can create and track their favorite company stocks live, in real time, with access to integrated charts and related news headlines. Users can also set up a custom CNBC Ticker with a playlist of favorite stocks, or choose from "CNBC Stocks to Watch," "Indices" and "Top Headlines/Videos" lists.

CNBC's global editorial team also supplies a stream of breaking news alerts direct to the iPad app, keeping users up to date on what is moving the markets.

Staff training and scheduling

Remote monitoring of staff may seem a trifle Orwellian, but aside from the safety and security side of things, this form of mobile interaction with staff has other benefits – not least that it can be used as a remote training tool, as well as a way of scheduling staff across multiple locations, running appointments and meetings, planning overtime and other cost-sensitive aspects of running a business. In fact, mobile can deliver a raft of benefits on the corporate side in management, training, staff morale and more.

Mobile also offers a quick and easy access point to company information, staff data and a messaging tool to help manage shift workers, call for extra staff, manage overtime and more.

It is being toyed with as a way of delivering some training internally, within companies. Many businesses, especially in the retail sector, have widely dispersed staff at branches and stores across a country or even the world. Many of these businesses have already implemented online-based training, webinars and video link-ups to provide vital information cheaply and efficiently. Mobile, while not ideal for doing in-depth remote training, can augment this, offering a chance to update workers on small changes to company policy, details of special promotions, access to handbooks and manuals, as well as being a portal to human resources and other functions within the business that many workers are keen to make best use of.

There is also the chance to use mobile internally to help improve staff morale. Simple things such as letting everyone know who employee of the month is, or letting people vote on who employee of the month should be, is one way to do this. There is also the chance to offer employees to join in things such as fantasy football games across the company.

On a more prosaic note, mobile lets workers and managers communicate with one another remotely, from making a voice call to using text, e-mail or even instant messaging. Developments in corporate private networks – which are mobile voice and data networks that are usually built using public network infrastructure and the web, but are run so that they appear to be private networks – can make using mobile a cheap, effective and secure way to link stores, staff and suppliers together across wide geographies at minimal cost.

Many retailers already use mobile messaging to help managers stay in touch with one another and the home office, and the arrival of tablet computers and video calling, iPad 2 for instance, means that businesses have the chance to allow video conferencing between remote managers cheaply across private networks.

Case study

Mobile to go at McDonald's

Fast food chain McDonald's has long been an advocate of remote training and interaction with staff. It has, in the UK alone, 1,200 restaurants, 80,000 employees and serves 2.5 million customers a day, producing a £2bn ($3.23bn) annual turnover. On the consumer front it has already embraced mobile, with an app that features store finders, deals and all sorts of other content, but it has recently decided to extend what it does with mobile to interact with its huge and widely dispersed workforce.

The company already has a range of online services for both branch managers and staff, offering employee handbooks, staff training, details of new promotions, employee discounts and details of the company's benefits scheme. In developing its mobile offerings for consumers, the company decided to also look at how it could use mobile to target this business to enterprise (B2E) area more effectively and more personally with mobile.

The result has been an app and platform agnostic m-web site for staff who don't have an iPhone, which allows the company and its staff to interact with one another and keep the business running smoothly. The app and m-web site let managers run staff scheduling and the staff self-service scheduling, as well as manage their own absence notification. The app and m-web service also lets managers initiate shift alerts and reminders to staff, and generally allows for more efficient use of staff across the company.

The service also lets employees calculate their earnings, and provides details of training, company policy and the introduction of new offers.

ACTION POINTS

- **Control your mobile management.** If you have remote workers – both remote to the office and in remote locations – there is the risk that mobile connectivity and monitoring can turn Big Brother-esque and create tension.
- **Check that mobile coverage and sturdiness is fit for purpose.** If using mobile in rugged industrial environments or hostile geographies, check devices and ask your service provider. For example, are iPhones suitable for an offshore oil platform?
- **Keep message file sizes as small as possible.** When disseminating company information such as training, consider the size of the screen, the network limitations and where and how the user will be accessing it.
- **Don't make company messages too long, too wordy or too data heavy.** Video may be tempting as an early-morning inspiration, but might be too long, too data heavy and simply too much.
- **Make communication two-way.** Mobile offers a huge opportunity to cheaply, easily and conveniently keep in touch with your workforce. Internet-enabled, it also gives staff a convenient tool to access company intranets and to contact you.
- **Don't overspend where you don't have to.** For a small business, simple business tariffs are enough, and no complex messaging or management technology is needed to operate these services.
- **Use third-party suppliers and network operators to build mobile operations.** For medium and large enterprises, the challenges of running a company-wide mobile information service are greater. Ask your current supplier what's possible.

CHAPTER 9

Mobile payments

ℕ What are the simplest ways to utilize mobile payments and where does WAP billing fit in?

ℕ How close is the average consumer to using the mobile phone as a wallet?

ℕ Where are the security threats to switching to mobile payments?

Mobile, as we have seen in previous chapters, is not only an ultra-personal commerce tool, but one that comes with the potential to allow secure and flexible payments. This can be through use of the fact that the phone is connected to a phone bill, making it easy for charges to be put onto that phone bill; or because it is connected to the Internet, and so can use all the billing and payment tools already working successfully online.

The rise of social networking and the commercialization of social media – in particular the use of virtual goods on such sites as either credit for games or gifts to woo other site users – has seen a growing need for getting money into the Internet. The people using these sites typically don't have bank accounts or are too young to have credit cards, and so a cottage industry in using mobile as a means of getting money into the system has grown into a multibillion dollar industry.

But mobile has yet more to offer in the money-moving stakes than just acting as a way of getting money from a prepaid phone account into a website. It can transfer money from device to device and, thanks to some ground-breaking technology that is starting to come on stream, it can be used as a bank card or electronic wallet, closing the loop on the whole process of discovery, review and purchase from the comfort of your own phone.

This has seen mobile attract a lot of attention from banks, as well as network operators, handset makers, credit and debit card companies, merchants, retailers and a host of third-party billing providers – both online and off – as a means of not only moving money about (and skimming small percentages from each of the prospective billions of transactions worldwide), but also as another way to own the customer.

For network operators, faced increasingly with the prospect of just becoming dump pipes that only carry the data, mobile payments offers a way for them to truly add value using the billing technologies they already have in place. For the likes of Apple and Google, Nokia and Microsoft, it offers the chance to enhance their devices and make them even more indispensable to consumers. For the banks, it offers the possibility of creating new ways to sell their services to consumers and merchants; and for third parties, it offers a lucrative chance to cash in on the growing demand for m-commerce related offerings.

How this will play out is anyone's guess, but a battle royal is about to commence over who owns the customer in a financial sense. So what is on offer and who are the major players?

Using the phone's bill

As we have seen in early chapters of this book, the mobile phone comes connected to an operator's phone bill — or if it's prepaid, is already credited with money that sits on an operator's server — which makes mobile the ideal payment tool.

Exploiting this for commercial purposes is nothing new. The fixed-line telephone world has been doing that since the mid-1980s in the US and Europe, offering premium-rate telephone numbers to call that incur a higher than normal charge. These are still used today — from fixed line and mobile — and they allow consumers to pay for things with the phone. Typically this has been paying for content of one form or another — from sex chat lines to cricket scores to even listening to the top 10 records — that was deemed to have some added value. Today, most premium-rate numbers are tied to things like information lines. From a regulatory perspective, actually using a voice telephone call to pay for anything substantial has been frowned upon in most geographies (because of the potential for fraud, money laundering and all sorts of other nefarious things), so typically, premium-rate voice calls are a way of generating money from the need to call a number.

On mobile these voice-activated billing calls tend to be even more expensive, and in many markets, the charges levied by the operators to call these numbers are very high, differ from operator to operator, and are largely opaque to the consumer, since the operator applies different charges to individual number sets. Typically, the only warning you get when calling one of these numbers – usually in the small print on the ad on which they appear, or in rushed and hushed tones on TV shows – is that "calls from mobiles are substantially higher than from landlines and operator charges vary." It is one of the rare instances where you are charged for something and yet you have absolutely no idea how much it is going to cost you until you have actually paid it.

For this reason, the use of premium-rate voice calling is something that, while done on mobile, is not often considered by most businesses to be a clear enough payment channel to warrant being used to charge for things specifically. As we have seen in previous chapters, many TV shows that encourage user voting use PRS voice calls, terminated by automated response, or IVR, systems. These are not explicitly targeted at mobile, but due to the mobile-centric nature of most of the target audiences of these shows, substantial revenues come through this channel.

pSMS

More pertinent to the mobile commerce field is the role of premium rate SMS (pSMS). Much like premium-rate telephone calls, this uses text messaging to either deliver content, or allow consumers to text a specific number (usually a five-digit shortcode) and incur a higher than normal charge in return for some sort of premium content or service. It can be broken down into two basic forms: MT (mobile terminated) and MO (mobile originated).

Mobile-terminated short messages are typically used to deliver digital content such as news alerts, financial information, logos and ringtones. The first premium-rate media content delivered via the SMS was the downloadable ringtones, launched by Saunalahti (later Jippii, now part of Elisa Group) in 1998. Initially, only Nokia-branded phones could handle them. By 2002 the global ringtone business had exceeded $1bn, and nearly $5bn by 2010.

The value-added service provider (VASP), or content provider running the content service, submits the message to the mobile operator's message center, or SMSC. The SMSC delivers the text using the normal MT delivery procedure. The subscribers are charged extra for receiving this premium content, with the revenue typically divided between the mobile network operator and the VASP, either through revenue share or a fixed transport fee. The proportion of who gets what varies from operator to operator. It used to be stacked very much in the operator's favor, but things are changing.

Mobile originated (MO) messages may also be used in a premium-rated manner for services such as televoting. In this case, the VASP providing the service obtains a shortcode from the network operator, and subscribers send texts to that number. The payouts to the carriers vary by carrier; percentages paid are greatest on the lowest-priced premium SMS services. Most information providers should expect to pay about 45% of the cost of the premium SMS to the carrier.

The submission of the text to the SMSC is identical to a standard MO short message submission, but once the text is at the SMSC, the Service Center (SC) identifies the short message as a premium service. The SC will then direct the content of the text message to the VASP, typically using an IP protocol such as SMPP or EMI. Subscribers are charged a premium for the sending of such messages, with the revenue typically shared between the network operator and the VASP. Shortcodes only work within one country; they are not international.

Case study

The world of alt.billing

Many ways of using the mobile bill are starting to take shape in a market that is being dubbed alternative billing (or for those with a country rock bent, alt.billing). These are typically melding some of the benefits of on-bill billing, pSMS and the web to create ways of using mobile to buy things online.

One example is alt.billing mobile company BOKU, which formed a partnership with listings company Gumtree to offer users a convenient way to pay for classifieds listings via their mobile phone number. At checkout, users simply click "pay by mobile" and enter their mobile phone number. They receive a text that confirms the payment, and the charge either appears on their mobile phone bill or is deducted from their pay-as-you-go credit.

Gumtree originated in the UK and now offers online classifieds postings for 60 different cities spread across six different countries: UK, Ireland, Poland, Australia, New Zealand and South Africa. Gumtree users in the UK alone post more than 250,000 new ads every week, and 2.3 million ads are live on the site at any given time. Gumtree.com users spend an average of 72 minutes on the website each month.

In the US, BOKU competitor Zong is also leveraging the fact that rather than memorizing credit card numbers, most people know their mobile number. It does much the same thing as

BOKU, only it is targeting not only mobile phones, but games consoles, Internet-connected TVs and tablets. It has also opened up its platform to Android developers, so that it can become a billing tool for the purchase of things in-app.

PayWizard is also starting to emerge as an interesting take on how mobile payments can carve out a niche for themselves in the content-consumption market - by making the most of mobile payment's ability to handle small micropayments, by working fairly instantly and acting as a two-way delivery channel. The user preregisters his bank details with PayWizard to set up an account, and then can access the service on mobile, online or on TV. Merchants wishing to sell digital content or collect money for services online, on TV or on mobile then put their PayWizard logo at the point of access. The user clicks it, the money moves from consumer account to merchant, and access to the content is given immediately.

The aim is to give users instant access to paid-for content online, on mobile and on TV, and offers merchants the chance to micro-monetize their content and services. In theory, PayWizard, BOKU and Zong can all be used for anything that requires purchasing, not just online goods. We expect to see more of these sorts of services arrive in the next 24 months, which will allow for quick paid-for access and even the purchase of tangible goods, via mobile and other devices.

As we can see, pSMS and on-bill services are typically used for virtual goods that are "consumed" digitally on the phone, or for televoting and other media interaction. There are plans to try to open up these – and all other operator-run billing services – to the payment of bills, and for the purchase of real-world goods and services not consumed on the phone. However, there are still a number of hurdles.

First, most network operators run only a limited and fixed number of tariffs, so price points for goods and services have to fall into these rigid limits or multiples of these tariffs (typically 50p ($0.81) per message, or £1.50 ($2.43) per message or multiples thereof). This makes the pricing of pSMS-purchased goods hard to keep in line with the same goods being purchased in other ways.

Second, the fact that the network operators take a slice of the revenue, which is usually in double-digit percentile terms, means that again, a retailer can't sell through this payment mechanism for the same price as goods purchased using cash or credit cards. For example, a coat that costs £100 ($162) to buy in a shop with cash or credit card costs just that. To buy it using pSMS with an operator cut of 45%, would mean that the retailer would have to either lose almost half of his profit on the coat, or charge anyone paying via pSMS £145 ($234) for the same coat.

In the early days of mobile, when it was largely looked upon as an expensive method of communicating and so all things mobile were charged at a premium, it appeared that this model would work: people might pay £145 for a £100 coat for the convenience of using mobile. However, the rise of the debit card (which typically charges 3% or less for transactions, which can be swallowed by the retailer) means that there are now in place many different ways of purchasing goods in a shop, all of which keep the price of the goods the same.

However, as I write, the lure of the billions of pounds, dollars and yen that could be made through a simplification of the mobile purchasing process has got many network operators thinking that, to get their slice of this almighty pie, they should cut their revenue share to debit and credit card levels. The logic is that by making it only cost 3% to use mobile to pay for things, through pSMS and other mobile-operator billing tools as discussed below, they can extract a multibillion dollar slice of the retail pie. Or they can keep things as they are and get nothing.

There is a long way to go on getting it to work, and for the operators, retailers and consumers to buy into the move, but it could yield a new way to pay. Operator billing has the huge advantage that the user either already had his credit checked when he got the phone, or he has credit on his phone if the phone is prepaid. That cuts out the risk of charges going through at, say, a weekend on a card, only for the bank to find on Monday morning that they have no credit or money.

That said, as it takes both retailers and mobile operators glacial amounts of time to work through the policies and politics of making such dramatic changes to how they operate, there is a pretty good chance that they may well miss the boat. While the procrastination continues, other ways of using mobile to pay for things, which consumers are already familiar with from the online world, are finding their way into mobile. And they are more flexible and, frankly, better value to the consumer, and so operators could again be cut out of the loop altogether.

WAP billing

Before the advent of the Internet-enabled, Wi-Fi-toting smartphone, the future of mobile online services appeared to be something called WAP, or Wireless Application Protocol. WAP is basically a low-rent browser technology, developed as a cut-rate way of accessing the Internet from mobile devices, back in the day when mobile devices were pretty low powered, memory and processing-wise. It was seen as the way we were going to access the web, until Apple decided that it wasn't and phones became more like computers. Anyhow, the developers of WAP realized that within WAP there needed to be the ability to bill for stuff consumed via the mobile web, and so developed a billing mechanism for consumers to buy content from WAP sites that was charged directly to their mobile phone bill. It was and still is marketed for people to use as an alternative payment mechanism to debit or credit cards and premium SMS for billing.

Using WAP billing, consumers can buy mobile content without registering for a service or entering a username or password. Users simply click on a link and agree to make a purchase, after which they can download content. Since it is tied to their phone bills, the users are either already credit checked or have credit on their prepaid accounts.

WAP billing, like pSMS, is particularly associated with downloading mobile entertainment content like ringtones, mobile games and wallpapers. Some commentators have suggested it could compete with premium SMS as a leading payment channel for mobile content, although it faces many of the same challenges outlined above that pSMS does – namely operator revenue shares and lack of retailer awareness. It is also beset by problems from each operator having its own WAP billing products and setups. Any retailer, brand or business looking to add this as a payment tool would have to implement different versions for each operator in the geography in which they operate.

In mainstream mobile markets in the US, as well as European countries, including Spain, Italy, Scandinavia and the UK, attempts have been made to create cross-operator WAP billing platforms that can support the purchase of products on any mobile network. Unfortunately, it is challenging getting operators to agree to any third party essentially agglomerating competing network billing infrastructures.

The UK has so far seen the most successful attempt at this with the PayForIt service, which aims to provide a safe and trustworthy environment for consumers buying mobile content.

Here a Trusted Mobile Payment Framework governs how merchants, accredited payment intermediaries and mobile network operators cooperate to make mobile payments a secure and seamless process. A set of screen-style rules govern how payment pages look and function, so consumers can purchase content via a standardized interface presented on their mobile phones.

PayForIt was first announced in March 2006 and is supported by all licensed UK mobile operators. Initially, it supported micropayments – generally less than £10 ($16) – for services purchased on mobile portals, and in May 2007 the scheme was extended to support web transactions as well. The Ericsson IPX Internet Payment Exchange cross-network WAP billing solution was the first mobile payment system to host a live payment service complying with the PayForIt scheme in the UK, on the T-Mobile service.

The benefits cited for WAP billing include the ability for under 18 year-olds to pay for goods without holding a credit card or bank account, and an improved customer experience, including single click purchases, where transactions are completed without consumers having to send or receive a text message or remember shortcodes.

It has been claimed that WAP billing also reduces the possibility of fraud when paying for mobile content. Another benefit cited for WAP billing is the assertion that users have the same browse-and-buy experience they are used to on the Internet via their PC.

Similarly, though, many of the same challenges apply to getting PayForIt and other WAP billing tools out there in the market: operator revenue share and customer and retailer buy-in.

The biggest challenge, however, seems to be that since it was first introduced, after having had five years with zero publicity, things have moved on. Consumers now use more online-oriented payment tools, offered by brands they trust and that they have worked with online for years. WAP billing has failed to ignite a great deal of interest and, through the woeful lack of publicity and any clear branding, has simply not attracted the numbers of users that many thought it would.

As with anything in mobile though, don't write it off. It might just be that its time hasn't yet come, or it hasn't found the niche where it is the best fit as a billing tool. The search continues as many other billing models and products have much more to offer the mobile consumer. Some clever branding is putting WAP billing at the forefront of the mobile storefront for a number of industries, as the case study below reveals.

In the US, the approach has been very different. Here a number of third-party companies have set themselves up as billing hubs, creating a single point of contact for merchants to allow billing across any network signed up to that billing. Offered by a number of companies, including OpenMarket and Bango (a UK-based company that is striking out as an international billing and WAP billing specialist), these services. offer to make the processing purchase for the consumer more straightforward and, from a merchant's point of view, easier to manage.

According to OpenMarket, a simple, non-SMS-based mobile-payment tool that still bills to the phone bill is something that the US market has been crying out for. It offers a seamless one-click purchase, the simplicity of which makes for higher conversion rates at the point of purchase.

US use of WAP billing has grown exponentially since about 2007, topping more than 160 million users by 2010. In the UK it is also growing, albeit slowly due to lack of any marketing push. However, its use in simple everyday things such as car parking charges, as run by billing company ImpulsePay, has seen it start to gain users almost by stealth.

WAP billing also has the advantage of offering an experience much more akin to web browsing and web purchasing – something that consumers in the US in particular are much more used to – and is thus viewed as one of the key tools in getting consumers in that market to start using their mobiles as a payment tool.

WAP billing also has another advantage. Unlike SMS-based billing, the user doesn't have to leave the billing page of a mobile website to complete the transaction and get a code from their SMS inbox. This simplicity is one of the saving graces for WAP billing and why, given time, it may just start to see widespread adoption around the world.

Case study

ImpulsePay makes a case for WAP billing

PayForIt WAP billing is a key tool for billing for things on websites, where being out and about also has relevance. Through a third party called ImpulsePay that offers cross-network UK companies such as SpareRoom.co.uk (the UK's most popular flat- and house-share website) and beepbeep.ie (a website dedicated to the buying and selling of vehicles and vehicle parts) are letting their customers pay for the services they offer remotely, from their mobiles.

Using ImpulsePay's mobile purchasing service, mobile users can pay for access to early bird ads on SpareRoom.co.uk and get a head start on finding their next room with just one click. The cost, which is taken directly from the user's mobile phone bill or available credit, is just £3 ($4.85) for 24 hours access, or £10 ($16) for 10 days access.

Meanwhile, mobile users of beepbeep.ie can use their phones to create an ad, with payment again being taken from their mobile phone bill or available credit. The ImpulsePay solution means that beepbeep.ie's advertisers no longer have to enter credit card details, or be registered for services such as PayPal. Instead, they can click on the pay-by-mobile button to have the £5 ($8) charge for five weeks' advertising (£1 or $1.62 per week) taken from their mobile phone bill.

PayPal, 1-Click and store accounts

While the mobile phone lends itself to using its own inherent payment tools, smartphone technology means that mobile devices have started to come toward the payment space from the online, e-commerce side of the fence. This side tends to see smartphones and tablets as just portable devices that are connected to the Internet, rather than devices that are connected to a mobile phone operator's network and, therefore, its billing tools.

This means that for many coming late to the m-commerce marketplace, particularly from the retail sector, the obvious choice of billing solution lies firmly with what they already offer their customers online – especially when it comes to offering a mobile-optimized version of their website. (Things are a bit different with apps, but again network operators lose out here too, but we'll come to that.)

The most prevalent online billing tool is, surprisingly, credit card payments, capturing 43.5% of the total online payments volume, according to research firm Javelin. It estimates that consumers spent $205bn online in 2010, although it predicts the share of credit card payments will decline to 39.4% in 2014.

Debit cards also will represent a smaller share of online payments, declining to 25.6% in 2014 from 28% in 2009. Meanwhile, prepaid and gift cards will account for 10.7% of online payments by 2014, up from 6.6% in 2009; while PayPal, Google Checkout and other alternative payment methods will capture 19.2% of online purchases in 2014, up from 15.9% in 2009. The remainder, about 5%, will come from store-brand credit cards.

By 2014, prepaid and gift cards will have the highest compound annual growth rate for online payment forms between 2009 and 2014 of 26%.

On mobile, similar models, albeit with much smaller revenues attached (for now), apply. Credit and debit card are still dominant, but with most payments that use this method taking a minimum of 68 keystrokes (often with three more for the QVC code on the back of the card: the lowest form of security available), this is becoming a cumbersome interface for many users. Also, many websites' card payment pages, when not properly mobile-optimized, simply don't work or are far too awkward to use on a small screen and keypad.

Instead, many consumers are turning to other ways of paying by card on mobile, mostly based on services where you register a bank account, debit or credit card online once and then use that billing tool when on the handset.

Typical examples of this are apps stores (which are cornering the market in in-app billing), PayPal and, increasingly, Amazon's 1-Click. In the case of Amazon, the simplicity of its billing mechanism, combined with its enormous range of stock, is acting as a differentiator above the usual reason people shop around: price. It is interesting to note that the ease of use of the payment mechanism on Amazon's mobile site actually means more people use it to shop than if based on price alone.

These preregistered billing tools make life much easier for consumers on mobile, and make it much easier for retailers to extend all the benefits of their online payment tools to the mobile channel — a key driver in the uptake of multichannel retail.

So let's take a look at some of the most popular preregistered shopping experiences on mobile.

PayPal

PayPal has 232 million accounts worldwide, 83 million of them active users, and processes $29.5bn annually online. It handles 24 different currencies and operates in 190 different market geographies around the world. In the UK, 95% of people that shop online have a PayPal account, even if many don't actually use it. Penetration is similar in the US and Canada, and varies in other regions.

How does it work? For those of you not in the know, PayPal is an online account that allows you to receive and send money electronically with your bank account and credit cards. It is owned by eBay, and is used mainly for buying and selling through auctions. The user and the merchant simply register bank account or card details with PayPal and, when a payment needs to be made, PayPal moves the money from one PayPal account to another. In this way, the seller has no access to your financial details and no one needs to enter any complicated account numbers and so on, once logged into the service.

This makes it ideal for online and mobile transactions, as it is secure, quick and easy to use. Unsurprisingly then, PayPal announced a two-click mobile payment system called Mobile Express Checkout back in October 2010 at its developer conference in San Francisco. The system allows for payment on mobile using just two clicks, and promises to get over the problem that besets all mobile payment tools: the balance between ease of use and security. PayPal Mobile Express Checkout uses all the security of PayPal that has made it so popular online and transfers it to mobile, so that merchants of any stripe can add a simple, quick and secure payment tool to their mobile offerings — something that is crucial to getting m-commerce up and running.

It will allow users to opt into the service and stay logged in between various mobile apps. PayPal says the new product is also easy to use for existing merchants who already use PayPal Express Checkout on their web-based stores.

Starbucks, one initial partner for Mobile Checkout Express, will use PayPal's newest mobile payment product to let customers quickly reload their Starbucks cards from within the company's iPhone app. Many of PayPal's beta-tester merchants for Mobile Express Checkout have reported double-digit sales growth on their mobile stores since adding the feature. PayPal plans to give Mobile Checkout Express merchants the ability to accept credit card payments in addition to PayPal (through a VeriFone partnership) in early 2011.

Amazon

One-click purchasing – one fewer click than PayPal Mobile Express – is pretty much the Holy Grail of mobile payments, and Amazon was one of the first retailers to crack it. The service relies on the user preregistering his card details, delivery address and all other information online (though you can also do it on mobile, through Amazon's app). This means that when you are shopping on mobile on Amazon and you want to purchase anything, you simply click on one button labeled Buy with Amazon 1-Click and that's it.

So long as there is money in your account or balance on the registered card, you have bought the item. It is simple, fast and uncomplicated, and is just what is needed for mobile commerce.

Patented by Apple as 1-Click, the process is a boon to mobile shoppers, as it makes purchasing simple and easy. There are plans as we go to press for Amazon to white label the product to other merchants, starting with Hallmark Cards in the US.

Apps stores

Apps stores, as we saw earlier in this book, are also turning out to be a great way to purchase things on mobile. Again, like PayPal and 1-Click, they rely on a card or bank details being preregistered, primarily so that you can easily buy apps. This, however, lends itself to adding in-app billing, which then lets you purchase things, real goods or digital goods, such as credit in games and so on, from within the app, all using the secure app stores setup.

On Apple and Android stores this process isn't quite "one click," as you have to also enter your password to make it work. But the security screen for doing this is optimized for the device, so it is relatively painless (until Apple suddenly decides, randomly, not to recognize your password, but that's another story), and quick and secure.

It is worth noting here that there are also other ways of doing in-app billing that don't rely on the apps store.

In-app billing

As mobile apps across all major platforms continue to flourish, a missing link has been a comprehensive mobile billing solution that works across all of them. Billing company Bango has joined a range of companies launching billing solutions that will let apps developers bill for things in-app across all the platforms they may find their app operating on. Bango claims that its in-app billing solution works seamlessly across Nokia/Symbian, Android, BlackBerry, Windows Mobile and iPhone.

The new solution is completely open, giving developers complete control over the experience, from how they charge consumers to pricing and currency, allowing them to sell content, virtual goods and add-ons from within their apps. This opens up a wide range of commercial opportunities no matter the platform developers are using.

Apps developers can collect one-time payments or start ongoing subscriptions within their app, using operator billing, credit cards or even PayPal. The goal is to provide consumers a simple and consistent application payment experience on operator networks, as well as over Wi-Fi. The new solution is aimed at developers who would rather have greater control over in-app billing and purchases, rather than relying on apps stores to provide the functionality.

A recent study by Bango found that 45% of developers plan to monetize their apps directly, outside of apps stores, making the case even stronger for an independent third-party solution. Though Apple and Google have launched their own in-app billing solutions that are tightly integrated with their corresponding apps stores, as more and more platforms become popular for development, a third-party solution that works across all of them will become more attractive.

Case study

In-app billing takes Virgin Media TV catch-up service mobile

Buying content within apps is becoming a crucial revenue stream for many companies - not least to pay for the development of the apps themselves - and mobile payments, naturally, are becoming a key way of billing for such services. A prime example of this is UK-based multimedia TV company Virgin Media. It developed an app for mobile and tablet that brings its TV catch-up service to those on the move. The only thing was, Virgin Media wanted to bill for access to this content in a quick and on-the-fly way, without the consumer having to leave the app.

The company worked with leading international billing company OpenMarket to develop an in-app billing tool for charging for pay-per-view. This allows consumers to put the charge of watching the service onto their phone bill quickly and easily. The key driver for this choice is the simplicity of mobile payments over alternative methods, which would require the user to enter more information to make a purchase, the company says.

The service uses a bespoke billing system designed and implemented jointly by Virgin Media and OpenMarket, called Customer, Pass Purchase and Subscriptions (COPPS). COPPS provides typical billing functionality with Virgin Media's content partners, as well as Network Lookup, geoblocking and customer care integration functionality. In order to enable mobile charging, Virgin Media uses OpenMarket's MSISDN (mobile subscriber ISDN number) passing and direct-billing capabilities to give the best possible user experience. Basically, this means the ability to pass on the unique ID of the phone, somewhere between a serial number and the mobile phone number of the SIM.

In-app billing infrastructure enables a content provider to carry out cross-network billing, and collect single payments as well as recurring subscriptions. It can easily be integrated into future applications, and Virgin Media is already planning the launch of a Music Player application that also allows in-app purchases of new singles.

In-app billing requires no development work by mobile network operators, as existing technology is used. OpenMarket has control over the SMS receipt, so the user will be informed of exactly how much he has been charged. The payment screens follow the PayForIt model, which is the standard set by UK network operators for on and off-portal charging.

. . . and the rest

Mobile payment is such a huge area that there are also many services that are hard to categorize, combining a bit of banking with some lateral thinking. As we shall see further on in this chapter, mobile is ideally suited to electronic wallets and the joys of turning your phone into a bank card and using it to pay for goods and services in shops and elsewhere.

But before we get there, it is worth looking at some of the other novel ways in which mobile is being used as a payment tool. Mobile payments have entered the retail market with an unexpected bang, as coffee giant Starbucks announced plans to let caffeine-seeking consumers pay for their coffee using mobile payments on selected smartphones in the US through the company's loyalty app. In effect, creating the largest mobile payment program in the world to date.

Starbucks bucks the trend in how coffee chains use loyalty. Its card doesn't accrue points as others do, but rather is used as a charge card to pay for drinks at point of sale. The coffee drinker charges the card up with money, and then uses it to spend. The loyalty aspect comes from repeat use resulting in cheaper coffee, so less money comes off the card. In 2010, $1.5bn was put on Starbucks' cards worldwide.

Some time ago Starbucks realized that this process could be streamlined and turned into a USP (a unique selling point) for the company if it was combined with mobile. Its research found that one in five of its customers had a loyalty card, and that more than a third used a smartphone, the vast majority toting iPhones and BlackBerrys. So the company has worked on how to get these users to start using mobile to pay. And the obvious place to start was with an app.

Customers use the app to pay with their smartphone by holding their device in front of a scanner on the countertop, which scans the Starbucks card mobile app's on-screen bar code to make a purchase.

In addition to the mobile payment capability, the app allows customers to manage their Starbucks card account, check their card balance, reload their card with any major credit card (iPhone users can also use the PayPal feature), check their My Starbucks Rewards status and find a nearby Starbucks store.

Test markets in Seattle, Northern California, New York and more than 1,000 Starbucks in US Target stores have seen extensive use of the app, and the company plans to roll it out across all 6,800 US branches and eventually into Europe.

The Starbucks example is interesting, since in one simple move – the creation of an app version of its loyalty card – it has created a working model of how mobile payments could work, without having to garner the involvement of operators or anyone else. It is, of course, a closed user group, and no one wants to have to use a different app for each store they shop in and manage multiple accounts. Still, it shows that there is a hunger for mobile payments and, when targeted at the correct user demographic, it can work.

Credit card companies strike back

Not to be outdone, credit and debit card companies are also maneuvering, albeit slowly, to offer forms of mobile payment. While many are betting the farm on contactless payments using NFC (see below), some are looking more speculatively as to how they can get their payment tools in front of users on mobile through some of the other facets of mobile retail.

MasterCard and CitiCards, the payment card arm of Citibank, are both using their brands to develop not only the payment tools for e- and m-commerce, but are also looking at how to create virtual shopping malls that combine loyalty programs and mobile payments in one offering.

CitiCards is developing a comparative shopping app that lets users buy at preferential prices when using their CitiCard. Similarly, MasterCard is offering a "personalized shopping platform with multiple deals all in one place." In other words, a shopping mall on mobile, where you have to pay using your MasterCard to get the best service and the best price.

Both these trials, localized around key US cities for now, are indicative of banks getting closer to m-commerce, offering both a storefront for merchants and a payment tool. However, while retailers may be threatened to a degree by the encroachment of banks into the retail side of business, the moves should be welcomed. One of the main pain points with mobile commerce is payments, and, if nothing else, these projects are getting banks and card companies involved in ameliorating that payment pain.

These are just two examples of how big brands in retail and banking are thinking laterally when it comes to mobile payments, and serve as a reminder that this is a very fluid and dynamic field, with many players – banks, card companies, operators, brands, retailers, merchants, handset makers, apps developers and third-party payment providers – all vying to get a slice of the vast revenues that mobile money is almost certain to deliver.

NFC and contactless payments

Near Field Communications (NFC) doesn't sound, on the face of it, like the next big thing in anything, let alone in the fabulously zetigeist-y world of mobile. Nonetheless, NFC is set to be something that everyone connected with mobile will be talking about in 2011 – not least because Apple and Google are likely to start using it in their next generation handsets. (The fact that Nokia already has in one range of its phones has been widely ignored, a testament to how the mighty can fall.)

To quote the Wireless Federation: "NFC is a short-range wireless connectivity technology based on magnetic field induction and is intended primarily for simple and secure communications between two electronic devices in close proximity to each other"; or contactlessly, if you prefer to make up words like I do. Already in use in some smart cards for payments (Visa payWave) and for ticketing (London's Oyster Card in the UK, not to mention on the Chinese Guangshen Railway Company and on Norway's state railways), NFC is becoming part of everyday life for a lucky few. It is also ideally suited to turning mobiles into payment tools. A simple wafting of the device near the right NFC receiver, and money can be transferred to make a payment. It is the ideal move toward turning the phone from a payment device to an extension of your bank account, and so NFC is one of the core reasons why mobile commerce is set to be so important to business in the coming years.

Nokia in particular has long been a champion of NFC in mobile, and has so far been the only handset maker to roll out a handset with NFC built in: the Nokia 6131 NFC phone. It has yet to set the public imagination alight, but is a start.

Google is also now pushing the idea of NFC, with NFC being built into the latest iteration of its open Android operating system. Outgoing Google CEO Eric Schmidt claims that NFC will make bank and credit cards redundant.

Microsoft is also rumored to be planning an NFC-enabled handset; a rumor given more weight by the company's partnership with Nokia to build smartphones with the Windows 7 OS built in.

Samsung is also planning a range of NFC-enabled handsets. It aims for an initial launch in 2012 in time for the London Olympics, which is set to demonstrate to the world that NFC and mobile together can be used for ticketing, payments and a host of other things.

And no one interested in mobile could have escaped the news that Apple's next iPhone, the iPhone 5, will also feature NFC; although this has been an on-again, off-again rumor that will only be resolved when the handset finally arrives.

Japanese operator SoftBank has managed to bring the iPhone and NFC together, developing an NFC payments sticker that covers the back of the iPhone 4. It doesn't connect with the phone, but is one of those nice developments that lets consumers be gently introduced to an idea before it really takes off.

Case study

Turkey: leading the way in NFC-based payments

One of the leading marketplaces where NFC-based mobile banking is actually up and running is Turkey, where Garanti Bank, the country's largest private bank by asset size, and Avea, Turkey's sole GSM mobile operator, have joined forces to provide Turkish mobile phone users with NFC-enabled SIM cards that remove the need to buy NFC-enabled handsets.

The SIM cards were developed in conjunction with MasterCard and technology company Gemalto. Geranti Bank customers simply get a new NFC-enabled SIM card from the bank – provided they have signed up with Avea, of course – that they pop into their handset and away they go.

The service leverages Garanti's existing Bonus Trink (pay pass) service, which already, thanks to an NFC sticker that can be applied to almost anything, allows users to make payments of up to 35 Turkish lira contactlessly. Mobile phone users will now have the option to make payments this way too, thanks to the NFC SIM card, which will take money from either the Garanti credit card they have assigned to the SIM or by using prepaid credit.

Consumers with the SIM card will also be able to use their mobile phone to pay for public transport where contactless functionality is available, as well as being used as identification to gain access to buildings, as a ticket to football games or concerts, and to pay for items at numerous vending machines across Turkey. It even allows users to download additional apps onto the phone to pay motorway tolls.

What this all means is that NFC is gaining momentum in the mobile sphere and could well start to become an accepted aspect of everyday mobile life.

In fact, according to the Wireless Federation, worldwide shipments of mobile phones with built-in NFC capability will rise to 220.1 million units in 2014, up by a factor of four from 52.6 million in 2010. In 2014, 13% of cell phones shipped will integrate NFC, up from 4.1% in 2010.

Much of this growth is expected to come from the developed world, and moves are already underway to start to launch NFC-enabled services. For instance, Monitise, which describes itself as "a global mobile money solutions provider," has joined forces with NFC software developer ViVOtech to deliver mobile phone payments services to banks across America. The partnership means customers of participating banks will be able to turn their handsets into mobile wallets (linked to registered bank accounts, credit and debit cards) and purchase items using contactless payments at merchants with NFC capabilities. They will also have the ability to transfer money and redeem coupons and vouchers.

Emerging markets such as China are also seeking to take a lead in this NFC boom. Nokia, HTC and TCL Communications are all planning to roll out NFC handsets in China in the second half of 2011, and are hoping for explosive growth in this huge market. They are working with China UniPay, the Chinese bank card industry association, to develop handsets and services, and expect to see the market grow from 2012.

But while NFC seemingly sits at the heart of many of the commercial offerings people want to make with mobile, not least payment, there are issues with it that may yet cause it not to be quite the hit that some are predicting.

The biggest hurdle NFC has to overcome, certainly as a payment tool, is that the infrastructure needed to let people use it in stores — particularly small stores — is not there, and it seems unclear as to who will be prepared to pay to roll this technology out to any widespread degree. Could the sheer weight of companies that are getting behind it force it to happen, with the banks, operators, phone makers and merchants all paying toward rolling out the redemption infrastructure?

The fact that NFC can also be used with other kinds of payment cards, as well as a much faster alternative for phone-to-phone file transfer than Bluetooth, mark it as a technology that, due to its wider reach than just as a mobile payment tech, may well make it more likely to gain the traction it needs to succeed.

Case study

Painting the town mobile

If you really want to know how well consumers from all walks of life will embrace contactless mobile payments - or not - you need to turn a whole town into a test site. And that is exactly what leading Spanish bank La Caixa did between May and December 2010 - they turned 500 shops and 1500 bank customers in the town of Sitges into contactless guinea pigs.

Each person was given an NFC-enabled Samsung Star Touch phone that effectively acts as a Visa card. The 500 merchants – everything from bars and restaurants to shoe shops and even market stalls – were given the redemption technology. After six months, the bank concluded that 80% of those involved in the trial – the average age of whom was 48 – were extremely satisfied with the service, and the trial has been extended due to popular demand. Of those that didn't give it the thumbs up, the main complaint was that not all the shops in the town accepted NFC payments, or that they didn't like the phone itself.

The majority (60%) of goods and services paid for with the NFC phones were under €20 ($28) – above that amount, a PIN was required – with the average spend per transaction coming in at about €10 ($14). The other 40% were above €20, averaging a sturdy €60 ($85). Interestingly, no instances of fraud were recorded, and most people involved in the trial – both users and merchants – said they would use it again.

What the trial showed is that with the devices and infrastructure in place, the general public finds these services easy to use and embraces them keenly. Many transactions – the 60% under €20 ($28)– point to most users seeing this sort of thing as being a cash replacement. But with 40% also spending on average €60 ($85) with PIN verification, many clearly also see it as an alternative to card payments.

What the trial doesn't quite show is how well this would pan out in the real world. It was, after all, a trial, and everyone involved would have been acutely aware of the novelty factor and that they were being monitored. Whether the success in Sitges can be replicated everywhere remains to be seen – especially the lack of criminality – but it is a good indicator of how NFC-based mobile payments is likely to work.

Mobile wallets

While there is much focus on how to use the mobile phone as a payment conduit, a lot of attention has been focused on how to turn the mobile into a connected extension of your bank account: the mobile electronic wallet (also known as the me-wallet or more commonly just m-wallet).

The premise is that you build into the phone a chip much like the eponymous chip of the PIN variety that you find on credit and debit cards, and then you NFC-enable it. This then acts, in conjunction with your bank account or credit card account, as a payment tool.

Using NFC you can wave the wallet around an NFC reader and pay for things, much as NFC is used in Oyster Cards in London to contactlessly check in and out of the London Underground. The advantages of this are that it connects your wallet to the network and all of your internal phone-based life – contacts, address books, apps and so on – and so makes it easier to pay for things, pay people and all that.

In practice, it does however offer some challenges, not least of which is, how do you call your bank to report your phone stolen?

The idea of turning your phone into a wallet is nothing new and has had a long and pretty unsuccessful history to date. The thinking goes that you have your phone and wallet with you all the time, so why not combine the two? (Apart from not having anywhere to put all my receipts, the thinking is sound.) But so far it has not really happened. Talk that Apple and Google are both now looking at it – thanks to the inclusion of chips (possibly) in their next generation of smartphones – makes the idea that storing money and card information on the phone is a great idea again.

But Nokia, which has sold more handsets than any other company, has already tried to NFC-enable one range of its mobiles, and has seen little or no interest from either the banks, the networks, nor the consumer in turning the phone into a payment device with a direct link to the bank.

Case study

M-wallets work for 15 million users in Japan

One place where mobile wallets seem to be a big hit is in Japan. NTT DOCOMO, the nation's leading mobile operator, announced recently that subscriptions to iD, its branded platform for using post-paid electronic money with DOCOMO handsets and compatible credit cards, had topped 15 million nationwide.

Launched in December 2005, iD reached five million subscribers in November 2007, 10 million in December 2008 and 15 million in August 2010, just four years and nine months since the launch. DOCOMO promoted the use of iD by offering an increasing number of compatible handsets and cards, as well as adding more opportunities to use the iD services. The number of subscribers using handsets equipped with contactless IC chips (Osaifu-Keitai) compatible with iD has surpassed 37.5 million, representing over 60% of all DOCOMO subscribers.

DOCOMO offers a credit payment service known as DCMX, and 67 credit card companies, such as Sumitomo Mitsui Card Company, Limited, are currently offering credit payment services via iD. A number of companies provide iD-enabled plastic credit cards in addition to Osaifu-Keitai handsets. Currently, there are approximately 481,000 iD-enabled payment terminals nationwide, which allow users to make payments just by waving compatible mobile phones or cards over them.

More than 90% of all convenience stores in Japan accept iD, including all ampm and 7-Eleven stores, which completed the installation of iD terminals in all their stores nationwide in December 2006 and July 2010 respectively. Seicomart plans to install the terminals in all of its stores in October 2011. Today, iD can also be used at McDonald's locations, Coca-Cola vending machines and electronics retailers, as well as in taxi cabs and shopping malls. According to a survey by the Japan Franchise Association, the average purchase amount is over 20% higher if the customer pays via iD only.

As a result of expanding opportunities and the benefits of using iD, over 16 million transactions were made in June 2010 alone. DOCOMO is also supporting stores using iD by implementing marketing initiatives and service enhancements possible only with mobile phones.

Having banking details built into the phone as part of an m-wallet means that should you be on the phone doing a bit of shopping, gaming, app-buying, gambling or any other commercial business, you can pay very simply, direct from your bank account, using the built-in banking chip. This may well, should it take off, put the kibosh on all other forms of mobile payment, as it is built in, easy to use and totally at the control of the phone user. We'll have to wait and see.

Do the bump

Just one last bit on payment tools before we look at what banks are hoping to do with mobile commerce: the bump. Version 2.0 of PayPal's iPhone payment app allows users to pay one another simply by bumping their iPhones together (though not too hard now, kids, as the screens can crack and they cost a bomb to replace and it'll void your warranty).

The app also allows for users to send money using PayPal to contacts in the phone's contacts list, the transfer of funds from PayPal to your bank account and a tip calculator.

Mobile banking

While mobile operators and the rest of the mobile ecosystem are eyeing mobile as a payment channel, a mobile wallet and so on, the banks are also looking at what they can get out of this newly mobilized audience of commercially minded consumers. It is set to be a huge market – not to mention a huge battle between the operators, the banks and, to some degree, the likes of Apple and Google, as to who owns you, the customer.

According to research by Berg Insight, the worldwide number of users of mobile banking and related services is forecasted to grow at a compound annual growth rate (CAGR) of 89%, from 20 million users in 2008 to 913 million users in 2014.

Asia-Pacific is expected to become the most important regional market, accounting for 65% of the total user base. Mobile banking is also anticipated to play a key role in bringing financial services to people in the Middle East and Africa. In Europe and North America, the technology will mainly serve as an extension of existing online banks as mobile handsets become more widely used for Internet access. By 2014, Berg Insight forecasts that mobile banking will attract 110 million users in Europe and 80 million users in North America.

Interestingly, a study by Simon-Kucher & Partners, a global strategy and marketing consultancy, found that, in the UK at least, 76% of people aged 18–26 want to do their banking via mobile. Even more surprisingly, many of these would be willing to pay up to £5 ($8) per month for the convenience of the service.

This means that the interest in mobile banking worldwide is not just a new channel for banks to worry about, but also one that could, in theory at least, deliver a new revenue stream.

So what do consumers want to do with mobile banking services? According to the Simon-Kucher study, it falls into three distinct areas:

- **Informational:** balance details, overdraft warnings and promotions were preferred by 80% of those surveyed, and balance checking was the most important informational service for 60%.
- **Transactional:** paying for things, moving money around and so on (69%), and blocking lost/stolen cards was the most essential transactional service (94%).
- **Interactive:** contacting the bank, fraud monitoring, security and other banking services (53%) and fraud monitoring was the most important interactive mobile banking service (87%).

Research by VocaLink, an international payment specialist, however, has found that the ability to make inter-bank payments immediately via a mobile phone holds a strong appeal for the modern consumer, due to its speed and convenience.

According to its research, rather than using cash, check or card, immediate payments would be the most popular payment method option for transferring money to friends or family (53%) and when paying urgent bills (44%). Consumers would also be willing to pay 5p (8 cents) per transaction to use the service.

The smartphone generation is already engaging with mobile banking services and is receptive to apps, mobile Internet sites and text messages; but it is also eager for banks to provide more proactive services to help them keep control of their finances, according to mobile marketing company Sponge. It surveyed 450 consumers via the mobile Internet in August 2010, and found that 44% claimed to already use the mobile Internet, apps or text messaging to interact with their banks; and more than one in four said they did so frequently.

Of those who didn't bank via their mobile phone (56%), two-thirds said they would be significantly more likely to use such services if they owned a smartphone. Smartphone penetration in the UK is growing at 70% per annum (source: comScore) and is likely to reach 25 million subscribers by the end of 2012.

Although the majority of respondents associated mobile banking with standard control features, such as checking their balance (almost half (49%) rated this the most useful function) Sponge's research also revealed a clear appetite for more proactive services. Specific areas of interest included a text-based customer service facility (48%), a mobile service that prompts customers to move funds around in order to maximize their rate of return (17%), and a location-based service offering consumers discounts or other rewards from retailers when they use their bank card (26%).

Awareness of and interest in mobile banking services is currently focused on standard features. Just over a quarter (26%) found viewing ministatements the most useful function, while 9% found bill payment options best. A further 9% felt the ability to transfer money between accounts most useful, and 6% preferred an alert function when they were about to overdraw their account.

Case study

Monitise powers up Ireland's first mobile banking app

Ulster Bank in Ireland has become one of the first banks in Europe to roll out a fully functioning iPhone-based banking app. The app, which uses the platform from mobile money network Monitise, will enable the bank to deliver a suite of services including:

- Balance checks
- Ministatements
- Automatic text alerts.

In addition to the iPhone app, Monitise and Ulster Bank plan to launch a range of SMS-based mobile banking options for customers in the Republic of Ireland too, so that the vast majority of the bank's customers who don't have an iPhone can also take advantage of Ulster Bank's move into mobile banking.

ACTION POINTS

- **Use mobile payments when selling digital and virtual goods.** If you run an online business selling digital or virtual goods, or are looking to try to make money through social media, you should be looking at mobile payments.
- **Shop around for the payment tool or tools to suit your customers' needs.** If your customer base is young, they will be mobile savvy but probably won't have a bank account, so look for on-bill mobile billing tools. If your customers are older, look for a mobile payments tie-in with a card, bank account or PayPal.
- **Factor hidden charges into your costs.** Network operators and billing service providers will each take a cut. Networks take up to 60% in some countries, while service providers typically ask for single-digit percentage commissions.
- **Put yourself in a position to negotiate terms.** If you're confident you'll sell successfully via mobile and can back it up, you'll be able to cut a favorable deal. See what's the best you can get from an operator billing solution.

- **Don't buy a mobile payments solution until you know what standards are going to be used and how.** If you want to sell real-world goods either online or in a store, then hold fire until the banks, network operators and card companies have worked out how it's going to work.
- **Keep abreast of latest developments.** This is a fast-moving space and currently there is a lot of heat around mobile payments, so keep tabs on the media and supplier websites for details of what's changing in this space.

CHAPTER 10

Present and future mobile technology

Mobile technology development moves so fast, it's often hard to keep up with it. In fact, in the time it took you to read that last sentence, something will have changed in terms of how a network works, or a new device will have launched, a new service or new strategy will have been devised somewhere in the world. And there goes another one. And another. You get the idea.

This of course makes future-proofing any mobile strategy you have very difficult, but it is essential. While many businesses stand at the threshold of taking that leap into the mobile world, most don't consider how quickly things change, and it is vital that any decision made today – especially if you are to invest heavily in it – at least tries to take into account what may happen in the months and years ahead.

Investing in a mobile commerce strategy can be expensive for both small and large businesses, and you have to carefully consider the return of investment (ROI) period in light of the fact that you may be investing over five years in something that, in two, will no longer fit the purpose.

However, knowing exactly what is going to change is very difficult. So anyone who is charging you to implement a mobile strategy must offer you a transparent view of how their solution can either be adapted or is scalable enough to cope, as far as is possible, with the unknown.

Typically, there are three areas where mobile technology can change the game:

Networks

The skeleton of mobile on which everything else hangs. These can be both operator-owned or, increasingly, things like Wi-Fi that offer alternatives to operator networks. Users demand more and more bandwidth to do evermore complex tasks.

Devices

The sexy bit that sits in the customer's hand. This has a habit of changing incrementally over a number of years, and then something comes along that completely reshapes the entire industry. Witness the iPhone. There is a distinct pre-iPhone world of mobile phones (very hard to use, designed by engineers in Finland and pretty much rubbish), and then the iPhone made everyone look at better user interfaces, touchscreens and more. Oh, and then there are tablets . . .

Services

The kind of things you can do with your handset. This incorporates everything from billing and payments, to apps, to mobile web and all that is likely to come in between. What third-party designers are going to come up with to run on mobile is anyone's guess, but the impact that has on a business is positive, as it offers new ways to engage customers and sell more things. This is the upside of the rapidly changing mobile world.

Networks

Networks are the bones that hold up the whole mobile ecosystem and are a good starting point for looking at mobile technological development. What the operators now find themselves up against is a consumer base that wants to use mobile networks for many things they were not designed for. These networks were designed for voice, with some non-time-critical messaging and web traffic over the top.

The iPhone and the creation of a true mobile-commerce platform has inspired consumers to want to access information from complex sources, get reams of data delivered to them, and even transact, live and securely, while out and about. This is not what networks were designed for and, as anyone who tries to use them on a regular basis as I do will find, they are simply not up to the job — and are getting worse.

But operators and network-technology providers, while slow to react, are well aware of the problems, and the technology is out there to make mobile networks extremely fast, reliable and capable of handling many millions more users than they do now. The trouble is, this is expensive. And at a time when users don't see mobile as something they will pay a premium for, but rather something of a right, operators no longer have the vast amounts to invest in new network technology.

So what is out there?

4G
4G is really a requirement rather than an actual technology, and has been defined by the ITU (International Telecommunication Union) as the "IMT-Advanced (International Mobile Telecommunications Advanced) requirements for 4G standards, setting peak speed requirements for 4G service at 100 Mbit/s for high mobility communication (such as from trains and cars) and 1Gbit/s for low mobility communication (such as pedestrians and stationary users)."

LTE (Long Term Evolution) Advanced
While there is still no definitive technology being implemented as 4G per se, there are many that are being rolled out and tested as candidate technologies for this role. One of these is LTE Advanced, which rather than being a new technology is an improved version of an existing one, and offers a level of service that is better than the ITU's stipulations for how 4G should perform, running at about 500Mb/s to 1Gb/s download rates.

LTE is also being rolled out commercially, with AT&T offering it as a new network service in some regions of the US. However, it is offering this, initially, as a mobile broadband service for laptops, with some plans to start running 4G devices on it when they are available (see Devices below).

Wi-Fi

Wi-Fi has been with us for many years and is essentially a local area networking technology that allows devices fitted with the right hardware to connect to a local router using the short-range capabilities of these radio services. Link all the Wi-Fi routers together into a network, however, and suddenly it becomes an interesting potential alternative to the mobile network operators.

And it has proved popular. Some 700 million people use Wi-Fi worldwide, according to the Wi-Fi Alliance, with some 4 million public Wi-Fi hotspots (places where you can connect to a Wi-Fi router publicly and get on the network from there). About 800 million new Wi-Fi devices come online every year, including smartphones, games consoles, computers and MP3 players, all of them mobile to some degree.

Not quite, then, a new technology, so where does it go next? Well, it gets more prevalent, is one way of looking at it. Rather than it being a massive technological leap forward that will impact on your mobile commerce offering, it could well be that more and more connectivity is done through Wi-Fi rather than network operators.

The impact of this on commerce is potentially huge. Much of mobile commerce, as we have seen, is predicated on using network operators' networks, and therefore their billing systems, to transact; and this means that the network operators can take a (often sizeable) cut. Wi-Fi connectivity means this doesn't happen. Wi-Fi connectivity of mobile devices puts them onto the web, and so the web's rules apply.

This could result in a much more e-commerce-like approach to mobile commerce: offering the same payment tools, same commercial rates and a similar experience (tailored to the screen and device limitations, naturally). This changes the dynamic of mobile commerce as we know it today – cutting out the markup needed on some goods and services that are in place to accommodate network-operator charges.

Second, increasing use of Wi-Fi also makes for more of an always-on culture within the mobile-consumer base. This means that they will do more and use more; and, so the argument goes, use more mobile network operator services too – when they find themselves in areas not covered by Wi-Fi.

This is why UK network operator O2, part of the massive Telefónica Group, has laid out plans to roll out its own free Wi-Fi network. O2 suffers from capacity issues on its mobile network, as it has a high proportion of iPhone users. The free Wi-Fi service helps alleviate this, but it also encourages more use of mobile and so more data use, which could, in theory, pay for "proper" network upgrades.

WiMAX

A sort of stopgap mobile broadband technology that offers around 40Mb/s data speeds, WiMAX was developed as Wi-Fi on steroids to deliver wireless coverage across, say, a city or a community, and to offer an alternative to cabling up residential or business areas at great expense. But, as the need for more mobile broadband connectivity has increased, some people are revisiting WiMAX as a way of delivering not quite 4G, but better-than-Wi-Fi coverage in defined areas.

WiMAX can also be rapidly deployed, and taken away again, and so it offers some interesting opportunities for setting it up around specific events, such as music festivals or sporting events. This gets around the issue of network coverage for advanced mobile services involving thousands of people in one place, and the potential cost of setting up something permanent.

The opportunity is huge, allowing, for example, a music festival the chance to offer advertisers and sponsors mobile channels to all those consumers over a broadband wireless network tied to that festival. In return, the mud-encrusted festival goers get free mobile broadband access in return for some ads or ad content from sponsors while at the festival.

The cloud

The launch of Apple's iCloud service – which took a disproportionate amount of headline space, despite being third out of the gate after Google and Amazon's cloud offerings – has once and for all focused minds on this thing called the cloud.

The cloud – short for cloud computing – has been with us for many years and is a simple concept: you stick all the software on a remote server that "dumb" devices then use via the web. Many businesses have been doing it for almost a decade, buying in Software as a Service (SaaS) from providers as a way of having the latest services that are maintained, updated and kept running by someone else.

Taking this public has become de rigueur in the late 2000s, and iCloud is just one more step along this path.

So what is the cloud? In mobile commerce terms, it is simply a way of putting software, data, content, products, payment tools – anything really – on a remote server farm somewhere in (to use Apple again as the yardstick) North Carolina, and letting devices with web connections use and access them from wherever they are.

The principle is simple and very appealing. Devices don't need massive and ever growing – and costly – memory storage, as all the content created and consumed, plus all the software the device needs, is stored somewhere else. This means that it can be held securely, can be backed up and, in theory, never lost. It means that software can be updated once for millions of users, and devices can become smaller, lighter and less expensive.

In practice all the above is true; the only weak link is the network. For a device to function if all its software is in the cloud, or for users to stream music or look at their photos, the device has to have a robust connection to the data server. And as more and more people do this over 3G, public Wi-Fi and even the fixed-line Internet, the connection speeds, and the effectiveness of cloud computing, become unworkable.

There is also the issue of security: that someone who is not you could get hold of your stuff is a large negative. But it is nothing to the network issues.

The fact that Apple, Google and Amazon, not to mention streaming services such as Spotify, all think that the cloud offers them something is heartening, but given the trouble most people have getting Google Maps to work at rush hour in a city center, I wouldn't like to be relying on the networks for everything else my phone does.

Devices

I have always been obsessed with mobile handsets, ever since I got my first one in the early 1990s. Looking back, it was horrible, and I suspect it appealed to the toy soldier in me in that it looked very much like a walkie-talkie from the 1970s. But over the decades mobile phones have morphed from ugly and expensive to things that, to my eye at least, are beautiful: the harmonious combination of form and function.

The advent of the smartphone (typically the iPhone, but I do have a roving eye for other brands, flibbertigibbet that I am) took this even further. These devices were now beautiful to look at, beautiful to use (touchscreens – why did we wait so long for you?) and very powerful. They were true multimedia devices that were no longer just about calling people, but could access the web, pick up e-mail, watch TV and videos, share stuff, and generally offer developers a platform on which to let their imaginations run riot.

So, it is no surprise that devices are very much the cornerstone of the technological future of mobile commerce. The tricky part is deciding what is in store for them in the coming years, and whether we have seen a step change, from handset to smartphone, and future changes will be incremental, or whether there are more radical step changes to come. Here is my take on it.

Smarter smartphones

Incrementally, smartphones will become more powerful, with better screens, better connectivity, greater storage capacity and better battery life — all in smaller bodies. They will rely more on the cloud, with some devices servicing the lower end of the market, becoming "cloud phones" only, with everything being online. This, I believe, will be the key to mass-market m-commerce, and anyone looking to have a mobile commerce presence will have to have an app, a mobile-optimized website and a cloud-based app service.

Step change-wise, I think that at some point in the next 10 years we will see devices with much greater intelligence. They will make decisions about what to access, how to access it and what to do with it for the user. I think we will also see a shift in how devices are interacted with, and hence, how content is interacted with, from jabbing with fingers, to speech-based, to, eventually, being thought controlled.

This last step is not as far-fetched as you might think. There is already a company called NeuroSky that is selling "brain-computer interface technologies" that take the form of a headset that puts thoughts into rudimentary actions on a computer. Aimed currently at the gaming market, these devices harness medical-grade technology to use brain impulses to control game play — literally thinking of what you want to happen. It takes a bit of practice, but is really quite astonishing once you get it working. It is but a short step to turning this into a computer controller – which encompasses our smartphones of the future – and this would radically reshape the device market.

Totally tablets

Rooted more in the here and now, the next evolution of mobile technology, and therefore mobile commerce, is the tablet computer. As we have seen throughout this book, tablets are like smartphones' bigger, more powerful sisters, and there is every possibility that they will replace laptops and PCs in the home environment in the coming decade.

Harnessing the portability and personal nature of mobile phones, these devices will become the portal through which we engage with brands and businesses when we don't want to do it via our smartphones.

Google's, Amazon's and Apple's cloud strategies all tip their caps at a PC-free future, certainly in the home; the office is a different matter, and one which uses the tablet as a content-consumption device.

Tablets in this instance are pretty revolutionary. Right now they are a high-end item used by relatively few people. But they look set to revolutionize how people consume, interact and entertain themselves. They are books. They are TVs. They are e-mail and social chat devices. They are shopping malls. They are bank accounts. They are, in fact, a window onto anything on the web and in the real world. They are very powerful indeed.

Well, that's the idea behind them, once they become mass-market. Are they the future of mobile commerce? Well, they are certainly part of it. Their development is likely to follow the same trajectory as the smartphone – better, more powerful, more versatile, and using a mix of apps, m-web and cloud computing. They will also see the move to mind control. Where else they might go is, like all of this, anyone's guess.

Libraries, shops, malls, planes, trains, buses, stations and many other public spaces may also start to see tablets cropping up. Stores in particular are likely to arm their shop assistants with them, and some may even start giving devices to shoppers, especially in malls. It could change the shape of how we shop.

On transport, particularly aircraft, tablets may soon replace in-flight entertainment systems, just so long as they can be locked so that if anyone takes them, they don't work.

Wireless appliances (and clothing)
All phones and tablets are personal to a large degree, but in the future I think we will see more and more "things" have Wi-Fi and even SIM-based wireless broadband connectivity. The intelligent fridge and even the intelligent trash have long been predicted, ever since computers connected to the web. The idea is that taking stuff out of the fridge or putting stuff in the bin tells the fridge or bin what you have used or thrown away, and it can order more.

This idea is likely to be taken even further, with all household electrical goods being connected to the web so that they can be updated, monitored and can communicate with the world – ordering shopping and so on.

Taking this idea further still, there could be web-enabled clothing to, for example, track children, or to allow your clothes to download music, or check in on social media, or communicate with friends. We can take the idea of communications to ludicrous new heights.

The benefit for retailers and advertisers is that these are yet more opportunities to engage with consumers and sell things. The benefit for consumers is that they get to feel evermore part of things (often while unknowingly drifting away from their fellow humans).

Linking all devices together

The real power of the mobile commerce world of the future is when you link all of them together: wirelessly.

Apple has started this with its iCloud service, which will let anyone with multiple Apple devices sync everything between them. So you take a photo on your iPhone, and it's immediately available on your MacBook, iPod and iPad.

Taking this one step further, linking all your devices, household appliances and TVs to the web is one thing. Letting them share everything among themselves starts to create a more joined-up vision of digital life. There is nothing that you can't access in some relevant form wherever you are. Buy once, use again and again and again. Keep tabs on everything you like, know and do.

This is the likely scenario for the home and life of the near future as the Internet becomes the fabric that holds everything together.

What a terrifying thought. The only chink of light is that networks will always remain so overloaded as all this stuff is added, despite investments in bandwidth, that it will never really work properly, and you can go about your business without having to watch *The X Factor* on your washing machine.

Wireless power

Okay, so to rein it in a bit, the devices, and their connectedness, of the future is all well and good, but we still have one massive problem (networks aside) to contend with when it comes to really exploiting mobile technology: power.

Batteries have improved, and continue to improve, radically every year. While your smartphone may have the computing power of around 10 space shuttles, they are power hungry; yet the battery life is still about a day of moderate use. That's progress.

However, this isn't enough in the long term. To have truly portable devices that are buried in everyday items or in your clothes, or even just to have better tablets and smartphones, something needs to be done about power. The obvious solution is to charge things wirelessly: taking power from the air wherever you are so that watching your battery bars decline becomes a thing of the past.

The science of delivering power through the air is not new: magnetic induction does the job already. Plans are already afoot to deliver power this way, but there are many hurdles.

What is challenging is getting it to work without upsetting the delicate electronics of the devices sucking up the power, or without harming people living and working in these fields. There is also the issue of efficiency: it is far from 100% efficient to convert electricity into magnetism, waft it about the place and then convert it back into electricity in a load of devices.

There are also plans to try to carry power using microwaves and even lasers – pioneered by NASA – so that electricity-hungry devices can work for days, weeks or months without being plugged in (or in space, where there are no plugs).

The other school of thought on this is to make devices much more efficient so that they use less power while doing more. This is the iterative approach to improving the future of devices, and the one that is really key to the short-term future of the mobile device.

A whole new media

Better devices and better networks will make content richer and easier to consume, and this won't be lost on what we used to call the newspaper industry. Already newspaper and magazine publishers are moving – some faster than others – to offering extremely rich media products. Increasingly this will combine the written word with video, diagrams and even 3D graphics to create living newspapers that you can almost literally climb into.

In fact, these devices and networks will reshape the media industry as we know it, removing the demarcations between TV, print, books, music and games. It will all just become content that is consumed in different ways and on different devices, packaged in different bundles. After all, it's all entertainment and people will pay to be entertained.

Everything will be held in the cloud and can be accessed on the fly by whatever device. The payment side will be based on packages of what you can do (wholesale) or per use, and will debited on the go using accounts that can be topped up by the user online.

This new new media will incorporate unparalleled levels of interactivity between user, content, content creators and other users. The idea of having a newspaper laid out with someone else's idea of what the lead story should be, or watching a TV program or movie at a specific time when someone else tells you to, will seem deeply odd. We will all be creating and editing our own content streams, intelligently tailored and managed by the devices and the networks and the cloud, giving us the feeling that we are in control.

What does this mean for you?

So what does all this mean for anyone looking to make money from mobile commerce? Well, better networks mean a better experience for consumers, which means more consumers using mobile to do commercial things, which means better ROI on your mobile investments. Simple.

Better, faster and "fatter" networks also mean that you can do more with your mobile offerings – so the whole mobile experience becomes richer and more rewarding for consumers. Take augmented reality, for instance. AR, as we saw earlier in the book, offers the chance to overlay images and information on the real world when viewed through the smartphone camera. The only problem is that it requires a lot of data and data processing. The processing is the preserve of the handset (see next section), but the data streaming that makes it work smoothly and as advertised comes from better network connections. Better networks will make AR suddenly worth investing in, as it will work well and offer a compelling service that people will come back to.

Similarly with mobile retail sites, mapping, price comparison, visual search – where you use a photo of an object to find out what it is – and much more. Better network connectivity suddenly makes all these things work. And once they work, consumers will want to use them. Once that happens, they become not only essential for business competitiveness, but also worth investing in, as they have a clearly defined ROI.

For anyone looking to invest in mobile commerce, the device end of things has everything and nothing to do with where you put your money. What all these future trends for devices do is make it easier for people to get online and buy things. More devices, and more variety of devices, mean that there is evermore opportunity to sell things to people.

Any sort of entertainment device or content-consumption unit can generate revenue through advertising and from direct sales of everything from digital goods to real-world bits and pieces. Connected household appliances allow for targeted sales of things pertinent to that device. In all, it opens up new channels to market, and while they may cannibalize some existing revenue streams, they offer the chance to sell more simply by giving the opportunity.

In-car connectivity also offers a new channel, and also a new captive audience that is liable to be susceptible to having certain things marketed to them: games to play on long journeys, facts about their destination, and even information about traffic, weather and alternative routes.

Again, what this does is offer a new place to try to reach consumers while they are doing something. Sure, most people cruising the highways and byways of mother earth have a mobile phone, but in-car systems, much like the connected household devices, add context. This makes marketing and, in theory, sales easier to achieve as you know the *what* and *why*, as well as the *when* and *where* of a consumer all at once.

The future

Thanks to augmented reality, visual search, voice recognition, intelligent cloud computing, powerful processors and, with the wind behind them, powerful wireless networks, mobile commerce of the future will be driven by sight and sound.

Bar code scanning will give way to image scanning, and this will be the jumping off point for a deep mobile-enhanced experience that will lead to seamless and painless purchasing.

You are walking along the main street of a strange town, between meetings, and you remember your son's birthday. You speak into the tiny Bluetooth mic woven into the collar of your jacket: "I want to see some 3D games consoles for the under-10s." You hold your smartphone up, and instantly you are directed to the nearest games shop – collecting a voucher as you go.

You pass a shoe shop and see some cool boots. You hold your phone up to them, and they appear on the screen surrounded by annotations about who made them, where, what sizes are in stock and how much they cost. You say "reserve," and the shoe shop owner's computer checkout gets a message saying, "Reserve the brown boots, size 9, for Mr. Skeldon."

You meanwhile have arrived at the toy store to be faced with a cut-price 3D games console and one that is almost the same price with the money-off voucher. Which do you choose? You hold up your phone and say, "Compare." Instantly you get a comparison website overlay that gives you the relative merits of each. You still can't decide. "It's for Elliot," you say into your mic. Your intelligent device then tells you to get the one with the voucher, as it includes games that feature my son Elliot's favorite X-Men characters. You say, "Buy." Seamlessly it is paid for, with the voucher applied, and you go and collect it at the counter, verifying who you are with a unique electronic "fingerprint" from your phone.

You leave with the console and head to the shoe store, where you try on the shoes. They are no good. You capture their image and ask your phone to find you similar boots, but with thicker soles. It does. You bookmark them to look at later.

Your phone tells you that it's five to one and that your one o'clock meeting has arrived at the restaurant you booked around the corner. You set off, your phone telling your colleague's phone you are on your way.

As you walk, guided by instructions in the discreet Bluetooth earpiece, your phone downloads all the relevant documents for your meeting from your cloud storage area, assembling them in order according to the agenda for the meeting that your colleague sent you. Your phone then asks you what you want to order for lunch, so that you can get going with business as soon as you sit down.

During the meeting you are sharing documents, e-mails and calling colleagues, all by voice command. All the documents you look at are AR-enhanced, so that you see who they are from and where they fit into the scheme of things.

Your meeting drawing to a close, you ask your device to get you a taxi to take you to the station. Your phone alerts you when the taxi arrives, and the taxi whisks you away to the station, your ride paid for as you exit, without your intervention.

You board your train home, your ticket embedded in your phone, and work out how to hide Elliot's present.

The remote control for life

The head of mobile at Spanish mobile giant Telefónica coined the idea that the mobile phone would become "the remote control for life." I think he was premature, but not wrong. Mobile devices — typically super smartphones and tablets — will become the devices we use to navigate the world, both real and virtual, forge relationships, consume entertainment, share our hopes and fears, and above all rely on to intelligently filter out what we don't want.

The mobile phone already sits at the heart of most peoples' lives and they feel lost without it, but we are only at the very beginning of what mobile technology can deliver to human lives. Mobile will become an integral part of everything we do. There will be no need for a book on mobile commerce in 50 years' time, because it will just be commerce. It will be part of life.

The journey starts here, and what I've discussed in this book gives you some pointers as to how to start on that great trip. Where we are heading who can say, but so long as you've got your mobile device with you, you can go anywhere.

Glossary

1G First generation analog mobile phone network and handset technologies, including AMPS, TACS and NMT. Coined after the arrival of 2G (see 2G).

2G Second generation and digital mobile phone network and handset technologies, including GSM, CDMA IS-95 and D-AMPS IS-136.

2.5G The enhancement of GSM that includes network and handset technologies such as GPRS and EDGE, and added higher speed data to the mix.

3G Third generation mobile phone network and handset technologies covered by the ITU IMT-2000 family.

4G The fourth generation of mobile phone network and handset technologies that look to add high-speed broadband data to 3G standards that will deliver as standard 10Mb/s for high-mobility communication (such as from trains and cars) and 1Gb/s for low-mobility communication (such as pedestrians and stationary users).

Android A mobile smartphone operating system (OS) developed by Google and then the Open Handset Alliance, which is based on Linux and therefore is considered open to developers the world over, so they can freely use the underlying technology to develop applications.

Analog The representation of information by a continuously variable physical quantity such as voltage, as opposed to digital (see Digital).

API (Application Program Interface) The tools needed to program applications.

ARPU (Average Revenue per User) How much money your business generates per user.

Apple Cupertino, California-based computer maker who used to be the also-ran next to Microsoft in the home computer market. The introduction of its iPhone in 2007 changed all that and lauched m-commerce as we know it.

App/s (short for applications) These are small, self-contained software programs designed to run on mobile phone operating systems (although Apple has long referred to all the software that runs on any of its operating systems as apps).

Bandwidth A term meaning both the width of a transmission channel in terms of hertz, and the maximum transmission speed in bits per second that it will support.

Bit The smallest unit of information used by computers. Made up using ones and zeros (on and off), all multiples of bits must be powers of two; ie, a kilobit is actually 1,024 bits and a megabit 1,048,576 bits. Transmission speeds are given in bits per second (bit/s).

Bluetooth A low-power, short-range wireless technology designed to provide a replacement for the serial cable. Operating in the 2.4GHz ISM band, Bluetooth can connect a wide range of personal, professional and domestic devices, such as laptop computers and mobile phones, together wirelessly.

Browser The software on a phone or computer that lets you access the Internet.

Byte A group of eight bits that operate as a single unit (*see Bit*).

Cell The area covered by a cellular base station in a mobile network. A mobile network is made up of cells connected to a land-based telecoms network.

CPU (Central Processing Unit) The processor at the heart of a phone or computing device that does all the work.

CRM (Customer Relationship Management) Looking after your customers. In the computer age this means using all the data you have on them to treat them all like individuals.

Digital The representation and transmission of information as ones and zeros, usually expressed as a sequence of bits.

E-commerce The buying and selling and associated technology done over the Internet using computers.

Feature phone A more functional device than a mobile phone and less functional than a smartphone. Feature phones were the forerunner of smartphones.

Gbit/s A unit of data transmission rate equal to one billion bits per second (*see Bit*).

Geo-fences Virtual areas covered by wireless technology. When a phone enters the geo-fence, it can be messaged. Used for marketing purposes.

GPS (Global Positioning System) A location system based on a constellation of US Department of Defense satellites. Increasingly being built into mobile phones to aid with location, although the mobile network can do a pretty good job of that too.

GSM (Global System for Mobile communications) The second generation digital technology for mobile phones. Originally developed for Europe, but now has in excess of 71% of the world market.

HTML (Hyper Text Markup Language) A set of elements used to write web pages and content that can be read on browsers.

HTML5 (Hyper Text Markup Language version 5) The fifth iteration of HTML that is more open for app development and allows mobile-compatible websites to be built that have the same rich user experience as apps.

I-mode A service developed by Japanese operator NTT DOCOMO to deliver a huge range of services to subscribers, and which has proved enormously popular with some 30 million regular users. The revenue-sharing model used for I-mode is being adopted by other operators as the basis for the new services enabled by GPRS and 3G.

Internet A loose confederation of autonomous databases and networks. Originally developed for academic use, the Internet is now a global structure of millions of sites accessible by anyone.

iOS Apple's mobile device operating system for iPhone and iPad (*see OS*).

IP (Internet Protocol) The set of standards that allow digital data to be transmitted and read over the web by devices.

ISP (Internet Service Provider) The company that gives you access to the Internet, usually via a PC. In the mobile world, network operators are sort of ISPs.

ITU (International Telecommunication Union) International group of telecom companies that seek to try to agree on standards for telecoms technology.

IVR (Interactive Voice Response) "Press one for . . ." telephone services: automatically handle voice calls.

Java A programming language developed by Sun Microsystems, characterized by not relying on an operating system, so it can be read by multiple devices.

JPEG (Joint Photographic Experts Group) Still image standard format (and the name of the group that set it).

LTE (Long Term Evolution) A next generation technology to make 3G networks faster and broader.

Mbit/s Data transmission speed equal to one million bits per second (*see Bit*).

M-commerce The mobile equivalent of e-commerce, where mobile devices are used to buy and consume things.

MMS (Multimedia Messaging Service) An evolution of SMS (Short Message Service) that adds various kinds of multimedia content, including images and audio and video clips to text messaging. Uses the mobile phone network, not the web.

Mobile Network Operator (MNO) The companies that build and operate the networks that mobile phones run on. They are also responsible for billing their customers for using these networks, as well as deciding, to some degree, what they can access (*see Network Operator*).

MPEG4 (Motion Picture Experts Group) A technology for compressing voice and video so that the information can be transmitted over normally difficult links, such as mobile radio.

NFC (Near Field Communications) A radio-based technology that allows for contactless communication between devices.

Network The bones on which the rest of the body mobile hangs. Networks are interconnected sets of wires, processors and other kit that carry all the voice and data traffic generated by telephones, computers and more.

Network operator The company that builds, operates, runs and bills for network use (*see Mobile Network Operator*).

OS (Operating System) The software that computer and smartphone programs run on. Think of it as a train: the software is the people, the carriages are the OS, the engine is the device and the track is the network.

PIN (Personal Identification Number) A private access key that only the user knows; used to lock devices and services so that only that user can access them.

Prosumer A portmanteau word made from professional and consumer; otherwise known as business users to you and me.

RAM (Random Access Memory) The processing memory of a device that stores all the software run by the OS.

Roaming The ability to make and receive calls on the same mobile phone when traveling outside the area of the home network operator.

Router A device that forwards information in a network on a connectionless basis.

SIM (Subscriber Identity Module) The SIM card is a smart card that makes a mobile phone yours and connects it to the mobile network and billing system. It contains the telephone number of the subscriber, encoded network identification details, the PIN and other user data, such as the phone book. A user's SIM card can be moved from phone to phone, as it contains all the key information required to activate the phone.

Smartphone A large-screen, voice-centric handheld device designed to offer complete phone functions, while simultaneously operating as a personal digital assistant (PDA), according to Gartner Inc., technology researchers. Palm Inc's definition is: "A portable device that combines a wireless phone, e-mail and Web access and an organizer into a single, integrated piece of hardware." It is basically a phone that thinks it's a computer.

Shortcode Five-digit access code to services on mobile that are more memorable than the standard 11-digit mobile number.

SMS (Short Message Service) A text message service enabling users to send short messages (160 characters) to other users.

SP (Service Provider) The company that offers you a service over mobile or the web that you pay for, in addition to your network operator.

Premium Rate Service (PRS) A service that is billed to the telephone bill, but charges more than the standard rate call charge.

UI (User Interface) The "face" of a device that the user uses to make things happen on that device.

URL (Uniform Resource Locator) The addressing system of the Internet.

VoIP (Voice over Internet Protocol) Sending voice digitally over the Internet and the coding needed to do it (*see IP*).

Voicemail A service offered by network operators, through which calls that are received when the phone is in use, switched off or out of coverage area can be diverted to an answering service to be accessed later.

WAP (Wireless Application Protocol) A *de facto* standard for enabling mobile phones to access the Internet and advanced services. Users can access websites and pages that have been converted by the use of WML into stripped-down versions of the original, more suitable for the limited display capabilities of feature phones.

Wi-Fi A trademarked name for radio-based, wireless local-area networks (WLAN). Wi-Fi connects computers and other devices to base stations that then link to the web. It is a way of wirelessly linking to the Internet without using a mobile network operator (*see WLAN*).

WLAN (Wireless Local Area Network) A short-range radio network normally deployed using Wi-Fi in hotspots such as airport lounges, hotels and restaurants. WLAN enables suitably equipped users to access the fixed network wirelessly, providing high-speed access (up to 11Mbit/s download) to distant servers. The key WLAN technologies are the IEEE802.11 family and ETSI HIPERLAN/2 (*see Wi-Fi*).

WML (Wireless Markup Language); aka HDML (Handheld Devices Markup Languages) This is the programming language that allows the text portions of web pages to be presented on mobile phones and other portable devices that run WAP. It is part of the WAP Protocol.

WWW (World Wide Web) A system of interlinked computer servers that all read HTML. Invented by Tim Berners-Lee in 1989 at CERN in Geneva. It is the reason I wrote this book (and possibly how you purchased it).

- groundswell s:18
- OS p. 26 Operating System

Nielsen net ratings →who does what
on Internet with what device